THE AMERICAN STOCKHOLDER

The American
STOCKHOLDER

By J. A. LIVINGSTON

J. B. LIPPINCOTT COMPANY
PHILADELPHIA AND NEW YORK

Acknowledgments

Writing is a lonely task. You can talk, you can consult, you can research, but ultimately, you alone, the author, must transfer the thoughts, knowledge and conclusions to paper. They are yours. You cannot blame them on anyone else. Yet, to any effort, such as this, many people contribute. Herewith I convey my thanks to those who have been generous with time and physical and mental effort and helpful with suggestions and criticism.

To my immediate associates in the financial department of the *Philadelphia Bulletin*: Eunice Bulla, a loyal and conscientious secretary; Arthur J. Boyle, A. Joseph Newman, Jr., and Peter Chrisafides, all of whom read the typescript in various drafts, many extremely rough; to Frank Donohoe, Bulletin librarian, and his associates, Helen Wells, Charles H. Martyn and Bernard Landolfi; to Robert McLean, publisher, and Walter B. Lister, managing editor for what are known in commerce as negotiable instruments; to Orval L. DuBois, the ever-courteous secretary of the Securities and Exchange Commission, and the several commissioners whom I have consulted; to Keith Funston, president, Philip L. West, Frank J. Coyle and C. Mac Coy, vice-presidents of the New York Stock Exchange and Edward T. McCormick, president of the American Stock Exchange; to Louis Loss, whose monumental work, *Securities Regulation*, is a concordance for anyone in such an endeavor as this; to S. Whitney Landon, secretary, and John J. Scanlon, treasurer, of American Telephone & Telegraph Company; to Corinne Friend, who helped me in my initial research and planning; to Lewis D. Gilbert, the stockholder's stockholder, for comments and reference material; to numerous attorneys, including Graham French in Philadelphia; James A. Farmer, general attorney for AT&T;

5

Acknowledgments

Henry Mayer, of Mayer, Weiner, and Mayer, New York, counsel to the Alliance of Independent Telephone Unions; Andrew B. Young, of Stradley, Ronon, Stevens and Young, Philadelphia; John Russell and H. Orvel Sebring and others in the Philadelphia firm of Morgan, Lewis and Bockius; Martin Horwitz, of Davis and Quat, and Julius Levy, of the firm of Pomerantz, Levy and Haudek, New York; and, especially, Professor Noyes E. Leech, of the University of Pennsylvania Law School for reading Chapter V; to Joseph E. Welch, executive vice-president of the Wellington Fund; to Lewis H. Kimmel, of Brookings Institution, for reading Chapter II in an early draft; to Lawrence M. Stevens, of Hemphill, Noyes & Company, and Merlyn S. Pitzele, both good friends, for serving as sounding boards and whetstones; to librarians at the Free Library of Philadelphia, the Federal Reserve Bank of Philadelphia, and the University of Pennsylvania; to Alfred T. Sprissler, proofreader of the *Philadelphia Bulletin,* who labored speedily and diligently on the Index, to my teen-age daughter, Patricia, who, in reading page proof, made a criticism of sufficient penetration to warrant a last-minute change; and, of course, to George Stevens, Howard K. Bauernfeind, and J. A. McKaughan, of Lippincott, for patience, encouragement, and the confidence of an advance payment.

To all the writers of newspaper and magazine articles and books I have read for this work; to the men whose ideas I have lifted consciously or inadvertently; in short, to all who have supplied help and material, some of which has been interpreted in a fashion the "suppliers" may not have intended. But this is the task of a writer: to be constructive when possible, critical when necessary. His duty is to his customers—those who buy the book—and not to his suppliers. And so, to all—those mentioned and those not—thanks.

J. A. LIVINGSTON

Subnote: Any person whose name appears above is entitled to take this acknowledgment into a bookstore and, on appropriate identification, to purchase *The American Stockholder* at the regular price.   J. A. L.

7

As every newspaperman knows, 30 is a magic number, signifying relief, the end of a story. It's the finis sign. The 30 that I put at the end of this book has a special significance. The typescript and the multifarious corrections were completed on the thirtieth anniversary of my marriage to a co-ed I met at the University of Michigan, Rosalie Frenger, of Las Cruces, New Mexico. I dedicate this book to her, not only in appreciation of her adroitness in putting up with me, but also because she's a typical American stockholder, who is described and analyzed in the following pages, and further because this anniversary is not, I pray, an ending but another beginning for both of us.

September 16, 1957

Contents

Contents

THE AMERICAN STOCKHOLDER

CHAPTER I

The Stockholder Versus the Slogan: Introduction

THE TEMPTATION in doing a book about stockholders is to call it *Hi, Sucker*—so many security buyers are bumpkins in Wall Street, prey to the sweet-talk of the sure-thing gamblers, like farmers a-holidaying at country fairs and circuses. Yet, there is likewise a practical realism about shareholders. They are suckers like the parasite that hangs on to the shark and, thereby, gets free transportation. Most purchasers of stocks know what they are doing. They are absentee owners who let somebody else work for them.

This is not a championing book, egging the stockholder on to fight for his legal and political rights in corporations. That is not what he wants. It is not a legalistic book, telling him how to use the law to protect himself in corporation infighting. That is not what he wants either. Nor does it give advice to the stocklorn, telling how to assuage an aching purse.

It is part expository—explaining what the stockholder can do and what he is likely to do. It is part descriptive—to show what does happen, as in the Ford stock flotation, in the New York Central proxy fight, and in the struggle for full disclosure by the Securities and Exchange Commission and the New York Stock Exchange. It is an attempt, without downbeats or cymbals, to indicate the kind of guy or gal the stockholder is— without making him a hero or a dunce, because he is neither.

If I were submitting this as a Ph.D. thesis, I would call it *The Rôle of the Stockholder in American Society*. You read that this is the land of "people's capitalism"—so many persons are the legal owners of industrial corporations, public utilities, mines, railroads, and banks, through possession of shares in major companies. You read that women are the majority owners of our enterprises—more women own stock than men. And so, we are told never to underestimate the financial power of the female.

But neither, it must be said in a quiet aside, should we overestimate women. Men run our corporations—and not too many men, at that.[1] They are the chairmen of the boards and the presidents and vice-presidents. They control—manipulate—the wealth. They are the husbands, or brothers, or sons who buy, sell, and send in the proxies for stock in their wives', sisters', or mothers' names. They are the trustees at banks who administer the estates of widows and orphans. They are the experts in investment banking and investment counsel firms and in brokerage offices who suggest to widows and single women how to manage their securities. The fiction that women control most of the wealth of America is chivalrous and useful. It makes women feel important and it serves the ends of men.

This book tries to go behind *The Folklore of Capitalism*, to use the title of Thurman Arnold's penetrating book. It examines the stockholder as a reality and not as a New York Stock Exchange slogan. Adolf A. Berle, Jr., a lawyer, and Gardiner C. Means, an economist, tore away the folklore of corporate ownership in *The Modern Corporation and Private Property*. They pointed out how great aggregates of men, machinery, materials, and money had been "captured" by a few control-

[1] *Poor's Register of Directors and Executives*, 1957, contains 75,000 names, virtually all men. *Who's Who*, which represents a broader cross-section of society since it includes artists, writers, teachers, scientists, contains 52,000 names, of which about 2,600 are women.

ling officers and directors of corporations. They wrote: "It is precisely this separation of control from ownership which makes possible tremendous aggregations of property. The Fords and the Mellons, whose personal wealth is sufficient to finance great enterprises, are so few, that they only emphasize the dependence of the large enterprise on the wealth of [the many]. The quasi-public corporation commands its supply of capital from . . . the 'investing public.' " [2]

Berle and Means documented the separation of control and legal ownership statistically and examined its sociological implications. After Berle and Means, James Burnham published *The Managerial Revolution,* in which he developed the theory of a new ruling class—the managers, the industrialists, who have a "special degree of control over . . . the instruments of production" and, thereby, obtain power and preference in our social order.

The managers of corporations control the proxy machinery, the ballot, even as a politician dominates a ward, a county, or a city. Stockholders pliantly return the directors and presidents to office year after year for their good deed—the payment of dividends. These managers mollify their personal and psychic needs with excellent salaries, nice bonuses, stock options, and liberal expense accounts. They have perfected financial devices to defeat graduated income taxes, as befits the corporate elite, a managerial class. Further, through their control of men, materials, machinery, and money—the corporate organization—these managers exert great power in American affairs—politics, society, and business.

It would be pretentious for me to suggest that *The American Stockholder* is in a class with *The Modern Corporation*

[2] *The Modern Corporation and Private Property* (The Macmillan Company), p. 5. Since the book was published in 1932, the Ford Motor Company has become part of the investing-public domain. But the control still vests—and most ingeniously, as will be noted in Chapter XIII—with the Ford family.

and Private Property, ground-breaking work that it was, or even that it is on the same plane of excitement and stimulation as *The Managerial Revolution. The American Stockholder* deals with a more modest subject, a group of people, who, in an analytical sense, can hardly be called a class. It concerns a group that is not and probably never will be homogenized, a group that has few champions but many exploiters, a group that seems naïve but which in the long run knows what it is getting and gets what it wants. This is an examination of the who, what, why, where, and how of 8,600,000 American shareholders—by New York Stock Exchange count.

The group is so diffuse and yet so narrowly based socially that once when I mentioned to a banker friend that I was working on this book, he said, "You're wasting your time and energy. The scope's too limited. Why don't you write about the nature of the economy? That's worthy of you." It was a shattering comment. For days I had doubts and misgivings. Was I researching an area of unimportance—a narrow corner of society of interest only to the Lewis D. Gilberts, Stock Exchange pedants, and legal and corporate technicians? Inertia—heaven bless it!—carried me on.

This book will have served a social end if it accomplishes one thing: Puts the stockholder in his proper place. In his massive work, *The Soviet Regime, Communism in Practice,* W. W. Kulski makes an observation which is useful for analogical purposes: "Often . . . people's emotions rule their judgment of the Soviet regime. Everyone [seems] to feel his ignorance excused by the famous statement of Sir Winston Churchill that the Soviet Union is a riddle wrapped in a mystery inside an enigma." In the United States, we are not shy of facts about our government, our economy, our social institutions, or our stockholders. We are so overrun with information that the average man cannot keep up with the deluge of data in depth. Consequently, facts surrender to catch-phrases. It is easier to construct slogans than to study, learn, and acquire understanding. It is less time-consuming to Madison-Avenueize than to investigate. We wrap up our knowledge with slogans and think we have understanding. Instead, we have half-truths, which are whole falsehoods.

I refer to the phrase "people's capitalism." The New York Stock Exchange uses it. The Advertising Council uses it. Great efforts are made to popularize it—to indicate that it is descriptive of our American way of life. The implied imagery is obvious: People—little people, big people, rich people, poor people—own a piece of American Telephone & Telegraph, General Motors, American Can, Allied Chemical & Dye, General Electric, and Kansas City Power & Light. Common stocks are widely dispersed in a nation of great corporations and little capitalists.

To me that verges on a pathetic fallacy and is a vicious image. And, in the course of this work, I hope to put the Q.E.D. to that statement. If I succeed, then this exploration of a dark enigmatic corner in American affairs will have been, for me, well worth the effort, worry, and multifold misgivings.

This is a great country, a wonderful society. Its wonders need no flannel-mouthed fictionalization by men in gray flannel suits. The power of the place is visible. A visitor from abroad who traverses a narrow sector along the Pennsylvania Railroad from New York to Washington, sees endless roads, strewn with endless lines of cars. He sees factories, automobiles parked at the factories. He sees cranes, derricks, hoists, shipyards. He sees America at work in a breathtaking panorama. If he has a chance to pause in any city, he sees a standard of living—a manner of eating, sleeping, dressing, and playing—unmatched anywhere. Ours is a consumeristic society. Incomes have risen steadily. Protections against old age and unemployment have developed and expanded since the depression 'thirties. Men and women feel more confident of finding jobs, earning a living, and having an income in their old age. They are more prone, therefore, to spend and borrow —to "live it up," so runs the phrase—to mortgage future income and buy homes, automobiles, household appliances, home furnishings, cabins in the woods and by the seashore, and kidney-shaped swimming pools.

> Once men worked from sun to sun,
> Now in eight hours work is done,
> Work was made to lead to fun.

But the means of production—the factories, the machines, the railroads, the trucks on the highways, the airplanes—which make this new aggregate of leisure possible, do not belong to workers en masse. The men who work at General Motors, the women who clerk in department stores or serve as stenographers, do not ordinarily own shares in corporations. Try telling one of Walter Reuther's United Auto Workers, or one of John L. Lewis's United Mine Workers that he is a "people's capitalist." He will laugh at you. Yet that is the stuff Madison Avenue sells Americans. It is the stuff America, itself, tries to propagate abroad. Any French, British, Belgian, or Italian economist who has studied the American structure of corporate ownership knows it is not true. He is aware of America's high standard of living—her consumeristic base.

He is not taken in by slogans, especially since share ownership in America is not "capitalistic" in nature. Shareholders own "paper," not property. Stock certificates are symbols of possession even as entries in a savings bank passbook are a record of title to a sum of money. But neither grants power to influence, direct, or control. Originally, a capitalist was both owner and manager. He owned a ship and captained it; he owned a store and ran it; he owned a farm and farmed it. (In farming old-style capitalism still persists.) The owner was a boss. Not so, or very much less so, today. Berle and Means and Burnham analyzed that.

A modern corporation is an island of power, a financial stronghold. Ambitious, wealth-minded men compete for top jobs in these economic fortresses. Sometimes this competition for power emerges as a proxy fight, which offers shareholders a chance to take sides. Sometimes a purposeful stockholder, sensing some overreaching, some dishonesty, will sue. And sometimes, the Securities and Exchange Commission may intervene—call a manager to account for violation of law or custom, suspend careless or misguided certified public accountants from practicing before it, as happened to two distinguished firms as we shall see later.

Historically—out of the common law in Great Britain—the stockholder has always had a bundle of rights, of protections from thievery, dishonesty, and double-dealing. But the bundle was tied together with rubber bands which could be skillfully stretched by ingenious executives and distinguished lawyers. Then, in 1933, President Franklin D. Roosevelt sent a message to Congress asking for the enactment of the Truth-in-Securities Bill, saying: "This proposal adds to the ancient rule of caveat emptor the further doctrine, 'Let the seller beware.' " Roosevelt was reacting to, recoiling from, the 1929 crash, the Great Depression, and the laxities of men in paneled offices with other people's money—men such as Albert H. Wiggin, of the Chase National Bank, Charles E. Mitchell, of the National City Bank, and—a later discovery—Richard Whitney, who for many years had been the untouchable president of the New York Stock Exchange and who went to jail for larceny after the failure of his firm, Richard Whitney & Company.

The 1933 Securities Act required issuers of stocks and bonds to tell the truth, the whole truth, and nothing but the truth. It was followed by the Securities Exchange Act of 1934, the

Public Utility Holding Company Act of 1935, and laws on investment companies, investment advisers, and the reorganization of companies in bankruptcy. The Securities and Exchange Commission (SEC), creature of this post-1929 revulsion, became the policeman of Wall Street. It determined the adequacy of information, rejected ambiguous statements, and denied sellers of securities the privilege of rosy, futuristic forecasts. The SEC formulated rules to help the stockholder help himself, and so fathered a new phrase, "corporate democracy."

In its own way, the phrase is as misleading as "people's democracy." It suggests a militancy among shareholders that does not exist.[3] It implies that the shareholder exercises his legal powers, and defends his own rights. A few shareholders —the large ones or aggressive ones—do. So does Lewis D. Gilbert, the self-appointed Stockholder Vigilante Committee, who is *sui generis*. But for the most part shareholders are scattered, unorganized, and indifferent. (And perhaps our system works very well for that reason. The managers are free to act quickly and decisively, without benefit of town meetings.) Ours is a plutocratic corporate system. When Leopold D. Silberstein, of Penn-Texas Corporation, battled for control of Fairbanks, Morse & Company, he did not rely on an appeal to the shareholders alone. He bought up Fairbanks, Morse stock in the open market. Then he could count on his purchased votes. Thus corporate democracy differs from political democracy. In a public election, to buy votes is a crime.

The SEC keeps this corporate plutocracy under control through rules and regulations. The accountants, lawyers, cor-

[3] This view would hardly be accepted by Frank D. Emerson and Franklin C. Latcham, who co-authored *Shareholder Democracy*, published in 1954 by The Press of Western Reserve University. They argue that "much evidence is at hand that the stockholder along with his fellow members of the general public [is] experiencing an awakening of . . . intellectual capacities for corporate as well as general understanding."

porate controllers and secretaries, and investment bankers and brokers who constantly lay bare their financial souls before the SEC create a framework, an environment, of rightness. An outside conscience has become part of Wall Street so that Wall Street has developed a new conscience all its own. Because of the penalties attached to misbehavior, corporate officials have become solicitous of the rights of stockholders. Thus, the mass of stockholders has become an institutional force in America—not because of what the individual stockholder does in his own behalf, but because of *what* others do for him as a class.

Louis Loss, in his book, *Securities Regulation,* wrote: "Congress did not take away from the citizen his inalienable right to make a fool of himself. It simply attempted to prevent others from making a fool of him." That has conferred on the shareholder a new dignity and status. The islands of economic power in the U.S. are greater than ever but misuse of that power has been channeled, funneled, filtered, and purified by statutory aeration. The stockholder's character has changed fundamentally from what it was one hundred and more years ago, in the early days of the corporation, when he was owner, operator, and active participant in the business. That change —the analysis of stockholders' mid-twentieth-century character—is what this book is about.

CHAPTER II

They Would Rather Not Be Bothered

DURING THE MONTH of May, 1947, the New York Stock Exchange splurged with heavy advertising in *Time, Look, The Saturday Evening Post, Collier's,* and other magazines. The ad showed a table covered with hats—the ten-gallon job of a man from Texas, the denim cap of the railroad fireman, the crushed fedora you might associate with a rushed physician, the white cap of the house painter, the derby of the stockbroker, the homburg that President Eisenhower has since made popular, the wide-brimmed straw the farmer uses in the field, the dashing cap of an airman, and, to represent the women, a fur neckpiece.

The title is, "Stockholders' Meeting." The copy says: "They come from everywhere . . . from every income group, from every community. They are women as well as men, employees as well as executives, farmers as well as businessmen. They are typical stockholders, the owners of business." And, it might have been added, a more ineffective bunch of Americans you never did see.

The advertisement, of course, wanted to convey just the opposite impression. Corporations are owned by everyone. Wall Street is not a rich man's preserve. It is where Main Street as well as Park Avenue puts its savings, where the millions of the millionaire and the tens and twenties of the widow and the schoolteacher commingle. And the stockholders' meeting, to which the owners of a corporation go to vote on its affairs, is the social leveler. An owner is an owner, even as at the polls a voter is a voter once the curtain on the booth closes.

The implication is that stockholders have something to say about their business. When they go to the meetings, the management sits up. Actually, as we shall see in the course of this analysis, the management is only as polite and attentive as it wants to be. Corporation executives know straw men when they see them.

Once upon a time, in the days of small companies, the owner and the manager of a business were one and the same. The stockholder controlled the affairs of the company because he was the management. In theory and tradition, he is still the boss. In theory, he provides the capital and hires the management. And managers of giant corporations like to perpetuate that convenient fiction. The fact is, though, that the stockholder hires nobody. He is the hireling—or, at least, his money is. A cynical economist would say, "Capital doesn't hire management, management hires capital."

In the days of the ad, when the Stock Exchange suffered from a sad case of giantism, L. O. Hooper, statistician and market-letter writer of W. E. Hutton & Co., reflected what Wall Street believed and wanted to believe when he wrote in the New York Stock Exchange's magazine, *The Exchange*:

"No accurate census has ever been taken, but the various experts who have studied the matter are agreed that between 15 million and 16 million Americans own stocks—approximately one person out of nine and about one family out of three." Hooper was under the influence of announcements by two New York Stock Exchange presidents, Charles R. Gay and Emil Schram, and they, in their way, were under his influence, too. All three were interested in emphasizing the scope and breadth of stockownership. It became mutual hypnosis.

Today we think we know better. Wall Street is not that big a puddle. It does not serve fifteen million frogs. Keith Funston, who succeeded Schram as president of the Exchange, asked the Brookings Institution, research organization of Washington, D.C., to find the facts. Brookings selected Lewis H. Kimmel, a thoughtful, careful research economist, for the job. After field studies and interviews with shareholders, Kimmel estimated the number of shareholders at 6,490,000.[1] Let's call it 6,500,000.

At first, Wall Street was shocked and shrunken. But then a new thought struck: Only 6,500,000 shareholders! In a country as big as America! My, we haven't begun to tap the market! The 6,500,000 estimate became a new credo, a goad to expansion, a promise to salesmen. It is the basis for the New York Stock Exchange Monthly Investment Plan—MIP [2]— which permits people to buy stocks for as little as $40 every three months. The Stock Exchange had just begun to fight!

Kimmel's estimate is now out-of-date. In the years since 1952, the New York Stock Exchange has made sample surveys and concluded that another two million stockholders have been added. Explanation: Vigorous sales promotion and good times. A bull market—rising prices—always brings in new investors.

Yet, even 8,600,000 shareholders, the official New York Stock Exchange number of July, 1956, is an economic commentary—a commentary on why Wall Streeters, in the last

[1] *Share Ownership in the United States,* published by The Brookings Institution, Washington 6, D. C., 1952.
[2] At one time it was termed the Periodic Investment Plan, but the initials were not flattering—PIP.

twenty years, have not made a deep impression in Washington, why their demands for changes in the capital gains tax and in reduction in corporation taxes made slow headway.[3] As a political bloc, Wall Street has never measured up to its own evaluation or its statistics. Congressional mail has consistently belied the well-reasoned briefs of high-priced Lower Manhattan law firms.

Why is that?

Eight million six hundred thousand people constitute a substantial bloc. It is 60 per cent larger than the total number of farmers and about half as large as the membership of the American Federation of Labor-Congress of Industrial Organizations. Large stockholders are willing and able with their checkbooks in campaigns. Yet stockholders, as a group, do not wield as much influence as labor organizations or farmers. Again, why?

Because the political power is not there. Farmers have a common interest. They are all in the same business—raising crops and livestock. They want high prices for what they sell, low prices for what they buy. When it comes to putting pressures on senators and representatives in Washington, they speak the same language, though livestock, cotton, or wheat farmers may differ on details and emphasis.

Similarly, with a union. Members have a common objective: higher wages and strong bargaining power vis-à-vis employers. They may not vote as their labor leaders tell them. But they will vote as their economic interests dictate. This makes for a large block of votes. Workers, like farmers, will defend their common livelihood.

Not so, stockholders. Those hats in the Stock Exchange ad

[3] The pressure for relief from double taxation of dividends has had some effect. In 1954, Congress granted a $50 dividend deduction ($100 for a married couple) plus 4 per cent of all additional dividends—with limits, however.

are a confession of weakness. These are the hats of men who are doctors, farmers, air pilots, house painters, merchants, and executives first and stockholders second. Stocks provide supplementary income to salaries, fees, or wages. Dividends are not, except in rare cases, their main income. For every Lewis D. Gilbert, who is willing to make a career of being a professional stockholder by guarding his own and other stockholders' interests, there are thousands of stockholders who are merely dividend collectors. They are "stockholders" only when directors omit a dividend. Then they wonder why it had to happen to them, ponder what to do about it, realize they can do little, and then pass on to other matters. Occasionally, a stockholder will write to the company even as an irate reader will write a letter to the editor. Stockholders are not stockholders. They are something else instead.

Indifference probably increases with stockholdings and education. This does not mean indifference to stock market fluctuations, to the value of one's stock market worth. Pride in investment success oftentimes mounts with the size of investments. I refer specifically to stockholder indifference to corporations as corporations rather than investment opportunities. The person who gets along in this world, who makes a success of his business or profession, is more interested in his own work, in what has made him a success, than in policing corporation executives and policies and safeguarding his legal rights as a stockholder. That implies that persons who in mass have much at stake as stockholders are least inclined to be legally exercised about it.

Anyone would accept as self-evident that stock ownership would follow the income curve upward. But Kimmel wanted to establish the facts. In effect, he sorted the hats. And he found more wearers of homburgs, derbies, and fedoras among shareholders than wearers of white or striped-denim caps. More than 65 per cent of all shareowning family units had incomes of $5,000 or more.[4]

The New York Stock Exchange, in its later surveys, found pretty much the same. However, the Exchange is so intent on publicizing the widespread ownership of stocks, of propagandizing the phrase, "people's capitalism," that it headlines: "Two-thirds of Shareowners Earn Under $7,500." The inference to be drawn is that only one third of America's shareholders are in the upper brackets. But you have to decide where the upper bracket begins—at $5,000 or $7,500. Further, it would be strange, indeed, if a majority of shareholders did not have incomes under $7,500. After all, nearly 90 per cent of the adult population is in the below-$7,500 income group. Only 10.4 per cent is in the above-$7,500 group. Yet, this 10.4 per cent accounts for 36 per cent of the shareholders by the Stock Exchange's own count.[5]

On a significant point the Kimmel and Stock Exchange data come close together: For shareholders in the $5,000-and-below

[4] The data are as follows:

Family Income	Individual Shareowners Per Cent of Total
Less than $2,000	4.3%
$2,000 to $3,000	5.4
$3,000 to $4,000	9.1
$4,000 to $5,000	12.8
$5,000 to $10,000	44.4
Over $10,000	24.0

[5] Here are the Stock Exchange figures:

Reported Household Income	Individual Shareholders Per Cent of Total
Under $3,000	11.6%
$3,000 to $5,000	26.1
$5,000 to $7,500	26.4
Over $7,500	35.9

income group, Kimmel shows 31.6 per cent, the Stock Exchange 37.7 per cent. The discrepancy—the higher percentage of the Stock Exchange—could well be due to the rise in incomes, the inflation between 1952 and 1956, rather than any important increase in the proportion of shareowners among the lower-income group.

We call the American economic system a capitalistic system. Yet, for the people at large, it is a consumeristic society, a high-standard-of-living society. The tendency of persons in the lower- and rising-income brackets is to save by spending— to purchase homes, autos, home furnishings, based on expected long-term increments to income. Our great corporations thrive on this propensity to spend. "Each year we build the best car we possibly can to satisfy the customer," said Alfred P. Sloan, Jr., when he was chairman of General Motors, "and then the next year we build another to make him dissatisfied."

Families with leftover income—unspent income—are the purchasers of common stocks. These are the better-heeled families. A sample survey by the Ford Motor Company of its shareholders supports this. Only 11 per cent of the Ford holders reported incomes of less than $5,000; only 31 per cent reported incomes of less than $7,500. In other words, 69 per cent had incomes of $7,500 or more. Four out of five purchasers of Ford stock (82 per cent) were already stockowners. Yet here was a security originally tabbed for the man in the denim cap, not the homburg hat.

The conclusion to be drawn is not that, increasingly, farmers and laborers own shares, but rather that as people ascend the income ladder, their savings spill over into the stock market. Kimmel's detailed tabulation in 1952, though not as up-to-date as that of Ford or the Stock Exchange, makes this point with great clarity:

Income	Per Cent of Families in Each Group Owning Stock
Less than $2,000	2.2%
$2,000 to $3,000	3.6
$3,000 to $4,000	4.6
$4,000 to $5,000	7.4
$5,000 to $10,000	19.8
Over $10,000	55.1

As a corollary, and as you would expect, the incidence of stock ownership improves with education. This does not mean you have to go to Harvard to own stock. But it helps. Persons with college training develop higher earning power than those who have not had such advantages. And college men and women are likely to come from middle- and upper-income families in the first instance. These would be families with a stockowning bias. The Stock Exchange survey shows that 29 per cent of college graduates are stockowners versus only 1.7 per cent of those who never went beyond grammar school:

Education	Per Cent of Each Group Owning Stock
4 years or more of college	29.4%
1-3 years of college	16.8
4 years of high school	9.6
1-3 years of high school	5.3
8th grade or less	1.7

Finally, a close correspondence exists between age and stock ownership. Youngsters starting a career do not earn wages or salaries sufficient to put aside funds for the purchase of common stocks. They have a hard enough time earning a bare living. As men and women grow older, as they become more experienced in their work, their earning power increases. Likewise, they have bought their initial homestake—beds, washing machines, refrigerators, autos, homes, and so forth. So, if they are of a provident turn, they have extra money. They can put it in insurance, savings bonds, savings institutions, or common stocks. Nearly 60 per cent of shareowners—4,810,000 out of the 8,280,000 whose age was indicated—are forty-five or more.

The correlation between age and stockownership makes a perfect statistical staircase until age sixty, as you can see in the following tabulation used by Kimmel: [6]

Age	Per Cent of Each Group Owning Stock
Under 21	0.2%
21 to 29	2.0
30 to 39	4.8
40 to 49	6.6
50 to 59	10.8
60 and over	9.1

So the pattern of the typical shareholder emerges. He tends to be a person in his late forties or early fifties. He has been relatively successful financially. And it is not too hard to guess which occupational group is most heavily committed to stocks. It is the—well, guess—and then turn the page upside down and see if you have guessed right:

[6] The Kimmel tabulation on age distribution of owners seems to me more inherently consistent than that of the Stock Exchange (below), even though it is four years older. The Stock Exchange tabulation shows a larger proportion of stockownership in the 21-to-34-age bracket than in the 35-to-44 bracket. This does not conform to my conception of common sense. For the record, here are the Stock Exchange data:

Age	Per Cent of Each Group Owning Stock
21 to 34	7.3%
35 to 44	5.5
45 to 54	9.1
55 to 64	14.2
65 and over	8.0

The business executive.

Kimmel notes that forty-five out of every hundred administrative executives own some stocks. The executive is in the high-salary bracket. After living expenses, he is apt to have funds for investment. Further, he is not afraid of common stocks. His own company is likely to be a stock corporation. He undoubtedly owns some of its stock. He may even have been given special incentives to purchase it—through stock option plans. He has, in his business life, been brought up with stocks and finance. And then, of course, there is that economic truism: "Them as has gits." High income and a big property stake in society are reciprocal. The high income helps to acquire property and property abets income.

Operating supervisory officials are next—nineteen out of every hundred of them are stockowners. In this group are some of the future business executives.

Next come professional men—the doctors, lawyers, architects, engineers, dentists—of whom thirteen out of every hundred are shareholders. Again, you can easily figure the reason. This is an upper- and middle-income group. Earnings would be well above a comfortable subsistence. So, there would be leftover income available for investment.

Next come sales representatives of wholesalers and manfacturers; next, merchants; then retired persons and dependents, with a proportion that at first thought seems surprisingly large—nine out of every hundred. Then you realize that many retired persons have built up substantial nest eggs, some of which would be entrusted to common stocks.

The next groups comprise white-collar workers, farmers, skilled, semi-skilled, and unskilled workers—this last with only two shareholders per thousand.

The largest single numerical group of stockholders consists

of 2,130,000 housewives—"nonemployed housewives" [7] is the technical designation—or nearly one third of all shareholders. But this is an arithmetical exaggeration. Many women are shareholders in name only. Stock may be owned jointly with husbands or registered in the wife's name for tax purposes. And it is the man of the house who has the say. He buys the stock, decides when to sell. Only the unusual housewife reads the reports, studies the statistics, cashes the dividend checks, and sends in proxies. In most homes, that is man's work. Still, facts are facts, and one out of every sixteen housewives has stock in her name. Here is the Kimmel occupational distribution of shareholders:

Occupation	Number of Shareholders	Per Cent in Group Owning Stock
Executives	300,000	44.8%
Supervisors	620,000	19.4
Professional Persons	670,000	12.8
Salesmen (a)	200,000	11.2
Merchants	250,000	10.6
Clerical Workers	590,000	7.6
Farmers	320,000	6.8
Skilled Workers—Foremen	410,000	4.4
Public Service Workers	40,000	3.4
Semi-Skilled Workers	210,000	1.4
Unskilled	10,000	0.2
Members of Armed Forces (b)	20,000	1.1
Retired, Dependents	560,000	9.1
Housewives—Nonemployed	2,130,000	6.0
Nonemployed Adults	30,000	1.3
Students & Pre-school Age	130,000	0.2

(a) For manufacturers and wholesalers.
(b) Living in households.

[7] Men, never say "nonworking" housewives! Not and keep your grace.

The Stock Exchange distribution by occupation is not as finely broken down—only nine classes versus Kimmel's sixteen. (Perhaps this is because of the smaller sample.) Proprietors, managers and officials are lumped together in a single group, of whom 24.6 per cent are shareowners. Kimmel, as you can see, was able to break out an executive category, of whom 44.8 per cent owned shares. Only 19.4 per cent of the supervisory group, which probably corresponds to the Exchange's "Officials," were classed as stockholders. The Exchange occupational break follows:

Occupation	Number of Shareholders	Per Cent in Group Owning Stock
Prop., Mgrs., Officials	1,140,000	24.6%
Professional & Semi-professional	1,010,000	18.0
Clerical & Sales	1,490,000	11.6
Housewives & Nonemployed Women	2,830,000	8.3
Nonemployed males	490,000	6.8
Service Workers	430,000	6.5
Craftsmen and Foremen	520,000	5.9
Farmers and Farm Laborers	230,000	4.9
Operatives and Laborers	140,000	0.9
Not Classified	350,000	

The very dispersion of stockownership is a partial explanation of the ineffectuality of stockholders, as stockholders. When doctor-stockholders get together, they are far more apt to talk about operations, or the incidence of cancer due to cigarette smoking, than about the stock market or corporate policy. Housewife-shareholders will be more interested in soufflés and garbage disposals than in the movement toward corporate democracy. Few shareholders, regardless of the hats they wear, have sufficient at stake financially to devote much time to the companies in which their money is invested.

A comparatively small group of persons, those in the $7,-500-and-up income group—and the "and-up" must be emphasized—have a major stake in common stocks. The Stock Exchange's own summary, as we have seen, shows that 36 per cent of the shareholders are to be found in a 10 per cent segment of the population—those with incomes of $7,500 and more. Butters, Thompson, and Bollinger, in *Effects of Taxation*, estimate that about 0.5 per cent of the nation's families hold slightly more than 50 per cent of all marketable stock owned by private investors. Roughly, this would represent about 250,000 shareholders. Yet, these are unlikely to be militant shareholders—guardians of the rights and prerogatives of the Stockholder with a capital S, which really means the small stockholder.

American society is an active society. Recognition and prestige come from doing, not from having. Doris Duke and Barbara Hutton make front page news because of their money and social exploits, including marriages, but they are not paid homage for that. You will not find their names in the 1956–57 *Who's Who*, but you will find the names of Betty Hutton, actress, Dorothy Shaver, department store executive, and Sylvia Porter, financial writer. John D. Rockefeller, Jr., and his sons have become symbols of American achievement—not because of their inheritance, but because of what they have done and are doing with it, including the construction of Rockefeller Center in New York and the judicious management of the Rockefeller Foundation. Henry Ford II is already far better known than his father, Edsel, because of his achievement in resurrecting the Ford Motor Company from an also-ran in the automobile industry. It is notable that the Rockefellers and the Ford brothers are all in *Who's Who*, that Tommy Manville, another scion of great wealth, who has devoted his life to wedding showgirls—he has had ten marriages in all—is not. In America, a man's work, not his dividends or dolls, distinguish him.

So it is with stockholders. The large shareholders are apt to be executives. In which case, they direct the policies of the companies. They are part of the managerial group, not the stockholder group. Their interests may coincide with stockholders as a group, but their interests may also diverge. As officers, they may be anxious to have liberal stock option plans for executives. These tend to dilute the equity of the great mass of shareholders. Or, being large shareholders and not needing dividends, they may want to plow back most of the earnings into growth, into development. Small shareholders, especially retired people, probably would be anxious to have substantial pay-outs for living expenses.

Economic self-interest does not create a large, earnest, "stockholder class" in America. In 1954, out of 3,681,000 taxpayers who reported dividend income, at least 3,039,000, or 83 per cent, had salaries, wages and other income in excess of dividends. In other words, less than 650,000 families, as a maximum, derived 50 per cent or more of their income from stocks.[8] The great majority counted on salaries or wages to keep the instalment collector away from the door. And, interestingly, most of the taxpayers who receive half their incomes from dividends are not the very, very rich.

For taxpayers with incomes between $30,000 and $50,000 a year, salaries will run two and a half times as much as dividends. Not until the taxpayer pushes into the $100,000-and-up bracket does dividend income exceed salary income. And in 1954, this involved only 17,187 returns. If you throw in the $50,000-to-$100,000 taxpayers, whose salary receipts are 50 per cent greater than dividends, you still add only 58,885 persons. And these $50,000-and-up recipients are often owners and con-

[8] *Statistics of Income, 1954.* U. S. Treasury.

trolling shareholders or managers of corporations. To many of them, their success as businessmen is more rewarding than guarding their legal rights as stockholders. They are professional businessmen, professional executives, professional behind-the-scenes policymakers. They are seldom professional stockholders.

Most of the half-million taxpayers whose dividend income approaches 50 per cent of total income are pensioners, retired persons (*see* Kimmel tabulation, page 32, in which he gives a figure of 560,000). They have the economic urge, the financial incentive, to be corporate watchdogs. But how many of the persons in this group would be competent guardians of their rights? A few who had been corporation officials would know how to analyze stock option and pension plans for executives and complicated financial statements. They would be able to ask intelligent questions at annual meetings of stockholders. However, by definition, by having been executives, they would probably be amply provided for in retirement. They might even have consulting salaries from the corporations. They would not be goaded by financial necessity to chaperone the officers of corporations in which they owned stock. Presumably, in retirement, they would prefer travel, golf, and good books to stockholder imbroglios.

That leaves the lower-income pensioners—those who have been successful, but not outstandingly successful, financially, those who may be getting by in their old age comfortably but not luxuriously. Obviously, they would be handicapped as corporate watchdogs. Retired doctors, farmers, mechanics or engineers cannot suddenly become conversant with finance. Their activities have been in different channels. And, by the time they have reached the age of retirement, they are hardly ready for a new career—notwithstanding their financial interest in what other people are doing with their money.

That is why stockholders, as stockholders, are ineffective.

The big stockholders are usually in the managerial group—protecting their personal interests. The middle-sized shareholders are preoccupied with careers. And the retired persons are too old to develop into effective champions of their own rights. So, in administering his property, in exercising his legal prerogatives, the average stockholder today is in the position of a depositor in a bank. If he does not like what is going on, he can get out. The depositor does it by taking out his money; the stockholder, by selling his stock.

In selling his stock, the shareholder abandons his right to make things right, to improve management. He "includes himself out." He passes on to someone else a stock certificate he regards as faulty, something he does not want. In which case, the only check on the management is the threat that the price of the stock will decline and some intruder—a Louis E. Wolfson or a Ben W. Heineman,[9] for example—may buy up the shares at a depreciated price and try to take over the company. If no such "raider" comes along, the average stockholder is left holding a bag of officials that Wall Street says are not very good.

America's a young country. George L. Schwartz, brilliant financial editor of the *Sunday Times,* of London, says that some day we will have a large capitalist class—"rich countries always do." We will have a great body of people who live off their investments, their stocks. Perhaps then, we will have a militant corps of professional shareholders. Perhaps Lewis D. Gilbert is the forerunner of such a corps. Perhaps they will develop into professional policemen for corporations—persons whose economic interest it is to see that the affairs of the companies they own are in order; persons who would adopt the motto, "Our company, right or wrong; if it's right, to keep

[9] Chicago lawyer, who captured control of the 1,400-mile Minneapolis & St. Louis Railway in a proxy battle with Lucian S. Sprague, chairman. Thence he vaulted into the chairmanship of the much-bigger and better-known Chicago & North Western with a show of voting power and without a fight.

it right; if it's wrong, to make it right." They will not include themselves out by selling stock. As yet, we have no such group in America. Stockholders, for the most part, are doctors, lawyers, executives, schoolteachers first, and stockholders second. They are investors, who, for the most part, do not wish to be bothered—except by dividends.

CHAPTER III

Three Positive Rights

DAVID McCORD WRIGHT, author, professor, lecturer in law, and economist,[1] was asked by the president of a large corporation what to do about indifferent stockholders. "Just don't declare dividends for a few years," said Wright. "You'll have plenty of interest then."

When something goes wrong with an investment—when the dividend is reduced or stops, when the stock drops sharply in price—the stockholder will suddenly take an interest in what is happening to his money, his investment. He becomes conscious of being an owner. He wants to do something. His property, his wealth, is in danger. He wonders, What are my rights?

If he were to consult a lawyer, he would find out he has quite a few rights, depending in part upon the state in which the company is incorporated. He has the right to share in the company's profits, providing the directors see fit to declare dividends. He has the right to elect directors. He has the right to receive annual reports of the company's earnings. He has the right to hold directors responsible for their acts—by lawsuit, if he wants to go that far. He also has the right to inspect the books of the corporation, to vote on mergers and consolidations, changes in the charter and, sometimes, the bylaws.

[1] As this is written, Wright is professor of economics and political science at McGill University, Montreal. Prior to that, he was a professor of economics and a lecturer in law at the University of Virginia.

In some states he has first rights—preëmptive rights—to buy new securities.

By the time the lawyer gets through, the stockholder realizes he is not lacking in rights. But if he is a small stockholder he is likely to find out that his rights are not exactly powers. He will find out that rights mean different things to different stockholders.

As I shall develop in the course of this book, stockholder rights vary with stockholders and the stockholders' purposes. To Robert R. Young, who took over the far-flung, $2,000,000,-000 New York Central Railroad in 1954 in a nationwide proxy fight, his rights as a shareholder were the means to get control of a company. To stockholders who follow the well-worn path of Clarence H. Venner, who made a modest fortune, as a New Jersey judge expressed it, "unsettling the nerves" and plans of giant corporations in the early 1900's, rights are something to be asserted in lawsuits. To banks, insurance companies, mutual funds, and similar institutions, rights are a check on management and a means to information. Such institutions exercise their rights decorously, discreetly, and quietly. And to a militant such as Lewis Gilbert, stockholder powers are the legal powers—by which the independent stockholder holds corporation officers and directors accountable to their boss, the Stockholder.

But for the average Joe and Jane Stockholder, the "Whereases" and legal trappings water down to three primary rights that he or she can exercise. They are:

1. The right to throw the officers and directors—the management—out of the corporation by electing new directors. That will take a proxy fight, a fight for control. This was Young's way in New York Central. That was what Louis E. Wolfson tried in 1955 with Montgomery Ward & Company—unsuccessfully; what Leopold D. Silberstein, German-born

president of Penn-Texas Corporation, tried in Fairbanks, Morse & Company in 1957, only to reach a compromise.

2. The right to sue officers and directors for misuse of powers, gross mismanagement, fraud, or dishonesty. This was Clarence Venner's way, but oftentimes he was accused of acting not for stockholders but for himself, as we shall see later.

3. The right to sell his stock, which means throw himself out. At that point, he "resigns" from the company. He ceases to be an owner.

Let's try to examine these three rights of stockholders. Are they real? Do they mean more to the large stockholder than to the small, to the institutional investor than to the individual investor? In short, let's see how they are used. What are the powers of stockholders—practical as well as legal?

Are the great majority of stockholders owners in fact, as the New York Stock Exchange likes to imply? Or, is this a Wall Street fancy, an advertising slogan?

We shall let the deeds and actions of stockholders, themselves, supply the evidence—the answers—in the following chapters.

CHAPTER IV

Throw the Rascals Out

"THROUGH THE INSTRUMENTALITY of the ballot, stockholders have effective control over management. They use this power in the election of directors and voting upon other important issues which are placed before them.

"If management is unsatisfactory, they have the means to remove it. Where the majority of stockholders are pleased with the results, they indicate their confidence by the reëlection of the nominees whom management recommends to them for the directorate." [1]

That statement was made by Harry A. Bullis, who, for many years, was the highly successful president and then chairman of General Mills, Inc. It is a typical statement of a corporate executive. It idealizes the stockholder. It has limited pertinence to reality.

It would be realistic if stockholders took an active interest in their companies; if they had a basic understanding of the issues to come up at annual meetings; if they had the capacity and energy to evaluate the performance of corporate managements intelligently and critically; if they read carefully the proxy material sent them. Mr. Bullis, himself, notes that some shareholders "resent the spending of money for the purpose of keeping them informed."

Substantial professional investors—the banks, investment

---

[1] *Corporate Democracy*, a compilation of *Virginia Law Weekly* articles, "Dicta," University of Virginia, 1952–53.

trusts, insurance companies, and well-to-do individuals or trustees—have the power to remove officers and directors. They do understand the issues. They actively analyze the earnings of companies in which they have investments.

The small stockholder, however, is in a separate pot. As the Temporary National Economic Committee of Congress pointed out in 1940: "Unless there is a powerful nucleus of some sort, it is practically impossible for the hundreds of thousands of scattered holders of a majority of stock of a giant corporation to get together even by proxy in order to exercise a degree of control. Moreover, 'the individual stockholder does not know the merits of those who contend for the control of the directorate; he has little or none of the materials which might enable him to judge by results. Earnings may be good or bad because of the competence of officers; but they may be good or bad, also, because of the good or bad conditions of business in general.' [2]

"Thus the small stockholder," continued the TNEC, "is not in a position to act decisively or even to know how to act. . . . So long as he receives satisfactory dividends or at least convincing reasons why such returns are not forthcoming, the average stockholder will return his proxy certificate to the existing management." Mr. Bullis concurs: "We realize that too many stockholders are not interested in company affairs so long as they are receiving satisfactory dividends." [3]

And that is why the ballot, as an instrument of control, is fictional. The right to vote in corporate affairs is not identical with the right to vote in politics. The right to vote implies an opposition. In politics, somebody is always ready and anxious to "throw the rascals out." But in corporate affairs, this right is usually latent. The small stockholder has to be offered a choice of candidates to exercise his right to change the man-

[2] *Modern Competition and Business Policy*, by H. F. Dennison and J. Kenneth Galbraith.

[3] *Corporate Democracy*, see page 42.

agement. Occasionally, but not often, he gets a choice, as in the New York Central fight. But such opportunities to "throw the rascals out" require special and unusual circumstances or individuals plus money.

Robert R. Young had an ambition to control an eastern railroad. He had become head of the Chesapeake & Ohio Railway Company in 1938 when he took over control of the Alleghany Corporation, top holding company in the disintegrating Van Sweringen empire. But he wanted a still bigger stake. He used Chesapeake & Ohio funds to buy 800,000 shares of Central stock. Later, he arranged for the sale of the Central stock to two friends, the oil-rich Clint W. Murchison and Sid W. Richardson of Texas.

Young had more than ambition. He was a millionaire in his own right. He was chairman of Alleghany Corporation, whose assets exceeded $50,000,000, and he spent $1,308,000 of his own and Alleghany funds to win proxies. (A group of Alleghany stockholders made such lavishness an issue in a lawsuit against him.) Clearly, such a struggle is above the financial competence of the schoolteacher, doctor, or farmer who owns ten, or fifty, or one hundred shares of stock in a company.

The struggle for economic power in a big company is far more costly than the struggle for a seat in the U.S. Senate. In the 1952 campaign, the highest outlay officially reported was that of John F. Kennedy, Democrat from Massachusetts, $234,000, of which $16,000 represented his own expenditures and $218,000 expenditures of others in his behalf. His defeated opponent, Henry Cabot Lodge, Jr., used funds—his own and others—of nearly $160,000. Their combined outlays were less than either Young or William White, deposed president of Central, spent.[4] New York Central's deposed management spent more than a half million.

[4] Kennedy's outlays do not approach those made in behalf of Frank L. Smith, who won the senatorial election in Illinois in 1926 as the Republican

A proxy fight costs money because the management, at the outset, has all the advantages. The officers have the list of stockholders. They control, as the saying goes, the proxy machinery. They can send out letters to shareholders extolling their own virtues, pointing with pride to their records, and detailing the company's long and successful history. They can describe the opposition as interlopers, trying to get covetous fingers in the corporate till. And all this is done with the funds of the corporation. The management does not risk personal funds to stay in office—as the challenger often does.[5]

Moreover, investors do not want to be disturbed. They prefer the *status quo*. Even in New York Central, the numerical majority went along with White. The small stockholder did not want to make a change. John D. Rockefeller, Jr., had the same experience in 1929 in his proxy campaign to unseat Colonel Robert W. Stewart as president of Standard Oil Company of Indiana. Again the small shareholder was apathetic. Yet, Rockefeller campaigned on a moral issue. Stewart, called to testify in Senator Thomas J. Walsh's famous investigation of the Teapot Dome scandal, refused to answer questions about bonds which had mysteriously changed hands. Rockefeller felt that was unbecoming to and improper for the chief executive of a major industrial enterprise. Hence his determination, as a large shareholder, to oust Stewart.

In the struggle, he enlisted the services of Winthrop W. Aldrich, his brother-in-law, one of New York's financial elite who later became head of the Chase National Bank and still

---

candidate, but was denied a seat because of overexpenditure of funds—$458,000, of which $203,000 came from officers of public utility companies. Smith had been on the Illinois Public Utilities Commission. In the same year, William S. Vare, Republican boss of Pennsylvania, was also denied a Senate seat. He had spent $785,000 to win the Republican primary. Smith and Vare were felt to have "bought" their elections.

[5] In the Central fight, to the extent that Young used Alleghany funds, it was a battle of corporate treasuries; neither principal suffered out-of-pocket loss.

later U.S. Ambassador to Great Britain under President Eisen-hower. Aldrich mobilized the support of the New York financial community and through it was able to throw Stewart out. Some $300,000 was spent in getting proxies. In those days, that was a respectable sum.

Rockefeller controlled, personally and through the Rockefeller Foundation, 13 per cent of Indiana Standard's stock. In the Central fight, Young, through his own holdings and those of Murchison and Richardson, owned 17 per cent of the shares of Central. The challenger for control of a corporation must not only be prepared to spend money in a proxy campaign, but he usually must have a large stock interest. (A detailed account of the Central fight is given in Chapter XI.)

Without a Young or a Rockefeller to make effective the stockholders' right to throw the ins out, the proxy is like a Communist ballot. There is only one slate to vote for. Nevertheless, the mere fact that the right exists, that occasionally a Young or a Rockefeller arises and is successful, is a boon to all shareholders in a political sense: No management can be complacent. No management can feel entrenched in its emoluments.

The haunting thought will rise: It happened in Standard of Indiana; it happened in New York Central. It might happen here. This threat is a constant goad to pay dividends, to make the stock highly prized in the market place—in short, to make it impossibly expensive to be challenged successfully.

Essentially, though, the power to control management through the ballot, as Bullis put it, is limited. It takes a man with money and ambition to make a fight for control of a company. If he wins a proxy contest, he must be prepared to manage the company or get someone to do so. Only when a challenger arises can a shareholder express approval or disapproval of the management and so make his vote effective.

Shortly after World War II, an outburst of stockholder

fights, of which the Central and Montgomery Ward made front page headlines, gave newspaper columnists and other writers an opportunity to indulge in blatant superficialities: "Stockholders have found their voices." "Stockholders are asserting their rights." "Stockholder democracy has burst into flower." The facts do not support such clichés.

Out of some three thousand companies whose stocks are traded on America's fourteen registered stock exchanges,[6] only twenty-four proxy contests occurred in 1956 and only twelve in 1957. Of the twenty-four in 1956, half were contests for outright control—in other words, fights to the finish. The other half were for representation on the board. That is, minority stockholders wanted a "say" or a "look-in" on management. In 1957, only seven were for outright control, and five were for representation.[7]

[6] The registered exchanges are: American Stock Exchange, Boston Stock Exchange, Chicago Board of Trade, Cincinnati Stock Exchange, Detroit Stock Exchange, Midwest Stock Exchange, New Orleans Stock Exchange, New York Stock Exchange, Philadelphia-Baltimore Stock Exchange, Pacific Coast Stock Exchange, Pittsburgh Stock Exchange, Salt Lake City Exchange, San Francisco Mining Exchange, and Spokane Stock Exchange. In addition, there are four exchanges which are exempt from registration, but whose members must comply, by and large, with the rules set forth for registered exchanges. They are the Colorado Springs Stock Exchange, Honolulu Stock Exchange, Richmond Stock Exchange, and Wheeling Stock Exchange. The New York Stock Exchange accounts for 87 per cent of the dollar value of stocktrading on exchanges; The American Stock Exchange, for 11 per cent; all the other exchanges, for 2 per cent.

[7] The SEC distinguishes between outright fights for control and efforts of minority stockholders to obtain representation on boards of directors. The statistics for the last six years follow; however, for 1952 and 1953 no breakdown on contests for control and representation is available:

Year	Total Proxy Contests	Fights for Control	Fights for Representation
1952	18	—	—
1953	14	—	—
1954	22	13	9
1955	18	11	7
1956	24	12	12
1957 *	12	7	5

* To June 30. Annual meetings occur in April, May, and June.

47

Most proxy disputes do not make national news, often are quiet, local affairs. Among the contests in 1956 and 1957 were Hercules Motors Corporation, Allied International Investing, Michigan Steel Tube Products, Parkersburg Aetna Corporation, Reda Pump, United Board & Carton, Western Air Lines. How many of these did you hear of or do you remember? Sometimes proxy fights take years to mature. In 1957, an opposition slate, supported by Robert R. Young and Alleghany Corporation, sought representation on the board of directors of the Missouri Pacific Railroad in the cumulative voting state of Missouri. One anti-management director was elected out of five.[8] This could balloon later into a full-fledged fight for control.

Often proxy contests are compromised. A court decree settled the bitter Fairbanks, Morse fight after Robert H. Morse, Jr., president, and Leopold D. Silberstein, who wanted to take over, reached a stalemate. This took the issue out of the hands of shareholders. They could not vote. In a dispute in Loew's, an SEC report makes this revealing observation: "By negotiation, opposition was given one place on the board; no opposition solicitation was made." Again, a vote of stockholders was made unnecessary. Corporate democracy is bypassed.

Obviously, shareholder voting muscles do not get much exercise. Twelve to twenty-four fights a year out of more than three thousand elections comes to far less than 1 per cent. Essentially, the shareholder vote is potent only when, as, and if the opportunity—the challenger—arises, which is not often.[9]

[8] The Missouri Pacific staggers election of its fifteen directors at the rate of five each year. This staggered election system became a subject for court action even as in Montgomery Ward & Company, which is discussed in Chapter VIII.

[9] Nor is that deplorable. If proxy fights were a corporate constant, going on continually, business would be in a turmoil. Management would not have time to manage. It would be too busy politicking, rustling votes.

CHAPTER V

Sue the . . .

No STOCKHOLDER has the right to good management. But he has the right to honest management. He can expect officers and directors to watch over the business and property of his corporation as if it were their own. Thus, Section 408 of the Pennsylvania Business Corporation Law states: "Officers and directors shall be deemed to stand in a fiduciary relation to the corporation, and shall discharge the duties of their respective positions in good faith and with that diligence, care, and skill which ordinarily prudent men would exercise under similar circumstances in their personal business affairs."

The law grants officers and directors wide latitude. They can make mistakes. They can exercise bad judgment. They can lose money. They can refuse to pay dividends if they can adduce a business reason for so doing. But they must not abuse their powers and privileges.

They must not be dishonest. They must not make profits at the expense of the corporation. They must not favor friends or relatives in business dealings to the detriment of the business. They must not pursue a dividend policy to their own ends. They must serve the stockholders, not themselves.

If they fail to do so, they can be sued. But a stockholder's suit is not so easy as it used to be—nor as profitable. Which brings us to the story of Clarence H. Venner and what may seem like a digression. . . .

Venner died in 1933. Eleven years later—in 1944—Governor

Thomas E. Dewey, of New York, signed a law which is a left-handed monument to Venner's life and work. It is designed to make it more difficult for others to do what Venner did so persistently.

The law provides that a stockholder who brings suit against officers and directors of a corporation in New York must put up a bond to pay court costs and the expenses of the defendant directors and officers unless he owns or represents $50,000 worth, or 5 per cent, of stock of any one class. Subsequently, Pennsylvania, Maryland, New Jersey, and other states adopted similar statutes. In signing the New York bill, Governor Dewey said: "A shareholder with a real grievance should have little trouble persuading enough other stockholders to join with him to meet one of these exemptions." [1] None the less, the law makes it harder for stockholders to sue.

Venner was a member of the New York Stock Exchange and a man of mystery. He died leaving an estate of $700,000 after having sued more corporate titans than any other non-lawyer. Among his court antagonists were Atchison, Topeka & Santa Fe Railway, Union Pacific Railroad, Pullman Palace Car Company, United States Steel Corporation, J. P. Morgan & Company, New York Central Railroad, Great Northern Railway, and its powerful president, James J. Hill, the Wabash, Guaranty Trust Company, Bethlehem Steel, New York Life Insurance Company, American Telephone & Telegraph, American Hide & Leather, and many more. To Venner, the bigger the opponent, the more lucrative the triumph.

He settled a suit against the Great Northern by selling Hill, its doughty president and no pushover, 980 shares of stock, for $513,000. Venner had paid $188,587 for the shares. He received $300,000 for bonds with a face value of $30,000 by withdrawing a suit against the Union Pacific. He was ac-

[1] From Laurens H. Rhinelander's "The Derivative Stockholder's Suit," in *Corporate Democracy*.

cused of selling for $250,000 "worthless stock" in a paper railroad, the Nebraska Central, to the Chicago, Rock Island & Pacific Railway. Venner said he had spent $75,000 in projecting the Nebraska Central and it was profitable for the Rock Island to purchase the franchise even though it was never used.

The above facts about his triumphs are not of Venner's voluntary revealing. His own lawyer, in a suit to collect a fee, brought out the price Hill paid for the Great Northern stock. An Interstate Commerce Commission investigator gave evidence in the Rock Island case at a government hearing.

Venner was tall, heavy-set, and always impeccably dressed in expensively tailored clothes. He wore a stiff collar and his tie was embellished with a pearl stickpin. He carried his noseglasses in a handsome silver case. His iron-gray hair and moustache carried out the impression of a purposeful man. Often he hid his identity as a litigant behind the Continental Securities Company, the General Investment Company, and the New York Central Securities Corporation,[2] which he controlled. These companies became known among lawyers of the day as Venner's "alter egos."

In 1925, when Venner was fighting American Hide & Leather Company's plan of reorganization, Laurence Stern, a reporter on the *New York World*, persuaded him to grant an interview. The following colloquy occurred:

STERN: "You are regarded as a man of mystery."

VENNER: "I will talk about my suit against American Hide & Leather. I will not talk about myself. I have one cardinal rule, and that is the rule of silence. It is unnecessary and useless to make statements to the newspapers and I prefer to do my talking in court. I seek no personal publicity."

[2] Not to be confused with New York Central's own New York Central Securities Corporation.

STERN: "What has moved you to oppose so many corporate plans?"

VENNER: "I have investments to protect, and it is a bad thing to permit large corporations to jam through plans involving millions. You see, the average stockholder's proxy means nothing. He sends it in slavishly at the call of his directors. His act does not mean he has studied the question involved or that he has any understanding of it.

"I am not a stockholder of this kind. I make it my business to be informed and I conceive it to be my duty not only to protect my own interest but those of unthinking minority security owners."

On several occasions he was rebuffed by officers of the American Hide & Leather Company, when he sought information to which, as a stockholder, he was entitled. This became an issue in court. Vice Chancellor John Bentley of the Chancery Court of New Jersey, commented:

"It is true that Clarence H. Venner, in his quest for particulars, met with many obstacles and some rebuffs at the hands of the defendant's officers. Some allowances must be made, however, for the weakness of human nature. I can conceive of no monster of the jungle . . . that could [so] unsettle the nerves of a corporation director . . . as the appearance of Mr. Venner in search of information."

When the Interborough Rapid Transit Company of New York, since merged into the New York City subway system, was in financial difficulties, Venner, as a bondholder, refused to go along with a reorganization plan approved by 96 per cent of the bondholders. He demanded the appointment of a receiver. De Lancey Nicoll, one of the numerous lawyers for the IRT, said in court:

"Venner sits here on my right and has many times in court heard me expose his litigious life. Could anything be plainer than that his action either as a stockholder, bondholder, or creditor is not for the benefit of his fellow bondholders, stockholders, and creditors but entirely for himself? The higher courts have held repeatedly that in such circumstances the court is under no obligation to embarrass a company which is trying to smooth out its affairs for the benefit of the stockholders and bondholders generally."

Later, when Venner offered to withdraw his request for a receiver in the IRT case, the company's counsel immediately told the court he was taken by surprise. Venner was not withdrawing his motion at the request or suggestion of any person associated with the IRT. Counsel felt compelled to make clear that Venner had not been bought off, that no deal had been made.

When Venner attempted to join in a suit already begun against the General Baking Company in 1927, the other plaintiffs withdrew. They said they did not want to be joint plaintiffs with him.

A 1916 suit against Venner revealed his method. Mrs. Retta Ellis demanded he return to her three hundred shares of Iowa Central stock, which he had borrowed in order to sue the railroad as a shareholder. If the suit did not succeed, she said she was to get her shares back plus $750 for their use. If the suit succeeded Venner could buy her stock under an option for $10,000.

Venner's technique was to discover some legal flaw in a company's plans. He would try to stop a merger, a reorganization, or a plan of action. It would be more costly to hold up corporate plans than to buy Venner out. There is one apocryphal story: After he was well known as a bringer of "strike suits," he held up the plans of a large company over a legalism, and was invited to talk things over with the board of directors. The board listened to Venner, then asked him to retire briefly. When he returned, the chairman said he was authorized to offer Venner $10,000 for his stock—a sum which would have yielded him a handsome profit. Venner stood up and said: "Gentlemen, you forget I have a reputation to uphold."

As the years went by, a common headline was, "Venner Sues New York Central," or "Venner Against J. P. Morgan," or even more revealing, as corporations found it necessary to contest his actions, "Venner Loses Again."

Assessing Venner's work in behalf of stockholders is not easy. August Belmont, the banker, called him a "practical blackmailer." Venner started a suit for libel. But when Belmont confronted him with a demand to take the stand and be examined, Venner dropped the action.

Supreme Court Justice James C. Van Siclen, New York, said:

"No weight or virtue can be added to the court's memorandum by indulging in invectives or branding the plaintiff Venner. . . . If heretofore the judicial record and published opinions of various state and federal courts tend to establish that Venner is an artificer of litigation and a menace to corporate society, an added curse will work no cure."

But to many small stockholders and opponents of big corporations, he was a darling and a protector. One of his admirers suggested a monument to him at Broad and Wall Streets, saying:

"Sacred to the Memory of Clarence Venner—the only man who ever made money playing a lone hand against the wizards of high finance." Instead, his epitaph is the law which curtails the rights of stockholders to sue.[3]

[3] "Perhaps someone will some day write a treatise called 'In Praise of Venner et al.,'" the late U.S. Court of Appeals Judge Jerome N. Frank wrote in the *Yale Law Review* (Vol. 42, p. 992), in the course of reviewing Berle and Means *The Modern Corporation and Private Property*. Frank went on to observe that when "strike suits" are disposed of by settlement for the sole benefit of the litigant without knowledge of the other shareholders, then the "action does nothing for the body of shareholders." Before ascending to the bench, Frank had been a chairman of the Securities and Exchange Commission.

Venner was called a nuisance, but he was also a legal Robin Hood, a protector of the ignorant. By constantly challenging the proposals of companies, by demanding to have stock "appraised out"—as the expression is—in mergers, by examining every legal loophole, he kept corporation officials and lawyers alert to their obligations to security owners. They had to observe the letter as well as the spirit of their charters and by-laws, or face Venner. He was like an auditing system in business, or a policeman on a beat—a restraint on people who might be tempted. True, he would sell his nightstick—at a price. But the mere fact that he wore a coat of mail, often called black, produced higher corporate morality. He raised the level of the corporate conscience. He made such a nuisance of himself that the phrase "strike suit" is associated with his name. And laws to protect corporations from strike suits have crystallized.[4]

Today, in New York State—and many other states—a stockholder cannot bring suit against a corporation unless he owned stock at the time of the alleged wrongdoing. The stockholder cannot buy into a suit, be a corporate ambulance chaser, or, to use the legal terminology, engage in champerty.

Furthermore, a stockholder who brings suit against officers and directors today in defense of his and other shareholders' rights cannot readily make a behind-the-scenes settlement. In

[4] "Strike suit" is defined as "an action brought purely for its nuisance value with the purpose of obtaining a settlement for the complainant's sole benefit—the amount of the proposed settlement being far greater than any possible injury suffered by the complainant." George T. Washington, *Corporate Executives Compensation.*

A note in the *Columbia Law Review* (1934, p. 1308) points out that "strike litigation" is a better term. The whole purpose is to avoid a suit. They are really "strike campaigns." The note says that Venner "conducted at least 23 such campaigns," which invited at least 50 separate actions, and left over 100 cases in [legal] reports. [His] campaign against New York Central extended over 14 years, involved 12 suits in four jurisdictions, employed four nominal plaintiffs [Venner had many alter egos], left 29 cases in the reports, and reached the United States Supreme Court five times.

Federal courts, a proposed settlement must be open, approved by a court, and stockholders are notified beforehand of the terms. In New York State, home of the biggest and most important stockholder suits, this procedure is almost invariably the practice, if not the rule. This is to prevent private dealing between management, on the one hand, and a particular stockholder or group of shareholders, on the other, at the expense of the majority. States are moving toward judicially approved settlements as a necessary safeguard against Vennerism. The rule in Pennsylvania is emphatic: An "action brought on behalf of a class shall not be dismissed, discontinued, or compromised . . . without the approval of the court in which the action is pending." [5]

This protection for the great body of stockholders was implemented in the famous case of Associated Gas & Electric Company vs. Greenberg. Howard C. Hopson, president of AG&E, who later went to jail, had engaged in many practices that would hardly stand the searching examination of an accountant. He became an easy mark for sharpshooting lawyers and stockholders: Bring a suit against him and he would buy your stock. And since Associated Gas & Electric securities were dropping steadily in the post-1929 markets, it was profitable for a stockholder who had lost money in AG&E to bring suit.

Adolph Greenberg and other shareholders settled out of court with Hopson, receiving $9,000 of AG&E funds for stock worth $51.88 in the market. Later, when AG&E went into receivership, the AG&E trustee sued for the difference and finally won in the Court of Appeals in New York. Justice Marion R. Dye held that when a stockholder brings suit in behalf of the corporation and other stockholders, the "amount secured is in behalf of and for the account of the corporation.

[5] Rule #2230(b), Pennsylvania Rules of Civil Procedure.

This is so because the action belongs primarily to it.[6] The manner and method by which success is accomplished, whether by judgment, settlement with court approval, or by stipulation of the parties, makes no substantial difference. The plaintiff-stockholder, in good conscience, should not be allowed to retain the proceeds of a derivative suit discontinued by stipulation."

This is in keeping with the feeling of the Securities Exchange Act. Congress provided that officers and directors who realize profits trading in the company's stock held less than six months are liable to suit—in behalf of the corporation, that is, all stockholders. It was also a triumph for ethics. No longer could shareholders hope to bring a suit and, by private settlement, make a profit.

But this was not enough, corporation attorneys argued. There are always lawyers with more time than practice, who will willingly bring suit—purely on speculation. If they win, they collect a fat fee from the company. If they lose, they have lost nought but time, of which they seem to have plenty.

So, New York, Pennsylvania, and other states have passed legislation to make it difficult for lawyers to bring suits on a shoestring. Here, again, the legislation favors the large shareholder. As noted, a suing shareholder in New York must be prepared to post a bond to cover court costs and expenses of the defendant unless he owns $50,000 worth, or 5 per cent, of the company's stock. In Pennsylvania, a suing shareholder may be required to post security for costs unless he owns or has joined with him owners of 5 per cent of the company's outstanding stock. Amassing that amount of stock in a company as large as the Pennsylvania Railroad, with 13,167,000

[6] Stockholders' suits against officers and directors are called "derivative suits," because they are derived from rights of the corporation and are brought, in behalf of the corporation, to enforce a right or cause of action when officers and directors, themselves, will not bring such an action.

shares outstanding, is tantamount to a prohibition.[7] Pennsylvania property laws are notable for their solicitous regard for the rights of large property managers and owners.

The American bar splits into two sections on anti-Venner laws. Lawyers for corporations declare they are necessary to stop frivolous suits. They contend it is relatively easy for any attorney, or group of stockholders, with a genuine cause of action to recruit $50,000, or 5 per cent, of stock in New York. But lawyers who bring "derivative suits" declare it is undemocratic, penalizes the small shareholder, and stops many legitimate suits. Some shareholders are just not in a position to post a bond. California tries to minimize the power of property by permitting a plaintiff to avoid posting a bond if he can demonstrate to a court in a preliminary hearing that he has a reasonable case and that the corporation and stockholders have a reasonable chance of benefit from the suit. (But some lawyers argue that it forces disclosure of their case to the defense before trial.)

These restrictions assume that the large stockholder will not indulge in a frivolous suit. They impose financial tests on the small shareholder, often the pawn of the lawyer who scents a wrong and will finance court costs, knowing that if he wins he will collect a fee. The small shareholder will seldom, from his own investigation of corporation affairs—reading reports, studying the financial pages of newspapers—discover wrongdoing. Nor are the small shareholder's benefits in winning a suit likely to be sufficient to warrant his being a principal litigant. It is trouble, even if the lawyer does all the work.

Lawsuits, like proxy fights, are primarily the large stockholder's game. Or the lawyer's game. You have to be sophisti-

[7] That would call for 658,000 shares. At a price of $20 a share, which prevailed in July, 1957, that is more than $13,000,000. Actual proxy solicitation would be necessary to pull together that much stock.

cated to go into them. You have to have a sufficient stake to justify the effort. And you cannot hope, as a stockholder, to be directly reimbursed. Your lawyer will get a fee, if you win, paid by the company.

All you get as the suing stockholder is your pro rata share of whatever is collected from officers and directors. And this goes into the corporate pot. You do not get a direct cash benefit unless it is later paid out in dividends.

Thus, in proxy fights, as noted in the previous chapter, and in lawsuits, the small stockholder is protected by the large stockholder who is willing to fight. But this happens haphazardly—and only when it is in the direct interest of the large shareholder: in a proxy fight, if he wants to take over control of the company; in a lawsuit, if he has a great deal to gain financially, or if he is a lawyer looking for a substantial fee.

Lawsuits or proxy fights (such as the Rockefeller fight against Stewart) out of pure righteousness are rarities.

CHAPTER VI

Throw Yourself Out

HERE's a natural question: If a stockholder is not satisfied with a company's management, why should he start a proxy fight, why should he sue, why shouldn't he just sell his stock and be done with it?

Answer: That is what most stockholders do.

It is the easiest, cheapest, and, from many points of view, the most practical way to express stockholder dissatisfaction with a management, a company, or an industry.

The right to sell is a vote. And the stock market—Wall Street—is the polling booth. If the price of a stock goes up, it registers stockholder—investor—satisfaction. If it goes down, it registers dissatisfaction in the market place.

Sewell L. Avery, as head of Montgomery Ward & Company, got his share of market-place votes both ways. At the suggestion of J. P. Morgan & Company, Avery, a successful Chicago executive and head of U. S. Gypsum Company, accepted the presidency of Ward's in 1931, a year in which Ward's went $8,700,000 in the red. In 1939, the company reported a profit of $27,000,000 and its stock registered approval of Avery's performance. From a low of 3½ in 1932 the common climbed to 57¾ in 1939. Avery was hailed as a master builder and executive.

But during World War II, Avery lost his constructive touch—and his favor with investors, shareholders. He got into a brawl with the government over labor policy and was bodily carried out of his office in Chicago by two soldiers when the U.S. Army seized the company to stop a strike. Later, he had a series of difficulties with top executives who quit, first in ones and twos, then often by the half dozen.

As a result, Sears, Roebuck & Company, Ward's principal rival in the mail-order and chain-store business, made up for ground lost during the 'thirties. Sears' sales, profits, and dividends expanded faster than Ward's. The Wall Street voting machine duly registered the difference. By 1953, Sears' stock sold higher than Ward's, even though in 1945 Ward's common was quoted 50 per cent higher than Sears'.[1]

This right to sell stock—to vote for or against a management in the market place—is different from a vote at a stockholders' meeting. When a stockholder votes against a slate of directors, he is exercising his right as a stockholder, as an owner. He hopes to change the management and improve the company. But a stockholder who sells says to hell with it. He is not going to reform the company. He is not an owner trying to increase the value of his property. He says, in effect, "Include me out."

In one case, the shareholder continues his interest in the company. In the other, he passes on his dissatisfaction to somebody else. The object is to get out of a stock while the price is still high. In this decision to sell or not to sell, the large stockholder has distinct advantages. He holds many shares. He is listened to by management. He has political influence in the company even though he is not represented on the board of directors.

Thus, just before the Montgomery Ward stockholders' meeting in 1949, Sewell Avery held court. Large shareholders —representatives of banks and investment trusts—could see

---

[1] Not until 1954, when Louis E. Wolfson organized a proxy fight to take control, did Ward's stock rise above Sears'. Buying for control undoubtedly had its effect on the market price.

him. Avery tried to impress upon them the wisdom of his policies by unfolding a long-term chart which showed that after the Revolutionary War, the Civil War, and World War I prices inevitably fell. Avery expected prices to drop again. He was not going to expand during a boom. He was battening down Ward's hatches—for a bust.

The point here is not whether Avery was right or wrong, but that he gave large stockholders personal insight into his reasoning. Small shareholders seldom have the benefit of a personal meeting with the chief executive of a major enterprise. They are handled by correspondence—remote control.

On this same point, consider the experience of Russell McPhail. One day in August, 1953, he dropped into the offices of L. S. Starrett & Company, at Athol, Massachusetts, and indicated to the vice-president and treasurer that he owned 10 per cent or more of the stock. The plush carpet unrolled. Arthur H. Starrett, the president, who was away on vacation, arranged to come back and meet McPhail.

McPhail had some radical ideas. He wanted the company, which was paying $4 a share in dividends annually, to halve the rate. He also felt that he ought to become a member of the board and an officer. Subsequently, he met Starrett and Starrett invited him to a meeting of the entire board of directors to present his arguments for a change in dividend policy and for his election to the board.

Can you imagine a holder of ten or one hundred shares receiving such elegant treatment?

McPhail, incidentally, used the same method in introducing himself to officials of Transue & Williams Forging Company. He was named vice-chairman of the board and chairman of the finance committee of Transue & Williams at a salary of $46,000 a year later boosted to $61,000. As a large shareholder, he got a direct voice in management and became the highest paid officer.

The Starrett board did not accept McPhail's views, did not name him to the board of directors, did not give him a top-level job. But he got his hearing.

And later, he went to court to demand a stockholders' list so he could communicate with other stockholders. He did not get it. A Massachusetts court decided that he wanted "access to the stock transfer books" in order to persuade shareholders to sell him their stock or enlist their aid in getting a paid voice in management and not for a proper corporate purpose.

A North Carolina-born rebel, domiciled in his spare time on a 56-foot, six-bed boat off Florida and with a candy business in New York City, McPhail was stubbornly undiscouraged. He was firmly determined to make the Massachusetts Yankees treat with him. Periodically, he conferred with Starrett, the elderly president of the family-run tool enterprise, a man as stubborn as McPhail, and determined not to let a Southern upstart run his company.

Starrett fathered a ten-year instalment plan to sell twenty thousand shares of stock to loyal employees. This was about enough stock to offset McPhail's holdings. McPhail wanted no part of the plan. The employees' stock might be used against him in a proxy contest. He managed to get hold of a stockholders' list—to fight the plan. When stockholders supported Starrett, McPhail went to court—this time to Federal Court. The plan was unusual. As soon as employees subscribed to shares, they obtained full voting and dividend rights. In most instalment purchase arrangements, voting and dividend rights either are held in suspense until employees own stock outright or their rights accrue as the stock is paid for.

Under the Starrett plan, if the stock was selling for $60 a share, an employee would have to put up only $6 of his own money in the first year. He could then not only vote the stock in a proxy contest, but also would be entitled to full dividends, which at the recent rate of $3 a year, would yield 50 per cent on his initial investment. The dividends would be applied to the purchase price of the stock. Of course, as the employee's equity in the stock increased, this would be reduced. For the first five years, the plan required an employee to pay 10 per cent a year on the purchase price. But at the end of five years, once an employee had put up 50 per cent of his own money, dividends might be counted as part of his 10 per cent annual payment. Thus, the actual purchase of the stock would not take a full ten years.

The Federal Court held up action on the plan for about two years, notwithstanding the approval of shareholders on three different occasions—first, when the plan was originally submitted, and twice when amendments were offered to the proposal. Informally, the Federal judge suggested that the issue might be settled by inviting McPhail to become a member of the board. But Starrett would have no dilution of the Yankee strain in his company. The full board of directors turned down that suggestion in October, 1957—leaving the issue still pending.

As the largest single holder in the company, McPhail philosophizes that Starrett is "making money for me. Every time he increases the dividend, I can buy more stock. And if he doesn't make money, and the stock drops in price, that suits me too—I can accumulate more at lower prices." Clearly, McPhail is an atypical stockholder. He is not an investor, but a contender for power. He had a big enough stake in Starrett to want to assert his rights as a shareholder. And he was sufficiently well off to finance the legal fees, running into thousands of dollars, demanded by assertion.

Because they have easy access to the top management, most large shareholders, and particularly, institutional investors, banks, trusts, insurance companies, and pension funds, seldom participate in proxy fights, seldom have representatives make speeches at stockholders' meetings, seldom make proposals on proxies for the consideration of other shareholders. They achieve their ends through direct consultation. And if they feel that the management is unconstructive or unwilling to listen to their ideas, they sell—they divest themselves of their rights as shareholders—and look around for another investment niche for their money. They act strictly as investors handling other people's money. They do not assume the rôle of champions of stockholders' rights.[2]

Sometimes small stockholders are afflicted with attachment —loyalty—in their decisions to sell or not to sell. Maybe they have acquired stock through legacy. "My husband bought this stock. He had a reason for wanting me to have it." Or maybe the shareholder has held shares for many years and has the attitude: "The stock's treated me well, I'll stick by the company." American Telephone & Telegraph Company, which has come to be known as the "widows' and orphans' stock," has built up a huge following of loyal investors. And it has earned it—by its consistent earnings and dividend performance.

An emotional and unbusinesslike approach seldom hampers the large investor—the bank, the investment trust, the pension fund. To the institution, investment is cold, hard, and matter-of-fact. Is the company doing well? Is the management good? Is the industry prospering? If these criteria are satisfied, the stock is bought or retained. If not, it is sold.

All investors, once they tear themselves loose from emotions, apply similar criteria in sell-or-hold decisions. But the large stockholder is in a far better position to make a wise decision than the small stockholder. Investing is a full-time job for him or his agent. He has a staff which is constantly studying the merits of the individual companies and securities. Still further, the best investment brains among banks and brokerage firms are constantly at the service of the large security

[2] The attitude of the institutional investor is examined in Chapter XII.

holder—individual or institutional—seeking commissions and other business. If anything, the large stockholder is surfeited with counsel. He not only must make a choice of securities but a choice of advice on the securities.

The small investor, as observed in the second chapter, is a part-time investor at best. His income from securities, relative to total income, is small. His primary economic interest is in his job or profession. Reading annual reports or proxy notices is a chore. Communications from management go unopened.

Therefore, his rights as a shareholder tend to atrophy, to be unused. He is a victim of his own indifference and innocence. And he cannot count on the sophisticated investor to fight for him and his rights.

When it comes to controlling management, the interest of the great mass of small shareholders is at variance with that of the institutional investor who wants only "out" when things look bad. It was no accident that in the New York Central proxy fight investment trusts, insurance companies, pension funds, and other institutions held little stock. Central stock did not possess investment quality. The stock fell to a price low enough for Robert R. Young to buy up a large block of it and fight for control. The market place voted against Central as an investment stock. And in the subsequent proxy contest, the decisive votes were in the market place.

The sophisticated investor takes this view: "Life's too short. If something goes wrong with a company or a management, I'll sell. I'm not a reformer, a champion of stockholders' rights. There are plenty of stocks and companies and industries to choose from. Why tie up money and time in a managerial problem?"

And so it is that the market place, the price of stock, often is a polling place. If a stock persistently declines while other stocks in the same industry rise, then it is reasonable to conclude that the smart investors—the insiders—are getting out, unloading. Ultimately, the stock may get low enough for some self-serving knight in financial armor to buy it up and try to take over—a Robert R. Young, a Louis E. Wolfson. In serving himself, such a knight serves the stockholders who remained holding and holding and holding.

Thus, the market-place vote has power. It is a positive warning, a financial warning, to an incumbent management, of stockholder dissatisfaction. It lets the officers know that dissatisfaction has got beyond the discussion stage. The "big boys" are selling. So, the management might bestir itself—make changes—to strengthen the company's position. For that reason, selling stock is not an entirely empty gesture. True, the big investors do not fight for a change; they do not stay with the company that is retrogressing. But their leave-taking has an effect.

CHAPTER VII

Those C.D.'s—Corporate Democrats

In answer to the questions: Where does the term "corporate democracy" come from?, and Who first used it?, Lewis D. Gilbert, who now becomes a central character for two chapters, wrote:

"May I blush and admit to being the author of 'corporate democracy'? I have used it constantly in my speeches, lectures, and at meetings."

Since no one else has put forth this claim of fatherhood, Gilbert has a preëmptive right.

This can be safely said: The phrase has been in the making ever since Congress thrust on the Securities and Exchange Commission the responsibility of helping investors in financial clinches.

In 1943, Robert H. O'Brien, a member of the SEC, spoke of the need to "create an informed and active group of shareholders who have a voice in the councils of their own corporation." He talked about the "democratic process" in corporate affairs and the importance of good management-stockholder relations "in capitalism under democracy." Commissioner O'Brien was laying the groundwork for "corporate democracy," a term which was unknown in the 'twenties and has become, in the mid-'fifties, accepted terminology among watchful, militant stockholders. The *Weekly* of the University

68

of Virginia Law School has a 144-page compilation of "Dicta" devoted to phases of "corporate democracy." [1] Among the contributors were Louis Loss, former associate general counsel of the Securities and Exchange Commission, a law professor at Harvard, and author of the monumental *Securities Regulation;* W. H. Grimes, editor of the *Wall Street Journal;* Harry A. Bullis, then chairman of the board of General Mills, Inc.; Judge George Thomas Washington, of the U.S. Court of Appeals, District of Columbia, and co-author of *Compensating the Corporate Executive;* Benjamin Graham, founder of Graham-Newman Corporation, and author of many works on securities analysis and stockholder problems; Jackson Martindell, president of the American Institute of Management; Lewis D. Gilbert, himself, who has made a career of being a militant shareholder.

The phrase has gained status even though it is a legal solecism. Corporations are not democracies. They are plutocracies. Democracy implies individual equality—votes without distinction as to property. But in a corporation, each shareholder votes not as an individual, but in accord with his stake in the company. A holder of ten thousand shares has one hundred times the influence in electing directors as the holder of one hundred shares.

When it comes to dealing with officers and directors of corporations, the large shareholders—banks, insurance companies, investment trusts—often have a far greater influence than their proportionate stock ownership. They are listened to with great respect when they make suggestions or ask questions.

In such an anti-democratic environment, the phrase thrives. Fiction prevails over reality. At any meeting of the Securities and Exchange Commission involving stockholders' rights, it is certain to come up. Gilbert uses it frequently. So did the late

[1] Frank D. Emerson and Franklin C. Latcham use the term "shareholder democracy" and published a book in 1954 under that title.

Robert P. Vanderpoel, financial columnist of the *Chicago Sun-Times*; so does Wilma Soss, suffragette among American stockholders.

That being the case, what does it mean?

With her flair for attention-calling to herself, Mrs. Soss told the American Federation of Women Shareholders in Business, which she founded in her own image:

"We shareholders own the corporation. All these Prussian-faced directors are just our employees—laboring people, you might say. Naturally, we the owners have the right to give the hired help a few constructive suggestions from time to time and I am always astonished that they aren't more appreciative. . . ." Corporate democracy to Mrs. Soss is a constant battle of the shareholder with the management.

Mrs. Soss has been a professional press agent. And sometimes it seems as if her principal client were herself. Her goal in corporate affairs is to place a woman on the board of directors of every corporation. She insists that corporations would fare better with the women's point of view represented at the top. Naturally, she was delighted when Robert R. Young, in his fight for control of New York Central, nominated Lila Bell Acheson Wallace, co-editor and co-owner of *Reader's Digest*, as a candidate for director.

One common purpose binds the advocates of corporate democracy together. They seek recognition from management. They want to be listened to; they want to feel that they have some say in the companies they own. They do not accept the argument that the board of directors was elected by the stockholders; that it has a fiduciary responsibility to protect all stockholders' interests; that it acts at regular meetings to check up on management as the stockholders' agent.

The corporate democrat will argue that if managements and boards of directors are not required to account for their stewardship to the real owners, the shareholders, then the managements and the boards become self-satisfied and self-perpetuating cliques that treat the property and business as if they were proprietors. He will argue further that out of shareholder indifference grow laxity, nepotism, carelessness, self-dealing, double-dealing, and loose practices associated with handling other people's money. Therefore, the owners must be alert. They must supervise and question management.

And management, if it is conscientious and able, should be willing and anxious to accept these efforts of the real owners to know what gives. In short, corporate democracy requires coöperation—active coöperation—of the management so that the small shareholder can exercise a supervisory rôle.

More and more managements are becoming coöperative. Yet, most corporation officers and directors will insist that only a few shareholders are true corporate democrats. The other shareholders, which means ninety-nine out of a hundred, are content to receive reports, proxy statements and dividends. They do not want to be sidewalk superintendents. They feel that the officers of the company are best informed about the long- and short-term needs and problems of the company—for the obvious reason that the officers devote full time to running it.

This is accepted by the large shareholders such as banks and investment trusts. And because it is not accepted by the militant, vocal fractional minority, by the Gilberts and Sosses, this question arises: Is it reasonable for managements to be required to devote undue attention and solicitude to a small group, thus diverting energies from the main job of running the company and making money for stockholders?

Garrard W. Glenn, of the New York law firm of Lord, Day and Lord, points out that most stockholders are not concerned about corporate democracy, and are not worrying about what the management is doing, because they already have made up their minds. The stockholder, Glenn wrote in "Dicta," "first voted on the management and the policies of the corporation when he bought his stock or when he failed to sell it after it first came into his hands. He continues to vote in favor of the management during each year he continues to hold his stock. . . . If he were opposed to the management and its conduct of the affairs . . . he would have sold his stock since the last meeting of stockholders." This is the market-place concept of corporation democracy: the price of the stock renders a bloodless verdict on the performance of the management and the company.

But the market has no conscience. It is unmoral. It does not, by itself, impose ethical standards of conduct on corporations. A decline in price may prick the managerial pride but it does not necessarily disturb the managerial conscience. Only the direct exposure to the praise or blame, the applause or boos, of fellow men will accomplish that.

The militant shareholders—the Gilberts and the Sosses and their allies—have performed a useful service for all shareholders as stirrers-up and gadflies. Their vocalism and histrionics have transformed annual meetings from routine nobody-shows affairs to town meetings. A thousand stockholders and more are common nowadays at meetings of large companies, such as Pennsylvania Railroad, American Telephone & Telegraph, General Electric, and United States Steel, even though U.S. Steel holds its meetings in Hoboken, New Jersey, a town not easily reached.

Corporate directors may hold the proxies, the votes necessary to put through the corporate business at hand, but before such a large audience they face a different test. They must answer pertinent as well as impertinent questions with dignity and reasonableness. Displays of ignorance or arrogance might appear in the newspapers. Annual meetings once ignored by newspapers as routine now are covered as routine. News is where you go for it. A financial editor never knows when one of the gadflies or one of the officers will create news.

The prospect of televised meetings—American Machine & Foundry Company used a closed circuit television between two assemblages of shareholders, one in New York and one in Chicago, in 1957—only accentuates the importance of good executive comportment. Stockholders' meetings have become spectacles, of which alert corporation executives, especially those in consumer goods industries, are trying to take advantage by converting shareholders into customers and salesmen for the company's product. A temperamental executive might suggest a temperamental washing machine or vacuum cleaner!

But the corporate democrats are not always concerned with accountability, supervision, and watchfulness. Sometimes, like Stephen Leacock's Lord Ronald, they fling themselves upon their horses and ride "madly off in all directions." They confuse stockownership, in which the shareholder is one owner among many, with full proprietorship, in which the owner is also the manager or operator of a business.

Thus, some militant stockholder-democrats insist that they ought to receive discounts on company products. They feel a stockholder in Philco should be able to buy a television set at a reduced price; a GE stockholder should be able to purchase a refrigerator, or an electric stove, or—if you want to carry the argument to the extreme—a turbo-generator for a power plant, or a jet engine for a passenger airplane for less than regular price.

The argument goes like this: Department stores often grant employees discounts on company products; so do many manufacturers. This is good labor relations. It is designed to pay dividends to stockholders. If employees get discounts, why shouldn't stockholders, owners?

This is corporate throwbackism. The stockholder, who owns a tiny part of a company, is putting himself in the same position as the corporate owner of fifty years ago—when management and ownership were one and the same.

Then, it was perfectly all right for the owner to take things from the store for himself or his relatives and friends. He was giving away his own property. He was not depriving other co-owners of their rights. But, the manager of a large corporation is a trustee. He must not favor one shareholder at the expense of another. He must recognize that stockholders derive their benefits through dividends—not discounts.

In some circumstances, it is good business to offer discounts. Years ago, McGraw-Edison Company offered a new electric iron to stockholders at a special price. This was strictly a business decision—to test the iron. As a condition of purchase, stockholders were asked to report to the company on the iron's performance. The company thus got a *quid pro quo* for its discount. All shareholders, not just those who bought the iron, would be beneficiaries. If a discount to shareholders enables a management to make correct decisions, thereby enlarging profits, it is desirable. If discounts are granted as part of corporate democracy, then corporate democracy is being mocked and perverted.

Corporate democracy is sometimes a cloak for special pleading. For many years, the American Federation of Telephone Workers, which owned one share of stock in American Telephone & Telegraph Company, persistently petitioned shareholders to vote for increased pensions for employees, members of the union.[2] The union, as a stockholder, hoped to obtain through stockholders what it had not been able to obtain through collective bargaining. When Wilma Soss argues for women on boards of directors because a large proportion of shareholders are women, she is for women as women, not for

---

[2] This was done in proxy statements sent out by the company until the SEC decided this was not a proper subject for stockholder decision. Subsequently, the Federal Court in New York sustained the SEC.

women as shareholders.[3] By the same reasoning, you could demand children on the board, because many children own stock, or Presbyterians, or Democrats, or Republicans, or retired persons.

Oftentimes, stockholders introduce social concepts into corporate affairs as owner-democracy. Thus, a stockholder demanded that a company use its efforts to change the tax laws so as to eliminate double taxation of dividends. Another shareholder demanded that Greyhound buses do away with segregation. Now it so happens that Congress has reduced the impact of double taxation of dividends, and the Supreme Court has ordered an end to racial segregation. Nevertheless, the Securities and Exchange Commission, in applying its proxy rules, has felt that stockholders have no right to direct officers to fight for tax law changes or social improvements. Those are not, per se, business purposes.

In spite of the confusion that develops, the corporate democrat always comes back to one major objective. He wants representative management. He wants to feel that he has a responsive group of officers and directors. He wants the means to communicate with other shareholders. He is opposed to any policies or actions which make a management unapproachable and keep shareholders apart.

Wilma Soss has periodically asked the United States Steel Corporation to change its annual meeting place from Hoboken, New Jersey, to New York City. Why make shareholders take a ferry ride? she rightly asks. Yet, U.S. Steel, year after year, has refused to grant a request which seems entirely reasonable. The effect on shareholders who are sufficiently interested to attend meetings is imaginable. They wonder why the company is stubborn. Doesn't the management want

[3] Mrs. Soss says boards of directors need a woman's point of view. Yet, men have managed for many years to cater successfully to the wants of women—as merchants. The intelligent male cannot get away from the woman's point of view.

to meet as many shareholders as possible? Isn't it anxious to have shareholders attend meetings?

Accessibility of annual meeting places has become a rallying issue for corporate democrats. If managements have sales and executive offices in major financial centers, such as New York, Philadelphia, Chicago, or San Francisco, cities which are handy to officers and customers, why should they force shareholders to go to small, out-of-the-way localities such as Flemington, New Jersey (Republic Steel, American Tobacco); Watertown, New York (Woolworth); Wilmington, Delaware (Columbia Gas & Electric, Southern Pacific); Dover, Delaware (Cities Service, General Dynamics); Hoboken, New Jersey (U.S. Steel). Once upon a recent time, Southern Pacific held its meetings at Spring Station, Kentucky, a town known only to Wall Street for that reason. But Kentucky imposed a tax, and Southern Pacific fled to Wilmington, much to the annoyance of Gilbert, who argues that Los Angeles or San Francisco would be more sensible. On the West Coast, company officials would be able to court thousands of shareholders and shippers. That is the area it serves.

Corporate democracy may be defined as the shareholder's right to speak, congregate, communicate with other shareholders, and to know what is going on. To this end, corporate democrats will usually be found plumping for these ten points:

1. Unlimited freedom of speech at stockholder meetings.

2. Accessible meeting places so that attendance at meetings will not be kept down because of lack of convenient transportation.

3. Cumulative voting, which enables minority groups of shareholders to gain representation on boards of directors, by concentrating—cumulating—all votes on one or two candi-

dates. If, for example, nine directors are to be chosen, a share-holder can cast nine votes for one candidate or five votes for one candidate and four for another. Under straight voting he casts one vote for each of nine candidates, so the majority can completely freeze out the minority.[4]

4. Elimination of the stagger system for electing directors —for example, three directors one year, another three the following year, and another three the next year. The corporate democrat wants all directors elected each year. (*See* next chapter, pages 92-93.

5. The appointment of professional or public directors, who will represent a broader viewpoint on the board than the strictly management viewpoint. As a corollary, the corporate democrat opposes boards of directors consisting solely of company officials, such as, Bethlehem Steel, American Tobacco, Liggett & Myers, and Standard Oil of New Jersey. Standard Oil carries its policy of employee-directors so far that when a distinguished president retires, he resigns from the board. Example: Frank Abrams, and when he attends sharehold-

[4] In his *Cumulative Voting for Directors*, published by the Graduate School of Business Administration at Harvard, Charles M. Williams gives this example of a board of nine directors, in which one group of shareholders controls 5,100 shares, and an opposition group 4,900 shares. "If cumulative voting is authorized, each voting shareholder is entitled to votes equal to the number of his shares multiplied by the number of directors to be elected. . . . The group with 5,100 shares would be entitled to 45,900 votes and the [opposition] to 44,100 votes. By distributing its 44,100 votes among only four candidates, the minority could give . . . four men 11,025 [each.] No matter how the majority distributes its votes, it can elect no more than five directors since it cannot give [a] sixth man 11,025 votes."

In straight voting, the group controlling 5,100 shares, would be able to cast 5,100 votes for each of nine candidates, and thus elect the entire board.

Williams gives this formula for cumulating votes to elect a maximum number of directors:

$$X = \frac{Y \times N^1}{N + 1} + 1$$

X = Number of shares needed to elect a given number of directors;
Y = Total number of shares at meeting;
N^1 = Number of directors desired to elect;
N = Total number of directors to be elected.

ers' meetings he sits in the audience, like any other stock-holder, not at the executive table. The policy of inside direc-tors only leads to provincialism—inbreeding of ideas, so it is argued.

The counter-argument is that an outside director, no matter how discreet, might inadvertently disclose company ideas, methods, or policies that are best kept in the family; further, who is better suited to direct a company than those who know most about it, those who live and breathe it every day?

6. The naming by shareholders of independent auditors, who will be responsible to the shareholders, not the manage-ment.

7. Freedom of shareholders to nominate on proxy state-ments candidates for director other than those nominated by management. This sounds reasonable and feasible; actually, it is extremely hard to accomplish. If shareholders were to nominate directors freely, company proxy statements would become unreasonably long—especially since some biographical data about each candidate would be needed. In proxy fights, the opposition group sends out its own proxies.

8. Freedom and scope to originate proposals on proxy state-ments for other shareholders to vote on. This, to the corpo-rate democrat, is the heart, soul, and muscle of democracy. A stockholder at an annual meeting speaks to a few hundred shareholders and a pile of proxies. The proxies are the votes. Therefore, it is necessary, if stockholders are to have a voice in the affairs of the company, to communicate with share-holders before they send in their proxies. You reach your fellow owner through his eyes rather than his ears. (Chapter XV and Appendix III.)

9. Post-meeting reports. This is a demand fostered by Lewis D. Gilbert to have the corporation send an account of the meeting to all shareholders. The theory is that absentee

shareholders are entitled to know what goes on at the one meeting a year at which their word is legally final.

10. Management ownership of stock. If the officers and directors do not own stock, then presumably they do not have sufficient interest to run the company.

Corporate democrats have one common and, at times, unfortunate quality. They seem to believe in activity for activity's sake. It does not matter what you propose, or what questions you ask, or what you say—participate! The corporate democrat wants the shareholder to make his presence felt. Therefore, you will find stockholders repeatedly proposing the same ideas—discounts on company products, women on the boards, higher pensions for employees. And the proposals will win the support of the same group, regardless of the merit of the idea.

Lewis Gilbert, for example, will support Mrs. Soss on having women on a board of directors; he will praise a shareholder for wanting discounts; and he will back the Federation of Telephone Workers in its demand for stockholder support on the union's bargaining demands for higher pensions—even though higher pensions would come out of profits and hence affect American Telephone's capacity to maintain its $9 dividend.

At the General Electric meeting in 1956, Louis Brusati, another corporate vigilante, introduced a resolution requiring that compensation to executives be paid in cash in the year earned. This would make it impossible for executives to defer taxes or to receive stock options. Gilbert regarded the proposal as too drastic. "How and when the compensation is paid," said Gilbert, "should not be a concern of the public stockholder . . . as long as a ceiling is maintained." Nevertheless, Gilbert voted his stock for the Brusati proposal because "we thought the warning vote a good one for the management."

A corporate democrat must attract a following. He can get nowhere leading a void.

So, like a young politician, the ardent C.D. is apt to be indiscriminate in his expenditure of energy. And aims often seem conflicting. No better example of these conflicting aims is to be found than Gilbert, himself. He epitomizes what is both good and bad in the corporate democrat, and he will be discussed in the next chapter.

But this you cannot take away from him. He started out as a G.D. C.D. Now he is just a C.D., whose advice on stockholder relations is often sought by corporation executives. He is respected and respectable. Thus have Gilbert and persistence wrought.

CHAPTER VIII

The Care and Feeding of Stockholders

Lewis D. Gilbert has earned the title of America's No. 1 Militant Shareholder—partly by default, but mostly by perseverance and dedication. Stockholders are known for their indifference to everything about the companies they own except dividends and the approximate price of the stock. Not Gilbert. Sometimes he gives the impression that dividends are incidental, and straightening out the management—by Gilbert—is the purpose for which corporations and Gilbert exist.

In January, 1957, Gilbert, as he has done in many previous Januaries, published a list of 1957 annual meetings he, personally, would attend—health, weather, and transportation permitting. They numbered ninety-three. Attendance at such meetings, appearances before the Securities and Exchange Commission and the Senate and House Banking and Currency Committees, petitions to the Interstate Commerce Commission, and speeches at various colleges and forums on the rights of "public shareholders" comprise the task Gilbert sets for himself in behalf of shareholders.

He does not go it alone. His brother, John J., goes to meetings too. The 1957 list indicated that John would be the shareholders' voice at thirty-four meetings, and that John Campbell Henry, an associate in this business of minding management's P's and Q's, would be present at ten. Thus, the three would be present at 137 [1] meetings in all.

If Lewis Gilbert or his brother were extraordinarily large shareholders in any one company, or if the bulk of their assets were in two or three corporations, their attendance at annual meetings would be self-explanatory. But the Gilbert family fortune is spread among six hundred different companies. Holdings vary from ten shares of Decca Records to 324 shares of Union Carbide and 179 of Chase Manhattan Bank. Fortunately, Gilbert's wealth is sufficient to permit him to give unremunerated attention to corporations. It is inherited wealth. And the Gilberts take care of it by protecting stockholders.

The lower a stock's value, the more impressed is Lewis Gilbert with the company's need for his family's care. This fits Lewis Gilbert's investment method. He marries a common stock for better or for worse. If the company is faring poorly, Gilbert will not sell. He will fight to make it better. And if it is doing well, he will try to keep it doing well.

Each year Gilbert publishes a report of his activities—and the progress of what he calls the "independent shareholder" movement. His 1954 report, released early in 1955, was his fifteenth. In it, he dispenses praise and blame freely. As he puts it, "A drama critic goes to plays; I go to annual meetings."

Gilbert was pleased by the record turnouts at so many annual meetings in 1954. American Telephone & Telegraph would have to find larger quarters; the management of Loew's felt that the 1955 meeting might have to be held in Loew's State Theater; Tide Water Oil moved to an uptown hotel. And so on.

[1] In 1955, Lewis had ninety-six stockholders' meetings on his schedule, John J. thirty, and John Campbell Henry nine, or 135 in all. So this is a steady diet.

He continued to pan "lost corporations" which hold meetings away from stockholder centers but do not elude Gilbert —F. W. Woolworth & Company (Watertown, New York), Republic Steel (Flemington, New Jersey), U.S. Steel (Hoboken, New Jersey), Pepsi-Cola and Avco (Wilmington, Delaware), Servel and Coty (Dover, Delaware).

Of Servel, Gilbert commented: "No wonder its sales are so poor that it has difficulty in even meeting a preferred dividend payment if its salesmanship thinking is conditioned on meeting as few instead of as many potential customers as possible." Of Coty: "This is hardly the way to increase sales of perfume."

Gilbert listed as a triumph the transfer of the International Telephone and Telegraph meeting from Baltimore to New York. "Some 1,800 owners swarmed into the meeting room and met the officers," commented Gilbert, "although there was heady competition from the New York Central and Standard Oil of New Jersey meetings the same day." When meetings conflict Gilbert tries to get a change. One of his complaints against William White, former president of New York Central, was that he was unwilling to shift Central's traditional meeting day. But Robert R. Young, who beat White in the proxy contest, showed "keener insight into small stockholder thinking" by voting "his own large holdings in favor of the change."

He is enthusiastic because Bristol-Myers, American Airlines, International Minerals & Chemical Corporation, Wisconsin Power & Light hold regional meetings for stockholders. This was innovated by General Mills in 1939. He noted that "some 160 owners turned up for a Beatrice Foods meeting" in Hawaii and "participated in the question and answer period." Such a meeting somehow seems more like a tax-deductible vacation for shareholders and an expense-paid vacation for officers than a useful contribution to corporate understanding between management and shareholders. But Gilbert felt it afforded an opportunity for officers to meet shareholders—something that cannot happen too often, in his judgment—at a place where Beatrice has extensive operations, embracing a dairy farm and milk distribution.

To Gilbert, one test of an executive is how he presides at a meeting: "If he gets along with his shareholders, makes friends of them and shows he is flexible in his thinking, then we feel he does have the executive abilities his friends and public relations men like to say he has. If he is able to make quick decisions and to handle unexpected emergencies well, we know he can make rapid decisions in his day-to-day business planning.

"On the other hand, if he goes constantly out of his way to antagonize people, if he always says no to a stockholder suggestion, if he is afraid to give credit in an open meeting to those who make suggestions which worked out well, then we wonder just how much executive ability he really has."

John A. Hill, of Air Reduction, meets the Gilbert test. And C. R. Smith, of American Airlines, is "becoming a better executive in his handling of his meetings" because of the practice he gets at regional get-togethers. Similarly, Juan T. Trippe, president of Pan American Airways "enjoys" the sessions. But Eddie Rickenbacker can "never rise in stockholder esteem" so long as Eastern Air Lines meetings are held in Wilmington, Delaware. And Cleo F. Craig, former president of American Telephone & Telegraph, which has so successfully paid dividends for so many years to shareholders, did not assay pure gold in the Gilbert crucible when he refused to read letters from stockholders to the annual meeting.

For the benefit of stockholders who do not attend meetings, Gilbert expects managements to provide an account of proceedings—a "post-meeting report." His specifications are rigorous. There should be a summary of the management's statement. Then the report should print in full or summarize questions, answers, and discussion. The names of persons who ask questions should be given. Forehanded printers, therefore, will be supplied with the letters, t, r, e, b, l, i, and g. Gilbert also recommends pictures of the meeting. Corporations that take his advice will display the Lewis Gilbert physiognomy as often as movie magazines once showed the picture of John Gilbert (no relation) in his Hollywood heyday.

There's a strategy in Gilbert's method. The more often his name is mentioned and pictures appear, the more conscious will passive stockholders become of the efforts of the militant. That Bell & Howell, manufacturer of photographic equipment, does not have pictures in its post-meeting report is to Gilbert a source of absolute astonishment.

Forty-five companies get the Gilbert Oscar for the best post-meeting reports of 1954.[2] General Electric missed despite spending "a good deal of money," because the company omitted the name of a stockholder who protested the three-for-one stock split. In contrast, Lockheed Aircraft merited Gilbertian approbation because it published this dialogue between Chairman Robert E. Gross and a shareholder:

SHAREHOLDER: "I hope you don't get [a stock option]."

GROSS: "I don't think it is important whether I get it. I would just like to deserve it."

[2] Aeroquip, Air Reduction, Alleghany Corporation, American Encaustic Tiling, Angostura-Wuppermann, Atlas Corporation, Beatrice Foods, Bristol-Myers, Celanese, Chesapeake & Ohio, Columbian Carbon, Congoleum-Nairn, Consolidated Natural Gas, Continental Can, Eastern Industries, Fairchild Camera & Instrument, Fairchild Engine & Airplane, General Foods, General Refractories, General Stores, Lamson Corporation, Lockheed, Lorillard, Lukens Steel, Matson Lines, Maytag, Merritt-Chapman & Scott, New York Shipbuilding, Northeast Capital, Philadelphia Transportation Company, Pitney-Bowes, Radio Corporation, Royal Typewriter, St. Joseph Lead, Seattle Gas, Southern Railway, A. G. Spalding, Standard Oil (N. J.), L. S. Starrett, Todd Shipyards, Twentieth Century-Fox, United Fruit, Universal Pictures, Waitt & Bond, and F. W. Woolworth.

Gilbert's report offers counsel to executives on the proper conduct of meetings: Start promptly at 10:30 or 11:00 A.M., hear from the chief executive, have about an hour or so of questions and open discussion of resolutions, and about 1:00 P.M. have luncheon. This gives stockholders time for informal discussion of corporate affairs with officers. Gilbert is a firm believer in breaking bread with officials, but resents officers who use "A collation awaits" to cut short a meeting. And for food companies, he considers a collation an opportunity for dispensation of wares. Standard Brands Corporation is "backward"—the only food company to Gilbert's knowledge that does not serve its products at an annual meeting.

Gilbert gives the impression—not necessarily a true impression—that he can be taken in by forms, that he will accept good manners from management in lieu of satisfactory earnings and dividends. Certainly, Gilbert is attracted toward executives who are gracious in answering shareholder questions, who serve lunch, talk informally with him and other stockholders, and who make post-meeting reports and seek his suggestions.

Gilbert went all out in supporting Robert R. Young in the proxy battle for New York Central. Why? Young put a woman on his slate of directors; he promised to change the date of Central's annual meeting, so as not to conflict with those of International Telephone and Standard Oil (N. J.); he also said he would favor cumulative voting, and announced he was voting his own shares for cumulative voting at the Central meeting. But when the showdown came, the Central board unanimously voted against cumulative voting. Gilbert has since become disenchanted with Young, felt he conducted the 1957 annual meeting without grace or consideration.

Gilbert is a watchdog over executive compensation. He singled out du Pont, General Motors, and Bethlehem Steel for paying excessive executive compensation in 1953. Du Pont paid Crawford H. Greenewalt, president, $501,293, and more than $250,000 each to nine other officers. GM paid Harlow H. Curtice, president, $573,036, plus 1,050 shares with a cash value of $64,197, and six other officers received more than $350,000 each. At Bethlehem Steel, Eugene G. Grace, chairman, and Arthur B. Homer, president, received $456,654 and $375,544 respectively. Other winners of wrath were Spyros P. Skouras, Twentieth Century-Fox, $247,660; Edward H. Little, Colgate-Palmolive, $325,779; K. C. Towe, American Cyanamid, $326,900.

"What a good contrast it is," wrote Gilbert, "to pick up the proxy statement of an equally successful and profitable corporation, Scott Paper, and find that President Thomas B. McCabe [3] actually serves without any remuneration whatsoever! Or that of Merritt-Chapman & Scott, where we find that Chairman-President Louis E. Wolfson waives any bonus payments and keeps his salary to a comparatively nominal $37,552.

"We do not expect every corporation top executive to be in the financial position of these individuals, able to serve the interests of their fellow owners with nominal or no recompense, but we have the right to ask that those who preach the doctrine of free enterprise show a little moderation when it comes to bonus payments and incentive compensation. The lion's share of such bonus payments should be for junior executives."

Gilbert is wont to refer to corporation executives as "hired hands," responsible to shareholders. Yet, if chief executives forego salaries or have incomes which render them independent of their income from corporations, they are hardly hired

[3] McCabe, who served the government with distinction during World War II and later as President Truman's surprise nominee for chairman of the Federal Reserve Board to replace Marriner S. Eccles, did not accept a salary from Scott Paper when he was in government service. After he returned to the company, he did not want to be tied down to a full-salaried basis. He wanted to be free for extracurricular activities. McCabe has a substantial stock ownership in Scott.

87

hands. Then they do not have to be responsible to the owners. They will not be economically destitute if thrown out of their jobs. Gratuitous service to a corporation—to the stockholders—is out of place in a profit-and-loss society. Stockholders should be more inclined to be suspicious of free-for-nothing hours than grateful. But uncompensated work fits into the Gilbert complex. After all, he is working free for all shareholders!

Gilbert's four main points on compensation are:

1. That cash compensation, salary and bonuses, ought to be reasonable—he sets a limit of $200,000 a year. Reason: The tax on incomes above $200,000 is so prohibitive that it is better for the corporation to have the money than the executive. (However, large salaries offer emoluments beyond mere spendable income. The executive can dispense large sums to charity. He can set up his own charitable foundation. He can assume capital gains risks—make investments which can be chargeable against income. Digging for oil is a case in point. Furthermore, pension and profit-sharing plans are usually based on salaries; hence, the higher the salary the greater will be the ultimate non-salary benefits to the executive.)

2. That bonus plans should have limitations—ceilings—and be correlated with stockholder income. Thus, the management of Celanese Corporation agreed to a stockholder-proposed amendment to its bonus plan providing that no bonus payments would be made to executives in any year in which dividends amounting to $1 a share are not paid. The company's dividend, $1.25 at the time, has since dropped to half that. So the limitation has been effective. David Sarnoff, chairman of RCA, agreed to submit the company's bonus plan to shareholders every five years, though he opposed a limitation. Still, this was a victory for Gilbert. Congoleum-Nairn also put a limit on its incentive plan. The bonus would not

amount to more than 100 per cent of an executive's salary, and aggregate compensation would have a $200,000 ceiling. Similarly, Lockheed Aircraft's incentive plan limits extra pay to 50 per cent of base salary.

3. That ceilings be put on pensions. Gilbert mustered 5,024 proxies (434,365 shares) against the du Pont proposal to raise its pension ceiling above $25,000. But the management had an overwhelming majority in favor—81,426 proxies and 37,898,563 shares. (This total would include the vast du Pont family holdings.)

At American Telephone & Telegraph, Gilbert also carries on an annual campaign for pension ceilings, pointing out that Walter Gifford, former president, receives an annual remittance of $91,000. Companies with ceilings include National Dairy Products Corporation, $30,000, raised in 1954 from $25,000, and American Encaustic Tiling, $25,000. U.S. Pipe & Foundry introduced a $35,000 ceiling into its plan. Commented Gilbert: "While this may be a few thousands higher than we would have fixed, the far more important principle of a ceiling is recognized." Gilbert does not insist on the last tithe.

4. That stock option plans be used sparingly, if at all. Gilbert argues that stock options dilute shareholder equity, that they are exercised only when the stock has appreciated in value, and that if they are granted, the optionees should be required to hold the stock for at least three years after acquisition. The optionee should be a bona fide investor, not a capital gains grabber. Gilbert quotes a letter he received: "If management does well they say it is their superior genius, but if they fail to produce it is simply economic conditions beyond their control."

Furthermore, Gilbert is a firm believer in management ownership of stock. He is wholeheartedly in favor of the proposal of Louis E. Wolfson, who has ruled publicly that officers who have been employed for two years by companies he controls must purchase stock equal to a year's salary. Explained Wolfson:

"None of these stock purchases will be made under any stock option purchase plan. I do not believe it is necessary to give corporate officers or directors any advantage over other investors. The men with the companies with which I am connected buy at the prevailing market price—without discount —without concession—without favor."

Whether this is a good policy, whether an employer should dictate how an employee should invest his own money, is subject to debate. And to put a year's salary into a company constitutes an extremely large sum for many executives. It could constitute 50 per cent or even more of their assets. The effect is to force a person to put too many eggs in one basket. Not only is he dependent on the company for dividends but also for his salary. This is particularly so when he borrows money to pay for his stock. The executive becomes dependent on Wolfson. He owes his job to him. He owes money on the stock. And he has all his eggs in Wolfson's basket. Thus Wolfson builds a coterie of vassals—yes-men. Is this a device to enable Wolfson to keep control of companies he has acquired? The men beholden to him for their jobs presumably would be on Wolfson's side in a proxy battle.

Of course, if Wolfson were ever to have a falling out with the officers, then he has established beforehand a group which has a stake in fighting him for control. This might lead Wolfson to hesitate to use his power as chief executive officer to fire inefficient officers who hold large amounts of stock. So, a program of executive stockownership is not unfailingly in the stockholders' interest. Circumstances alter cases. Suppose a dunderhead executive has bought a great deal of stock and the stock is down in price. Can you fire him—just like that? Or do you have to keep him on out of pity?

In any case, Wolfson is being paternalistic. He might quite properly look askance at officials who never acquire stock. But dictating that the officers must own stock equivalent to a year's salary is the old-time yellow-dog labor contract in reverse. The yellow-dog contract forbade a worker to join a union. In a Wolfson company, stockownership becomes the officer's union card.

Stockownership is a matter of judgment, not loyalty. Executives often acquire shares when they are optimistic about business, about the operations of the company. But they might decide at other times to sell their shares—because business generally was heading downward or because they felt the company's sales and profits were likely to decline. Those are strictly investment decisions. Stockownership is not a measure of industriousness or loyalty. As I see it, it is better to have a smart executive who gauges business prospects shrewdly and adjusts the company's operations and his own investments accordingly than a loyal lump who holds on to his stock regardless of economic tendencies.

After all, an executive job offers its enticements: membership in swank clubs; esteem in the community; a good salary, often with fringe benefits such as stock options, liberal pension plans, bonuses; an ample expense account; and opportunities for the family. People just "naturally" want to do things for an executive because of his power to do things for them. The son or daughter of a corporation president will be given serious consideration by the admissions officer of leading colleges. Grades are important, of course—but so are endowments.

Besides, an executive—if he is an executive—is a competitor. He wants to make a success of his business. It is part of the game. His personal prestige is at stake—in making good on the job and in holding on to it. So, it is reasonable to assume he will work equally hard—whether he has an investment stake or not. He has an important financial stake—his income —and a social stake—recognition by his peers in the business community.

When Gilbert attends an annual meeting you can expect him to bring up other items. At the 1953 meeting of Remington Rand, he chided General Douglas MacArthur, chairman, for not being a shareholder. MacArthur remarked that what he did with his money was his business, not Gilbert's. But the 1954 proxy statement showed that the General had acquired eight hundred shares. A triumph for Gilbert's insistence that directors own stock! General Lucius D. Clay, chairman of Continental Can, also hearkened to Gilbert's suggestion that as a director of Marine Midland Corporation, New York State bank holding company, he ought to own stock. Clay acquired one hundred shares and Gilbert's fealty. In his 1954 report, Gilbert, who never permits a mixed metaphor to limit his enthusiasm, said: "Every time a problem in stockholder relations has been presented to General Clay he has picked up the ball and led the company forward. Which is a far cry from the days when this company [Continental Can] met in Millbrook, Dutchess County, N. Y., where stockholders found only one train a day to get there!"

Gilbert considers it both proper for and incumbent upon officers and directors of corporations to be present at all annual meetings to "meet their constituents and learn first hand what other segments of ownership are thinking." He constantly adjures managements to adopt cumulative voting in states where it is not mandatory.

He protests staggered elections of directors, say one third each year for three years. This enables a "defeated" management to retain office. It takes two or more elections to get control of the board of directors. Staggered elections water down cumulative voting. Louis Wolfson, in his fight for control of Montgomery Ward & Company, won a dramatic victory in getting the Illinois Supreme Court to declare Ward's stagger system unconstitutional. But in Pennsylvania, the Supreme Court ruled that staggered election of directors was entirely consistent with the commonwealth's cumulative voting provision in the constitution.[4]

Gilbert argues for independent auditors, who report to shareholders rather than directors and officers. And he insists that stockholders be given preëmptive rights to subscribe to new shares of stock. Ownership or control cannot be sold en

---

[4] The Pennsylvania decision was handed down by Chief Justice Horace Stern on an appeal from a lower court which upheld the Philadelphia Transportation Company's system of electing eight directors every other year instead of sixteen each year. The Pennsylvania Railroad, Curtis Publishing, and other corporations tendered briefs and took part in the argument in support of the PTC as friends of the court.

Joseph N. Janney, a PTC shareholder, contended that the staggered election violated the Pennsylvania constitution by impairing the cumulative voting power of minority shareholders. Instead of needing a little less than 6 per cent of the vote to elect one director, under the PTC eight-a-year plan, they'd need over 11 per cent.

"Plaintiff relies in great measure," ruled Justice Stern, "on the decision of the Supreme Court of Illinois in Wolfson *vs* Avery. . . ." That case, he noted, turned on the phrase in the Illinois constitution that each stockholder should have the right to "as many votes as the number of directors." If there are nine directors, the stockholder is entitled to nine votes for each share.

But the Pennsylvania constitution says: "In all elections for directors or managers of a corporation each member or shareholder may cast the whole number of his votes for one candidate or distribute them upon two or more candidates, as he may prefer." The word "candidate" contrasts with the phrase "number of directors."

Justice Stern emphasized that the right to cumulate votes does not require the courts to guarantee a "maximum effectiveness to obtain minority representation on a board of directors." He observed that corporations can dilute the power of cumulative voting by having small boards, electing directors infrequently, or issuing non-voting stock. If the law permits such devices, then clearly cumulative voting is not a transcendent right, but merely one right among many.

To professional defenders of "corporate democracy" and cumulative voting, Justice Stern's decision was a setback. It put the Illinois decision in a provincial perspective. Each state's constitution or laws individualize—make specific—covenants covering cumulative voting. Hence, an Illinois or Pennsylvania decision is unlikely to set a national precedent.

93

bloc if shareholders have first call on Treasury or newly issued stock. Suppose a company has 500,000 shares outstanding; if it needed money and were to sell 500,001 additional shares all to one person, control would be transferred. Stockholders would have no say about the shift. Under the preëmptive rights rule, which grants shareholders the privileges of subscribing to new common stock or preferred stock or bonds convertible into stock, each stockholder would be entitled to buy an amount of the new issue in exact proportion to his holdings in the company.

Finally, he demands of management the right to use their proxy forms to communicate his resolutions on cumulative voting, pensions, or other matters. At annual meetings, a vocal stockholder, a Gilbert, can address only a tiny fraction of the owners. In the proxy statement, you reach shareholders before they vote. (*See* Chapter XV on proxy rules.)

Gilbert's operations—his demands—can be compartmentalized.

First, he wants the legal rights of shareholders preserved— so as to strengthen shareholders in dealing with management. He does not want the powers of shareholders whittled away. Thus, his insistence on cumulative voting and on preëmptive rights.

Second, he demands direct accountability of management to shareholders. Hence, his insistence on the legal formality that auditors report to the shareholders, not the management; he wants adequate post-meeting reports to supplement annual reports, so that stockholders know what goes on at meetings as well as what goes on financially and economically.

Third, he wants the officers and directors to manifest faith and devotion through stockownership.

Finally, he introduces moral sanctions: by examining what corporation officers pay themselves; and when the pay seems too high, he protests. Indeed, Congress introduced a subtle sanction in requiring the disclosure of remuneration of officers and directors of larger corporations.[5] Such disclosure is a conscience. Corporation executives know that their "take" is open to inspection and may be published in newspapers and be compared with the "take" of other executives. But such disclosure is silent.

Gilbert is not silent. At annual meetings he forces management to explain—to justify—to a jury of owners what it, the management, pays itself. Answering questions—even not answering—forces a corporation president to examine his remuneration by the world's standards rather than subjective standards. The executive must say to himself: How does this look to others? This had not happened before the Securities and Exchange Act. And it never had so vocal a public proclaimer before Gilbert.[6]

In the days before Gilbert and *The Solid Gold Cadillac,* large corporations often got through shareholders' meetings in three to five minutes. The president or chairman of the board would call the meeting to order. The secretary of the company would announce that the proxies present constituted a quorum for transacting business. The company's lawyer would move to dispense with the reading of the minutes. There might be a motion to approve the actions of the board of directors during the past year. The president would then offer the annual report of the company to be included in the minutes. A motion would be made to elect new directors. It would be seconded and passed—the stacked proxies being

[5] Companies whose stock is registered on a national stock exchange, such as the New York Stock Exchange, the American Stock Exchange, the Midwest Stock Exchange, are required to file annual 10-K reports with the Securities and Exchange Commission and reveal (1) salaries of the three highest paid officials and (2) total remuneration of all officers; also companies which have registered with the SEC securities valued at $2,000,000 or more must also file 10-K reports. In addition, listed companies must include data on major salaries in proxy statements to shareholders.

[6] Professor William Z. Ripley alerted the social conscience largely through his writings and as a teacher. Gilbert goes directly to shareholders.

more than sufficient. Thereupon, a motion to adjourn would be made, seconded and carried. Possibly no more than three or four persons—the president, the secretary, the lawyer, and one of the proxies—would be present.

Gilbert has made stockholders' meetings theatrical events. Stockholders go there for the fun, for the argument that might develop, or for the exchange of courtesies and compliments between Gilbert and the chairman, depending on their relationship.

To appraise Gilbert is not easy. When he started making his rounds of corporation annual meetings in 1933, he was resented as a speechmaking interloper, a waster of expensive executive time, a limelight-seeker. And he was thoroughly and abashedly naïve, as he himself told John Bainbridge, of the *New Yorker* magazine:

"I had inherited some common stocks, including a few shares of Consolidated Edison, and I thought I'd like to see what the company was like. I'd never attended a stockholders' meeting, so I expected to be welcomed cordially and to be treated like one of the owners. You can see how naïve I was. The meeting was a disgrace. After the chairman had wasted an hour reading the annual report,[7] which, of course had already been mailed to stockholders days before, I got up to ask a question, but before I had a chance to say anything, one of the officers sitting in the back of the room made a motion to adjourn. It was seconded and passed in no time. I was still standing there when the chairman said, 'And now a delightful collation awaits you in the adjoining dining room,' and everybody went for a free lunch. There I was, a part owner—I held ten shares—and I had been treated like a tramp by these people who were my employees. I was horrified."

[7] A rite often dispensed with; the New York Stock Exchange's listing rules require that annual reports to shareholders be mailed fifteen days before the annual meeting.

Thus began Gilbert's career as America's No. 1 Independent Shareholder.

Today at an annual meeting Lewis Gilbert is the icing on the cake, the champagne at the coming-out party, the éclat. If he is not there it is like a show that missed Broadway. Gilbert is likely to be pointed out—"There's Gilbert"—by fellow stockholders as frequently as the president or chairman of the board. Corporation executives no longer try to freeze him into a sitting posture with a stern look. Gilbert's persistence has won a following. When he supports a resolution, he can muster a fair-sized number of votes. He gets proxies tendered him. And he enlivens a stockholders' meeting.

Robert E. Bedingfield, able financial reporter of the *New York Times*, has referred to Gilbert and his brother, John, as "those experienced foes of serenity." Since the Gilberts are unshushable, many managements have found it useful to caress them with kindness, give them time for asking questions and airing their views.[8]

Gilbert is not averse to obstructionism. On March 28, 1955, after numerous frustrations, stockholders of the giant Chase National Bank were happily meeting to approve a merger with the Bank of Manhattan Company. But not Gilbert. The Chase had cumulative voting; the Manhattan did not. And since in this case the smaller bank, the Manhattan, was absorbing the larger bank, the Chase, stockholders might lose their cumulative voting rights under the Manhattan charter. Gilbert asked John J. McCloy, Chase chairman, to promise

[8] But not Robert R. Young, whom Gilbert so ardently supported in the New York Central proxy fight. Now Gilbert feels bilked that Young has not supported cumulative voting, and at the annual meeting on May 23, 1957, he brought the matter up numerous times. Finally, Thomas E. Dewey, former Governor of New York State and twice Republican candidate for President, who was acting as special counsel for Young at the meeting, said inelegantly to Gilbert, "Why the hell don't you shut up?" Applause from the audience, but disapprobation from Gilbert for unstatesmanlike and undemocratic behavior.

that the new Chase Manhattan Bank would have cumulative voting. McCloy said he could not promise; he was not sure of the legality under the Manhattan charter. Gilbert felt that was not enough. He moved to adjourn the meeting. McCloy ruled the motion out of order as "delaying and dilatory."

To the shareholders present, who were overwhelmingly in favor of the merger, Gilbert was a meddler. Most of them had never heard of cumulative voting rights. Not to have cumulative voting was not a deprivation. Gilbert was asking them to postpone something tangible, a profitable merger, for a legalistic trifle. But, to Gilbert, this was a precious basic right. He was looking to eternity, safeguarding Chase Manhattan shareholders forever and ever. Chase shareholders were interested in the now, the merger, and accordingly voted against delay. To them, Gilbert was obstreperous, frivolous.

Unquestionably, Gilbert has focused attention of some stockholders on their rights. And he has made corporation managements conscious of stockholders as stockholders. At meetings, amenities are emphasized. And officers are aware that annual reports and officers' salaries will be publicly analyzed if a Gilbert or a Gilbert ally attends a meeting. Some company officials solicit Gilbert's advice on what he, as a public shareholder, considers proper safeguards for shareholders, especially if pension or bonus plans are under consideration. This may be partly to forestall open conflict at a shareholders' meeting, which would make newspaper headlines and perhaps focus attention on something the executive would prefer to have pass unnoticed. It is possible that blandishments get executives somewhere in their dealings with Gilbert. After all, if you consult somebody beforehand and modify a plan or proposal to meet his likes and dislikes, you have gained an ally instead of an enemy. This is not so much a criticism of Gilbert—who, after all, gets his point across if an executive puts a ceiling on a pension plan or changes a stock option or bonus program—as a compliment to executives who have learned to handle a situation. (And Gilbert is a situation!)

Civilities, of course, do not produce dividends—and stockholders, as investors, are interested in dividends in the long run. Gilbert's contribution to managerial improvement is certainly contestable. He has improved stockholder interest in corporate affairs in the sense that more stockholders are interested in attending annual meetings and getting post-meeting reports than ten or twenty years ago. Still, most of the 8,600,000 shareholders are busier with their own careers than with the affairs of corporations in which they have investments.

Gilbert has managed to make some shareholders conscious of what management is doing and many managements conscious of Gilbert. And to the extent that disclosure manacles greed and piracy, Gilbert has had a modest effect on the affairs of corporations. But in the total impact on affairs of corporations, it is doubtful that Gilbert has had as much effect as, say one large investment trust which makes its ideas and interests known to managements in which it has investments. Gilbert's power is not commensurate with his energy, because he is trying to lead an army that prefers dividends and quiet to contumely in defense of rights they do not care about.

CHAPTER IX

Stockholder Relations in Capital Letters

A CORPORATION is not a lonely hearts society. The president and other top officers are not chosen for their ability to entertain shareholders. They have risen to five- and six-digit salaries and comforting fringe benefits because they have demonstrated a capacity to make money.

Whether by accident, experience, or systematic evaluation, top men in any corporation are likely to allocate their time and energies to:

1. Customers and prospective customers
2. Products, including research
3. Workers—good industrial relations
4. Suppliers—especially in a seller's market, when materials are scarce
5. Communities—being a good corporate citizen and neighbor

Finally come stockholders. The executive works for them, but only a small part of his energy goes directly to them.

This does not conform to the myth of "shareholder democracy," in which the shareholder is the boss, the officers his hirelings.

It does not fit the literature that corporations, themselves see fit to disseminate. Thus, the Pacific Gas & Electric Company sends a letter to a former shareholder, saying: "We regret that you have ceased to be a partner in this enterprise." The word, "partner," is a euphemism. More correct and straightforward would be: "We regret you have ceased to be an investor in this enterprise." But it is part of the tendency to cultivate shareholders—past, present, and future. It comes under the broad heading: "Stockholder relations."

Good managements look ahead. When dividends are highest and prospects brightest, trouble may be just around the corner. Trouble to a corporation executive is reduced sales, earnings, and dividends. At that stage, good stockholder relations can be an asset.

The stock will be low, making large-scale accumulation possible. And stockholders will be disgruntled, and, therefore, susceptible to promises. This would be the time for a Wolfson, Young, or Silberstein to launch a fight for control. Stockholder loyalty to the management would become critical.

The New York Central Railroad fight is illustrative. New York Central had not neglected its shareholders. But it had not cultivated shareholders either. Neither William White, who lost to Young, nor Gustav Metzman, his predecessor, was particularly interested in shareholders. They were railroad men, executives, not politicians. Neither was hail-fellow-well-met, anxious to turn a Central shareholder meeting into a great big party of common owners of a business, nor interested in writing letters to shareholders. To them, the annual meeting was a chore—something to be handled with dispatch.

The company did make some concessions to shareholders. Under the prodding of Wilma Soss, it arranged for a special train to take shareholders from New York to the annual meeting in Albany at a special rate. On the train was a "question car," which stockholders could visit to talk to officers. But the question car was for efficiency, not camaraderie. It utilized the two hours and forty-five minutes en route. If stockholders got hurt feelings off their chests in a private car, that would be less time consumed at the annual meeting. Also, the meeting would go off more smoothly.

Central did not send out letters welcoming new shareholders, as many companies did. It did not send out "regret" letters when stockholders sold stock. But it departed from a stodgy annual report. And shareholders were mailed copies of the company magazine and asked if they would like to receive it regularly. And thirty per cent said yes. So the Central was far from standoffish or indifferent to stockholders.

But, to many shareholders, the Central management was just what the word "management" implies—a group of faceless men running the railroad, reporting earnings annually, and meeting a few stockholders at the annual meeting. No quarterly summary of operations went to shareholders. Once in a while an enclosure would go out with the dividends. But dividends were erratic.

You cannot say that poor, inadequate, or impersonal stockholder relations were decisive in the Central proxy fight. Stockholders, in the final analysis, vote for the man they think will be able to pay the larger dividends. In this instance, Young promised a dividend of $7 to $10. White, much more literal-minded, would not promise what he could not foresee. Nor could he persuade shareholders, as he believed, that Young was tall-talking them.[1]

What if White, in his two years as president, had assiduously cultivated shareholders, had taken them into his confidence, letting them know in periodic letters, in regular quarterly reports, what the railroad's trials and troubles were— how passenger operations were losing money, how the railroad was trying to cut costs and increase revenues?

[1] Two years later, at the 1957 annual meeting of Central, Young repeated his promise with an escape clause: "Unless this country is crazy and turns its transportation system over to the highways and airways, the Central is going to be paying again an $8 a share dividend."

Would stockholders have had a kindlier personal feeling toward him—because he had become a personality to them? Would they have been more understanding of his problems? And would they, therefore, have listened much more sympathetically to what he said—on television, in his letters, and in press interviews during the proxy campaign? Would they have believed him rather than Young?

A proxy campaign is one man's word, one man's assertions, against another's. Young made the bolder claims. His promises paid off. White was not able to tear down those claims and establish his more modest promises as the more sensible and attainable. He entered the fight an unknown.

Young, with his great flair for public relations—his claims for the lightweight car, "Train X," he called it, thereby investing it with mystery; his espousal of competitive bidding for railroad bonds instead of private sales to preferred bankers, such as Kuhn, Loeb & Company, Morgan Stanley, or First Boston Corporation; his development of through coast-to-coast passenger trains (A Hog Can Cross the Country Without Changing Trains—But YOU Can't.)[2]—was the man most stockholders knew. And in a political campaign, which a proxy campaign is, being known is half the battle.

Essentially, White did not win because Central's dividend policy was erratic. Young played on stockholder dissatisfaction, particularly the dissatisfaction of speculative holders.

Furthermore, if getting ready for a proxy fight were the sole purpose of stockholder relations, most managements would not bother. Proxy fights are too remote as contingencies.

But good relations with shareholders are useful in two other ways:

[2] But every thirty-six hours the hogs have to be fed, watered, and rested, according to Interstate Commerce Commission regulations. So a layover is enforced in long journeys. Cattle must be taken out of the cars for feeding and watering.

1. If the company sells consumer goods and wants its share-holders to be customers and boosters.

2. If it wants to raise capital—new money.

All companies have relations with shareholders when they send out dividend checks, annual reports, and requests for proxies. Doing these tasks with finesse, flourish, and schmaltz makes Stockholder Relations in capital letters.

General Electric Company converts stockholder relations into "public relations." GE sells refrigerators, washing machines, coffee makers, television sets, electric stoves, oil burners, as well as heavy equipment for power plants. And 375,000 shareholders are worth cultivating. They are upper-income people; therefore, likely customers for GE household products. Hence, they are molders of consumer attitudes. They will influence others.

Suppose you have just bought a share of GE stock. Shortly, you will receive a letter, signed by the president, welcoming you "on becoming a share owner." The letter says that the company "attempts to keep its share owners not merely fully informed, but informed in a way that you will find stimulating and interesting."

Then the newcomer is told that the annual meeting, held in Schenectady, New York, the third Tuesday in April, affords an "opportunity" to gain first-hand impressions of the company in operation. If you cannot come, the letter says, a report of the meeting will be sent you. Stockholders also receive the annual report, and, with each dividend check, a special Share Owners Quarterly.

The next-to-last paragraph of the welcome letter expresses the hope that "you will come to feel that you are indeed a member of the General Electric family, conversant with its problems, proud of its contributions to our national economy, a user and advocate of its products." In his concluding paragraph, Ralph J. Cordiner, president, asks stockholders to send comments, suggestions, or inquiries "directly to me."

A month before the annual meeting a letter addressed "Dear Fellow Shareholder" goes out over the president's signature: "Once again I am pleased to invite you to our annual meeting." Quite a contrast with the letter sent out by Pittsburgh Plate Glass Company in 1955, addressed "To the Shareholders," and reading:

"If you do not plan to attend the annual meeting, please sign the enclosed proxy and return it promptly. A copy of our annual report has been mailed you," etc., etc. Sounds as if the company would just as lief have the shareholder absent.

GE encloses a reservation form for shareholders planning to attend the meeting, and waits till the last paragraph to ask the stockholder for his proxy, "if circumstances make it impossible for you to be present." To stockholders who say they are coming, GE sends advice on where to register, where busses will meet them, time of the business meeting, time of plant tours, time of lunch, where to park. . . . So the shareholder will not feel like a lost, lone freshman just arriving on a college campus for the first time.

When a shareholder registers for the meeting, he is handed a program—which gives him the schedule for the day. For the 1955 meeting, thought to be the largest ever held anywhere up to that time, 3,284 shareholders registered—more than could be comfortably accommodated at the Armory. Some shareholders, therefore, watched proceedings over closed-circuit television from a theater. The tours included seeing the plants, attending a magic show, at which General Electric scientific wizardry was unfolded, and, of course, seeing displays of GE products, including, for the benefit of women shareholders, an electric kitchen.

The schedule of the meeting was as follows:

8:00 A.M.	Registration at Radio Station WGY, from which busses leave for tours and exhibits
10:00 A.M.	Morning tours completed
10:30 A.M.	Annual meeting begins
1:00 P.M.	Box lunches served in seats at meeting
1:45 P.M.	Afternoon tours begin—buses leave from meeting area
3:00 P.M.	Tours completed

Here is careful attention to detail. The annual report is in keeping with this—full of charts, pictures. An attempt, if not entirely successful, is made to entice shareholders to read it. (For my taste, it is just a little too busy and magazine-like. I still think an annual report is a business document, not an inferior version of *The Saturday Evening Post*.)

A post-meeting report completes General Electric's stockholder-relations routine. The cover shows (1) a massive picture of the meeting, chock-full of shareholders, (2) President Cordiner chatting informally (there is always an informal picture) with one of the company's shareholders, (3) a view of a GE kitchen.

Inside, the report emphasizes that all sixteen directors were present. Criticisms of the company's stock option plan by a stockholder, Mr. Louis Brusati, were noted. Brusati's full name, address, and shareholdings were not given—an omission deplored by Lewis Gilbert, as previously noted. The president's address was printed in full. Discussion from the floor is summarized. Throughout were numerous photographs: a baby shareholder; shareholders eating their box lunches; Philip D. Reed, chairman, chatting with an elderly shareholder; shareholders looking over GE designs and products.

Intended effect: One big happy family sharing in a successful, friendly enterprise. A shareholder who attended such a meeting would turn against the management in a proxy fight only under great provocation—scandal or abysmally poor profits for several years. You also get the feeling that stockholders who read the reports regularly would become a part of the company by proxy. Thus, GE does it up brown.

The Scott Paper Company follows a like procedure—with this addition: It mails a package of its products—Scotkins (napkins), Cutrite wax paper, Scotties (facial tissues), kitchen towels with holder, bathroom towels, and three types of toilet paper—Waldorf, Scott, and Soft Weve—to new shareholders. With good results, as evidenced by this letter to Thomas B. McCabe, president:

"I wish to thank the Scott Paper Co. for the gift of various products, most of all, for the very friendly gesture on the part of a big corporation with even the smaller share buyers. Since I bought my few shares, my friends and co-workers now buy all Scott products."

Surveys by A. Weston Smith for the *Financial World* trace the growth of loving care of corporations for shareholders back to 1951. In that year, only 12 per cent of one thousand large corporations whom Smith questionnaired sent special invitations to shareholders to attend annual meetings. The proportion was 19 per cent in 1954, and 29 per cent in 1956.

The feeding of shareholders has also boomed, but not without its liabilities. James M. Symes, personable chairman of the Pennsylvania Railroad, lost a large part of his audience at the new Sheraton Hotel in Philadelphia when he announced that a lunch would be served in a near-by room immediately after the meeting. The shareholders believed in the breadline adage: First come, first served. At a Chesapeake & Ohio Railway meeting, according to the *Wall Street Journal*, "80% of the 3,000 shareholders present stampeded" for a box lunch and a two-hour free boat ride ten minutes before adjournment. Duplan Corporation, which shortly after the war feted shareholders with large profits and banquets, has eliminated the banquets as non-empathetic with low profits of the 'fifties. And Stix-Baer & Fuller, St. Louis department store, dispensed with coffee and sweet rolls after some stockholders grumbled about the unnecessary expense. Feeding shareholders arched from 5 per cent of total meetings in 1951, to 17 per cent in 1955, and then down to 14 per cent in 1956.

Some stockholders attend meetings with tote bags as evidence of their deep proprietary interest. They take the meeting home with them in the form of sandwiches, *petits fours*, and other memorabilia, just like citizens at a National Park or on a battleship. They own the place, don't they? Colgate-Palmolive customarily distributes samples to shareholders as a sales promotion, but the ownership instinct was so deep that the company's wall display of its products was vandalized like wild flowers by picnic-goers. At an International Telephone & Telegraph meeting, a hostess, passing around cigars, was startled when a hand emptied the box. "Aren't you ashamed of yourself?" she said. The man fastidiously put back one cigar.[3] Some of the more predatory are not stockholders at all—but free-loaders who come for the fun and victuals, saying they plan to invest in the company. Nevertheless, the trend of stockholder cultivation is still clearly up, as this *Financial World* tabulation of annual meeting techniques indicates:

[3] Lewis Gilbert might well write a sequel to his rules for the conduct of presidents at annual meetings consisting of rules for the conduct of stockholders.

Stockholder Relations in Capital Letters

Technique	Percentage					
	1956	1955	1954	1953	1952	1951
Special Invitations	29%	23%	19%	16%	14%	12%
Transportation Supplied	6	7	5	4	4	3
Feedbag	14	17	12	8	6	5
Regional Meetings	2	2	3	2	2	2
Minutes Mailed	28	26	25	22	20	19
Proxies Acknowledged	21	16	15	13	13	11

These are devices to give the stockholder a sense of belonging to the corporation that legally belongs to him. To foster this feeling of belongingness, sixty-two out of every thousand large corporations welcome new shareholders with letters. This in contrast to only thirty-seven per one thousand companies in 1950. And some corporations—about 3 per cent—still cling to letters of regret when a stockholder sells his stock. A General Motors stockholder I know was startled to receive a personal communiqué from Alfred P. Sloan, Jr., when he was chairman of the board. The letter said:

"It has recently come to my attention that your name no longer appears on our books as a holder of General Motors stock; and while I appreciate that in such a large family of stockholders there must be continual change of ownership, it is always with regret that we see any of our partners dropping out.

"I would not wish to appear inquiring into any personal reasons, voluntary or involuntary, that may have prompted you to relinquish this stock.

"However, if the disposal of your holdings was due, even in a small measure, to any unsatisfactory treatment on our part, I hope that you will do me the favor of writing me in detail, since it is our desire to retain your friendship." The letter went on to suggest that if this ex-stockholder had a wisp of continuing interest in GM, Mr. Sloan would be glad to put her name "on a special mailing list for a period of twelve months," to receive the company's periodic reports.[4]

GM has been sending out letters of regret since the 1930's. American Telephone & Telegraph, General Mills, and General Foods have discontinued such letters. Reason: Some people regard it as an intrusion on privacy or a suggestion perhaps of disloyalty. In 1950, the *Financial World* survey indicated that 10 per cent of the larger corporations sent regrets. It no longer compiles the data because of the decline in the practice.

AT&T has introduced a new touch. If officers notice that a particular shareholder has been adding to his holdings year after year, a letter signed by the president will be sent thanking him for his confidence in the company. Also trained personnel of the company will visit shareholders, selected pretty much at random, to obtain their views as shareholders. These interviewers are in search of knowledge and are not trying to "sell" the company. One interviewer saw a ninety-year-old grandmother, who started telling him about her several grandsons. The interviewer was there two hours and reported back to the company: "She was enjoying herself so much, I didn't have the heart to mention what I was there for." To this day he doesn't know whether she is a happy shareholder, but he does know she is a happy grandmother.

The regional meeting was an innovation of General Mills in 1939. If the stockholder could not go to the company, the company's officers would go to the stockholder. In 1954, the company held eight such meetings—from coast to coast. But the practice has its limitations. If a regional meeting is to be a success, the top man has to be on hand, usually with an executive retinue. The time away from home base must be measured alongside the value of stockholder relations. Closed-

[4] Mr. Sloan's successor as chairman, Albert Bradley, has continued the policy of sending out "welcome" and "regret" letters.

circuit inter-city television is a possible substitute. American Machine & Foundry conducted its 1957 annual meeting in New York and Chicago and speakers could be seen and heard in both places simultaneously. General Walter Bedell Smith, who after years of outstanding government service, became vice-chairman of American Machine & Foundry, presided over the New York meeting, the legal meeting; whereas More-head Patterson, chairman and president, presided over the Chicago meeting.

Regional meetings are more useful to consumer goods com-panies than to manufacturers of heavy machinery. They can be utilized as genteel, in-the-family sales whoop-de-doos. Of course, such meetings can serve dual purposes. Executives can talk to distributors, dealers, and large customers as well as shareholders as they travel about.

Good relations with shareholders also come in handy when a corporation is in pursuit of capital. American Telephone & Telegraph has made contented shareholders pay off in the money markets. Seven times between 1946 and 1955, it issued rights to shareholders to purchase convertible debentures and without Wall Street underwriting fees. In 1955 about 42 per cent of the shareholders subscribed to 55 per cent of the issue; the other 58 per cent sold their rights for cash. Between 1920 and 1930, AT&T offered shareholders rights to subscribe to new common stock six times, and in 1956, after a long lapse, resumed this method of raising money. For each ten shares held, a stockholder could subscribe to one additional share at $100. Since Telephone stock was quoted from $160 to $170 a share at the time, the rights were worth the equivalent of $6 to $7 on each share of AT&T stock owned. This constituted a nice reward—a small melon—to which stockholders had come to look forward as an addition to the regular $9 annual dividend. About 53 per cent of the shareholders took up 70 per cent to 75 per cent of the stock.

General Motors Corporation also has built up esteem among shareholders and investors. In February, 1955, it was able to float more than $300,000,000 of common stock by an offering of rights to shareholders. This was the largest single issue of common stock ever sold up to that time. Unlike AT&T offerings to shareholders, it was underwritten—by Morgan, Stanley & Company, and other investment firms. (Since then, the Ford Foundation has sold more than $600,000,000 of Ford Motor Company stock.)

Such esteem means favorable prices for stocks and bonds in the market place, in Wall Street. And many companies try to cultivate esteem by hiring experts in shareholder and public relations. Fifteen per cent of the companies in the *Financial World* survey reported they retained stockholder relations counsel in 1955.[5] Stockholder relations counsel are frequently ex-reporters who would rather eat well than meet interesting people. Such fugitives from journalism set up offices as consultants or go into the public or shareholder relations departments of large companies and offer advice on how to interest financial editors in a company's news releases and how to influence investors in a company's stocks and bonds.

This is a subtle operation. The market price for a stock or bond is determined by experts in security values—not by rank-and-file shareholders. Stockholder relations counsel must "get to" the professionals—the financial analysts. These analysts occupy strategic posts with banks, insurance companies, investment trusts, brokerage firms, investment bankers, foundations, university endowment funds, and investment counsel. They are the men who appraise securities—for purchase by their institutions or for recommendation to others. Collectively, they influence market-making decisions to buy or sell.

[5] The survey covers larger corporations. My guess is that the percentage would be lower for small companies.

Consequently, the alert stockholder relations counsel wants financial analysts to know about new products, plans for expansion, and other news and facts the company regards as important. Naturally, the better a company is known, the less he has to do. As a matter of course, analysts keep up with developments in General Motors, American Telephone and Telegraph, General Electric.

Anybody who appraises property is a financial analyst. John Jacob Astor, when he bought New York City real estate for long-term growth, was a financial analyst—and a speculator. Commodore Cornelius Vanderbilt was analyzing possibilities of New York Central when he bought control. But the financial analyst, as a professional man, is a comparatively new species in Wall Street and environs. His specific job is examining trends and individual securities for hidden values and growth potential.

The profession, if it can be called a profession, got its real start in the 'twenties, when American industry became more complex, when investors began thinking that industrial stocks were not too bad and might be included along with railroads in diversified portfolios. Institutions had to have specialists in steels, in coppers, in utilities, in textiles, as well as rails.

At first, corporation executives regarded analysts much as Stalin regarded visitors to Russia—*personae non gratae*. The corporate code then was strictly: Let the buyer beware, and tell nothing. As late as the 'thirties, Allied Chemical & Dye Corporation, then headed by Orlando Weber, refused to reveal to the New York Exchange its holdings of securities. After the Kreuger & Toll collapse in 1932,[6] buyers became more wary and got specialists in wariness to help them—the

[6] Ivar Kreuger, mysterious Swedish Match King, sold millions of securities in the U.S. through the highly respected firm of Lee, Higginson & Company, on earnings statements and balance sheets that were concoctions of a brilliant imagination. (Chapter XIV.)

113

analysts. An organization, the National Federation of Financial Analysts, is in existence, and the twenty-one constituent societies list 5,350 members.[7] The largest and most powerful group, as you would expect, is in New York.

These societies need a steady supply of speakers. In some cities, such as New York and Philadelphia, weekly meetings are held from fall through spring. The on-the-make stockholder relations counsel cultivates the officers or program chairmen of the societies in major cities so as to get "his man" or men on the platform to tell the company's story. What a change from the 'twenties, when corporation executives shied away from analysts even as from stockholders! After its slump in 1954, when sales dropped to as little as 12 per cent of the auto market, Chrysler Corporation sent the late George W. Troost, financial vice-president, on a tour of financial analysts societies to describe its plans to regain its traditional place alongside General Motors and Ford as the Big Three of motordom. Chrysler did not like being referred to as the half of the "Big 2½." Troost spoke to well-attended meetings, because the analysts were as interested in Chrysler Corporation as Chrysler Corporation in the analysts.

During the New York Central proxy fight, William White and Robert R. Young both appeared before the New York Society to argue their cases. Louis E. Wolfson made a tour

[7] The roster of societies belonging to the Federation in May, 1957, comprised: The Baltimore Security Analysts Society, The Boston Security Analysts Society, the Investment Analysts Society of Chicago, the Cleveland Society of Security Analysts, the Dallas Association of Investment Analysts, Denver Society of Security Analysts, the Financial Analysts Society of Detroit, Kansas City Society of Financial Analysts, the Los Angeles Society of Security Analysts, the Montreal Institute of Investment Analysts, the New York Society of Security Analysts, Inc., the Omaha-Lincoln Society of Financial Analysts, Financial Analysts of Philadelphia, the Providence Society of Financial Analysts, the Richmond Society of Financial Analysts, the Rochester Society of Investment Analysts, the St. Louis Society of Financial Analysts, the Security Analysts of San Francisco, the Security Analysts Association of Toronto, the Twin Cities Society of Security Analysts, Inc., the Washington Society of Investment Analysts.

during the Montgomery Ward & Company fight. He was a popular speaker. In Philadelphia, four hundred showed up at lunch, in contrast to the customary attendance of one hundred.

Officials of companies such as General Motors, General Electric, American Telephone & Telegraph always attract a good crowd because their stocks are so widely held. Hence, their slightest indication of interest will produce an invitation. And the logical man to throw out such a hint is a stockholder relations counsel, or one of the company's public relations men. Or sometimes a company official or a friendly banker will pass the word along to a friendly analyst. However it is done, the big companies seldom have trouble doing it. The smaller companies, which are seeking distribution of their securities, have a harder time.

Usually, the stockholder relations counsel or the company's public relations firm will get in touch with the newspapers before the speech—to get an advance announcement and thus "notify" interested analysts. And he will have a prepared text of the talk for newspapermen—if possible. Then, after the talk, the stockholder relations counsel will either send out the talk to other analysts or send a postcard offering to mail it on request. This is part of the we-want-you-to-be-acquainted-with-us formula. Theory: If you know us, you will be better able to appraise our securities and tell our story to the public.

Numerous companies make it possible for analysts to visit plants. Such visits are an important part of the fare at the annual convention of the National Federation of Financial Analysts Societies. Conventions are held in large cities—Boston, New York, Philadelphia, San Francisco, Cleveland, Los Angeles. The companies in the area turn on all the charm that money and the environment have to offer. When the analysts met in San Francisco, there was an airplane trip to Alaska, trips through vineyards, trips to the Kaiser Steel plant, trips

through utility plants. In Philadelphia, the local group introduced a new touch—meetings with top managements. Instead
of having analysts go to the plants, the executives came to the
hotel at which the convention was held. There were plant
visitations as well.

Regional meetings of analysts in New York, Boston, and
Chicago also provide opportunities for plant visitation. And
companies, themselves, will arrange special all-expenses-paid
tours for analysts or financial journalists. Thus, the Bank of
America brought newspapermen from the East to see the industrial development of the West Coast. Colorado Fuel &
Iron hauled Eastern newspapermen to Pueblo, Colorado, to
show its development. National Gypsum offered a private
plane trip to newspapermen to see its gypsum properties in
Nova Scotia. The Pennsylvania Railroad has had trips on its
right-of-way for both analysts and newspapermen.

Feting journalists is part of the technique of stimulating
interest in a company's shares. A financial editor, who knows
about a company, will be more interested in news releases
about it. You get mileage with the public through lineage in
newspapers. Furthermore, when financial writers go on plant
inspection tours, they take their typewriters along. The company does not ask for publicity. But a writer is a writer. He is
a victim of his trade. He sends back columns or stories. Such
articles serve to acquaint investors, speculators, and financial
analysts with the company and its properties under ideal circumstances. The newspaperman is a guest. His reports are
likely to reflect that status. For that reason, some newspapers
and newspapermen decline free junkets. They prefer to pay
their own way so as to eliminate the host-guest relationship.[8]

Companies also encourage analysts from Standard & Poor's
Corporation, Moody's Investment Service, brokerage firms,

[8] By carefully spacing trips, a calculating journalist could free-load for most
of the year. Only summer would find him wanting in fully paid tours.

banks, insurance companies, and so on, to feel free to ask questions. If an analyst cannot get to see the president, he is certain to see a vice-president who not only can talk but who understands what goes on.

The change in attitude is directly related to the change in the character of corporations. Stockownership is more widely dispersed. The dominant shareholder is a rarity rather than the rule for most companies. Major companies are subject to rules of the Securities and Exchange Commission. Information has become part of the public domain. This includes, in the case of companies whose stocks are listed on an exchange, the publication of salaries of officials.

Furthermore, the businessman has greater financial scope than in the 'twenties. Then, he relied on commercial banks for short-term loans and on investment bankers for long-term financing. Today, he deals with insurance companies, as well as with investment bankers and commerical bankers. When his securities are accepted, he has more alternatives in financing. He can drive a better bargain. So he plays up to the financial analysts who have the contacts and the power to influence investors—both those who own his stock and those who do not own the stock but might become stockholders.

Stockholder relations have become a marketing operation. In case of proxy fights, a management hopes it has sold itself sufficiently to repulse the challenger. In the case of new financing, a management hopes its securities are well enough known to command a good price. And wide stock distribution means customers. General Motors Corporation split its stock in 1950 because "an increase in the number of shareholders is considered an advantage." It has 685,000 common and preferred shareholders, but prints a million annual reports—the extra for the benefit of non-stockholders. GM shareholders would be partial to GM products. And, in January, 1956, when the Ford Motor Company stock was sold for the first time to the public, the Ford Foundation and the company urged the underwriters to sell stock in small lots. Object: A large number of shareholders—prospective buyers of Ford cars. The result was an extraordinary success—nearly three hundred thousand shareholders, which made Ford the fifth largest commercial enterprise in number of common stockholders.[9]

[9] The large companies have constantly added to the number of common shareholders in the bull market postwar era, so it is not possible, in a book, to give a total which will "stay put." As of mid-1957, the six largest stockholder companies were: AT&T, 1,500,000; General Motors, 657,000; Standard Oil (N. J.), 410,000; General Electric, 376,400; Ford, 292,000; United States Steel, 261,000.

General Motors had 27,000 preferred shareholders, and U.S. Steel had 64,500 preferred shareholders. There would be some overlap in the common and preferred.

Incidentally, two mutual funds—investment trusts—have got into the over-200,000 class: Investors Mutual, 240,000 shareholders, and Wellington Fund, 220,000. Among banking institutions, the Bank of America has the largest number, 200,000.

CHAPTER X

The Bonds That Separate

STOCKHOLDERS are odd fellows. Not members of the Independent Order of Odd Fellows. Just the opposite. Odd Fellows are joiners. Americans, as stockholders, are not joiners.

Yet America is overrun with organizations requiring joiners: Elks, Masons, Eagles, Odd Fellows, Kiwanis, Rotary; labor unions, political clubs, parent-teacher associations, college sororities and fraternities; medical, bar, and dental associations, veterans groups, farmers. Even psychiatrists go in for association with their kind.

And investors—well, it must be confessed that they, too, have their organizations. Three of them:

The Investors League
United Shareholders of America, Inc.
Federation of Women Shareholders in American Business

But, whereas the Elks or Odd Fellows or unions or fraternities have official public records of membership, the investors' organizations prefer adjectives to numbers in answering the question: How many members do you have? If you conclude from that that these are letterhead organizations, it is your conclusion, not mine. But that does not mean I do not agree with you. The trouble with stockholders as joiners is they have no common bond except sadness when a dividend is cut and joy when the market goes up. And we do not have an Association for the Improvement of Sadness.

Shareholders, as noted earlier, have economic pulls which are stronger than their attachment to securities. A doctor who owns stock will eagerly attend meetings of his county medical society, but he will ignore letters from a stockholder organization. An economist who is a stockholder will write articles for the *American Economic Review*, published by the American Economic Association, but he can be quite bored about a proxy fight in his own company. Somehow, the phrase, "Stockholders of the world unite, you have nothing to lose but your dividends," does not resound. The stockholder does not want to lose dividends. Yet if he did, he would be unlikely to be impoverished because dividends are rarely his main income. So he has no incentive for organizing.

Hence, what ought to be a long chapter, describing the character, influence, and composition of the three shareholder organizations, is, perforce, brief—for lack of substance. The 1957 *World Almanac* devotes sixteen pages to associations and societies in the United States, including the American Irish Historical Society, 3,000 members; the American Society of Biological Chemists, 1,266 members; and the Society of Women Barber Shop Quartet Singers, membership not given. None of the investor groups is listed. Yet all have headquarters in New York, the *World Almanac*'s home city. To correct this inattention, I append descriptions of the three stockholder groups:

INVESTORS LEAGUE, INC.

The late B. C. Forbes, publisher of *Forbes* magazine, writer of a syndicated column on business, and a friend of many corporation executives, was the founder and first president of the Investors League. The idea burgeoned on the golf course at Pinehurst in June, 1942, and immediately enveloped him. His partner was Joseph D. Goodman, a stockbroker and frequent contributor to *Forbes* magazine. Occasionally, they had talked about a league for investors, and this particular day, after a round on the fairways, Forbes was searching for a subject for his column. Goodman offered to jot down some ideas. Later Forbes reworked the thoughts—a proposal for a nationwide organization of investors. And after the column appeared, Forbes was "swamped," to use Goodman's word, with letters from people all over the country. Forbes tried to interest ex-President Herbert Hoover and Alfred E. Smith, who ran against Hoover in 1928, in heading up the league. They were not available. Forbes was stuck, and "took up the gauntlet himself." As initially incorporated in July, 1942, the name was Investors Fairplay League.[1] It took Forbes only a month to get going.

The idea was not original. Hugh S. Magill, a Chicago churchman, educator, and an Illinois state senator from 1911 to 1915, was head of the American Federation of Investors. Competition for investor loyalty was not considered desirable and the Federation was merged into Fairplay League. Forbes not only wrote about the organization in his column, but also devoted a page a month in *Forbes* magazine to the League. In 1945, the name was changed to Investors League.

In 1949, Forbes resigned the presidency and took the chairmanship. Allen M. Pope, retired president of The First Boston Corporation, became president for one year, and then William Jackman, an energetic, wiry man, whom Forbes called "Jacko," and who had been executive vice-president, took over. A year later, Forbes resigned but "continued his active interest and retained his membership." [2]

The League designates itself "A National Non-Profit, Non-Partisan Organization." Yet Jackman, in his capacity as presi-

---

[1] *Investors League Bulletin*, June, 1954, the first page of which is a memorial to Forbes, who died May 6, 1954.
[2] Same as above.

dent of the League, was openly enthusiastic about the election of President Eisenhower at a luncheon in Philadelphia at which Congressman Hugh Scott, Republican, was guest of honor. Jackman told the audience: "If we get those other people back" (referring to the Truman Democrats), "we'll have lost free enterprise. They have socialistic tendencies."

Jackman does not "go in for rabble-rousing at stockholders' meetings." He says: "We believe we can be most effective in the field of legislation." By legislation, he means getting taxes reduced. Specifically, the League has fought for elimination of double taxation of dividends, elimination of the capital gains tax, reduction in manufacturers' excise taxes, passage of the natural gas bill, which President Eisenhower vetoed in 1956, and adoption of the Hoover Commission's plan for reorganization of government.

National Biscuit, Allegheny Ludlum Steel, Glidden, Greyhound, and other corporations have distributed an *Investors League Bulletin* on the evils of double taxation of dividends. The League is happy to have corporations send its bulletins to shareholders, but corporations, as such, are not permitted to join—only individuals in corporations.

When he appears before committees of Congress, Jackman says he represents millions of investors. The membership of the Investors League is not published anywhere. Once when I pressed him, Jackman gave out a figure of "40,000 to 50,000," but critics will say these are paper names, not dues-payers. Total annual outlays run "to $100,000 a year," or $2.50 per member at the 40,000 figure. Yet, dues start at $5. In speeches, Jackman asserts that the League is "a national organization which spreads its tentacles through forty-eight states. We try to do what we cannot do as individuals." He, himself, is registered as a lobbyist because of his continuing interest in legislation.

The formal policy is (1) to keep its members informed

through a bulletin, newsletter, or other appropriate means of developments affecting the interest of investors; (2) to have its officers or other appropriate representatives appear before Congressional committees on matters of importance affecting the interest of investors; (3) to maintain contacts with Congress and with other governmental agencies for the purpose of keeping them fully informed on subjects relating to the interest of investors; (4) to supply at cost League bulletins or other printed material to corporations for distribution to shareholders whenever such distribution contributes to the advancement of the League or its policies.

The League urges: "Don't Be a Forgotten Man! The Investors League Can Help You . . . But You Must Help, Too!" This plea is accompanied by a membership application. An associate membership is $5, an annual membership $10, and then the rates stairstep up—$25, then $50, then $100, up to $499 for an "annual contributing membership." This odd amount is readily explained. Public Law 601, the so-called Lobbying Act, requires public filing of names of persons who give $500 or more to organizations that devote time and energy to legislation.

UNITED SHAREHOLDERS OF AMERICA, INC.

United Shareholders of America, Inc., is a split-off from the Investors League. Benjamin A. Javits, New York attorney and older brother of Senator Jacob K. Javits, had been long associated with Forbes and the Investors League. But he felt the League was "too close" to corporations. So he organized the United Shareholders in 1950. It, too, claims to be nonpartisan and its declared aims resemble those of the League. It opposes the capital gains tax and double taxation of dividends. It tells shareholders: "You own America, but you have no voice—no union, no lobby, no newspapers, no radio networks. You are the legion of the silent—the forgotten men and women of America."

In reply to a question on the number of members, a United Shareholders letter in April, 1954, says: "Our membership stretches across the country, both men and women, and our newsletters to the membership treat of subjects that should be of interest to them." Note the similarity to Investors League. A later letter gives six thousand as the "roster of members, men and women." But the annual income is put at $8,000 to $9,000 a year." Dues begin at $10. So a good many who are counted as members do not pay.

United Shareholders has opposed the stagger system of electing directors. It issues meritorious achievement awards to corporations judged to have good shareholder relations. A person invited to serve as a member of the advisory committee was asked: "At this writing, what corporations have your approbation for good stockholder relationship?" But no standard for determining good stockholder relationship was set forth. Among the companies receiving an award was American Tobacco, whose 1956 annual meeting, according to Lewis Gilbert, ended up "in absolute turmoil over the stubborn and arrogant refusal" of Paul Hahn, president, to give information which Gilbert felt stockholders were entitled to.

These awards, several hundred a year, have the merit of bringing to the United Shareholders glowing letters from presidents of some of America's largest corporations, an indication that courtesy and receptivity to approbation are not dead.[3]

When the cigarette-cancer scare developed into headline

[3] Excerpts: "My associates and I do indeed deem it an honor to have been awarded by the United Shareholders of America, Inc., their 1954–55 Annual Meeting Award for Meritorious Achievement in the field of Management-Shareholder relations and may I take this opportunity, both for myself and on behalf of my associates, to thank you and your committee in present-

news in 1954, United Shareholders of America sent out a bulletin to members quoting cigarette company assertions that no expert claims his research "to be conclusive." United Shareholders promised to "keep its members up to date on how the cigarette industry is meeting the serious problems before it." Somehow, this appears to be a problem for investment advisory firms, such as Standard & Poor's, and Moody's, not an organization designed to assert shareholders' rights. But shareholder organizations are hard put to find a unifying issue, to bring in members and dues.

Dues of United Shareholders also stairstep up to $499 for a "life membership." The United Shareholders promises (1) to represent shareholders "at Congressional hearings, before Federal, State and municipal agencies, departments, and commissions, and at stockholder meetings"; (2) to publicize shareholder "views through the press, radio, television, magazines, and all other public information media"; (3) to inform shareholders about "what you can do to protect your interests as a shareholder."

---

ing this award to Celanese Corporation of America. . . . HAROLD BLANCKE, President."

"We are most grateful for the award which we will display permanently and proudly. LUCIUS D. CLAY, Chairman, Continental Can Company."

"In our turn, I congratulate you and all others active in your organization for the definite service you are performing on behalf of shareholders and the entire system of private enterprise. . . . We prize your award, not only as a recognition of Merritt-Chapman & Scott's efforts . . . but as a symbol of a program that can achieve benefits for the economy at large. L. E. WOLFSON, President and Chairman."

"Your 1954–55 Annual Meeting Award has been received and we are deeply appreciative of the honor you pay us. It is our constant aim to keep our shareholders well informed . . . and we are gratified that your organization would feel we are doing a good job. L. L. COLBERT, President, Chrysler Corporation."

"Thanks for your recent letter presenting to The American Tobacco Company the 1954–55 Annual Meeting Award. . . . I am pleased to accept. . . . Your objective—encouragement of a broader and deeper base of shareownership in American Management—is a worthy one. We appreciate your recognition of our company's efforts in this field, which we have long considered important to the nation's economy. PAUL M. HAHN, President."

FEDERATION OF WOMEN SHAREHOLDERS IN AMERICAN BUSINESS, INC.

The third organization, the Federation of Women Shareholders in American Business, is less of an organization than a person, Mrs. Wilma Soss. She organized it, she became its first president, and she speaks for it. Her background is that of publicity agent and she functions in that capacity as president of FOWSAB, as the organization alphabetizes itself.

In testimony before the Securities and Exchange Commission in 1952, she declared: "The Federation of Women Shareholders is a national, nonprofit, nonpolitical, protective and educational organization for women. In 1947, Ferdinand Pecora, father of SEC,[4] signed the papers which granted our historic articles of incorporation. . . .

"Our members consist of large and small—chiefly small—stockholders. . . . Many are widows. Some are employee stockholders. Some were active in the women's political suffrage movement and now are pioneering in the exercise of women's economic suffrage."

The purposes of FOWSAB are to "enable women shareholders . . . to band together so as to help preserve the right of free enterprise, increase the productivity of our private enterprise system, and to combat influences detrimental thereto." The Republican Party, Democratic Party, American Legion, National Association of Manufacturers, Union

[4] Pecora occupied the post of counsel to the Senate Banking and Currency Committee, which, from January, 1933, to June, 1934, investigated banking and stock market practices prior to the stock market crash in 1929 and the subsequent depression. Congress then passed the Securities Act of 1933, known as the "Truth-in-Securities Act," and the Securities Exchange Act of 1934. President Franklin D. Roosevelt appointed Pecora one of the original members of the Securities and Exchange Commission on July 1, 1934. Pecora resigned in January, 1935, when Governor Lehman named him to a vacancy on the Supreme Court of New York.

League, Daughters of the American Revolution, the AFL-CIO, and the Americans for Democratic Action could subscribe without hesitancy to such a platform.

Mrs. Soss' point of view is radically different from that of Jackman or Javits. She is a corporate suffragette. She argues that women own a large share of the nation's wealth. They ought to be represented on boards of directors. When Robert R. Young named a woman to his slate of directors for New York Central, he promptly got the Soss vote. Mrs. Soss goes in for heckling managements, not for providing them with literature or issuing awards to them.

Once Mrs. Soss showed up at a United States Steel Corporation stockholders' meeting in a turn-of-the century dress. She was suiting her habit, she said, to the corporation's archaic custom of holding its meetings in Hoboken, New Jersey, out of the way of most stockholders. She appeared at a General Motors session in a golf outfit, because once, when Alfred P. Sloan, Jr., chairman, was asked why officers of the company were not present to answer stockholders' questions, he had said he had rather they were enjoying recreation—playing golf. Mrs. Soss' attire got her name and picture in the paper, which was just what she wanted.

Though Mrs. Soss waves the FOWSAB banner, she does not disclose FOWSAB membership. FOWSAB is described in a leaflet as a "nonprofit, nonpartisan association of women volunteers. No hidden masters. As American as apple pie." Dues start at $10 and rise to $15, $25, then $100, and finally to $1,000, which is called an "endowing membership." in May, 1955, FOWSAB operated from a postoffice box in New York City and Mrs. Soss' home. By the summer of 1957 it had graduated to a tiny two-desk office in the Hotel Shelton, New York. Mrs. Soss has not been able to whip women stockholders into a frenzy of financial enthusiasm for "their cause."

Americans, as stockholders, have a great deal of the inertia Mrs. Soss has so little of. And that is what makes the three investor organizations what they are. The bonds that bring Americans together as doctors, lawyers, or college professors, in unions as plumbers, bricklayers or auto workers, as music lovers, chess players, or members of barbershop quartets, as fund-raising alumni of Princeton, Michigan, and Stanford, pry them apart as stockholders.

Investors' clubs catch on, because they bring together people who are interested in investments as investments. These people do not brood about their rights as stockholders, or cutting taxes, or having representatives appear before Congressional committees, or granting awards to corporation presidents because they have good manners to stockholders. They analyze the market's ups and downs, industrial trends, dividend records, earnings possibilities. To get tax laws changed, Americans, including stockholders, prefer to go directly to their Congressmen or Senators, or local political leaders. Or they may work through trade organizations, or the various tax leagues, but not through investor organizations.

A stockholder organization can be easily torn apart by taxes as well as pulled together. A minority, but a large minority, of shareholders are Democrats. They are outraged by espousal of Republicanism. Many shareholders approve ability-to-pay taxation, so they are not appalled by compound levies on dividends or capital gains taxes. It is significant that when Herbert Hoover and Alfred E. Smith were asked to head up the Investors League, they declined. Is it going too far to suppose that this was a value judgment, a political judgment, on the viability of investor organizations as pressure groups?

CHAPTER XI

The Battle for The Century

ON FEBRUARY 10, 1954, fifteen directors of the New York Central Railroad Company unanimously voted to decline Robert R. Young's offer to become their chairman. The next day, Young declared war on these "powerful interests" in Wall Street, with whom, only twenty-four hours before, he was prepared to associate. Without benefit of a Gallup, Roper, or University of Michigan poll, Young announced he had the support of 90 per cent of the Central's shareholders on the issue of "whether the owners of the properties shall prevail in management over the selfish voice of the banking clique that brought on the 1929 crash."

Young considered himself an "owner." The directors who chose to resist his offer were "interlopers," and included such established financiers and businessmen as George Whitney, then chairman of J. P. Morgan & Company; Percy J. Ebbott, then president of the Chase National Bank, now the Chase Manhattan; Lawrence N. Murray, president of the Mellon National Bank & Trust Company; Alexander C. Nagle, president of the First National Bank, since merged into the First National City Bank of New York; William E. Levis, for many years president and later chairman of Owens-Illinois Glass Company; Earle J. Machold, president of Niagara Mohawk Power Corporation; James A. Farley, chairman of Coca-Cola Corporation, and an experienced political campaigner; Elton Hoyt, II, senior partner in Pickands, Mather & Company,

Cleveland investment and management firm in iron ore, coke and coal properties. Young picked on no patsies when he began the proxy battle for the Century, the New York Central's prestige New York-to-Chicago passenger train and all the wealth, tradition, and power it stands for.

Young's declaration of war came after he had told Harold S. Vanderbilt, largest stockholder on the Central board and great-grandson of Commodore Cornelius Vanderbilt, "grand old man of the Central," that he had been acquiring Central stock along with Allan P. Kirby, Young's long-time business associate. He also confided to Vanderbilt that he and Kirby were liquidating their holdings in Chesapeake & Ohio Railway Company; so was Alleghany Corporation, of which Young was chairman and Kirby president. Such liquidation would leave them free to serve as directors of Central and participate in the management.

Once before, in early 1947, Young had made a bid for a say in Central. He controlled the Chesapeake & Ohio through Alleghany. He had used C&O cash to buy enough Central stock to prompt Gustav Metzman, then president of Central, to proffer him two directorships—one for himself, as chairman of C&O, one for Robert J. Bowman, as C&O president. But in May, 1948, the Interstate Commerce Commission denied Young's application to serve on the Central board. The C&O competed with Central. Young controlled the C&O. Interlocking control would curb competition. The ICC went further. The C&O holdings of Central must be kept in an already established voting trust with an independent trustee. Young must not exercise his voting power; he must not select directors for Central. C&O could only hold Central shares as a simon-pure investment.

Young's interview with Vanderbilt took place in the cosy environment of Palm Beach where both had homes. They also were neighbors at Newport, Rhode Island. Young only wanted two seats on the board, he told his socialite friend. But one of those seats was to include a newly created post of chairman of the board. And the chairman was to be chief executive of the road. Young did not want to oust William White, president. White could continue as chief operating officer. Indeed, Young later invited White to lunch at the plush Cloud Club atop the Chrysler Building, in New York, and promised that if White remained on the job, he, White, would be given an opportunity to buy Central stock at a fixed price—and only if the stock went up. White turned down the proposal. When some one asked whether they parted friends, White answered, "Well, I didn't kiss the guy."

The proxy campaign, the strategy, of both sides quickly unfolded. White disclosed himself as the steady, hard-working railroad man—efficient, quiet, solid, decorous. When his public relations advisers advised: "Promise the stockholders a dividend," the best White could muster was a suggestion that maybe in the next few years earnings would recover sufficiently to warrant a $2 dividend. He was the archetype of all Young called him—a conservative banker's man.

Young had fewer inhibitions. He recalled that in the 'twenties Central had paid dividends of $7 and $8 a share. He saw no reason at all why the road, under Young, should not regain that glory. A $10 a share dividend was entirely possible.

He tried to get a Vanderbilt on the board—for old times' sake. Commodore Cornelius Vanderbilt had built the Central amid battles with "Uncle" Daniel Drew, Jay Gould, and "Admiral" Jim Fisk. But no Vanderbilt would play. He did nominate a woman, Lila Bell Acheson Wallace, as already noted, and this gratified Wilma Soss, president of the Federation of Women Shareholders in American Business. Young discovered a retired New York Central engineer, who owned eighty shares, and made him a candidate, supposedly to provide an employee point of view.[1] And he named William P. Feeley, president of the Great Lakes Dredge & Dock Company, because, in addition to his other qualifications, he was a Catholic. When Mrs. Soss had urged White to name a woman to his slate, he said that there was no vacancy on the board—a matter-of-fact statement that won no votes.

Young started out with only a slight advantage. He and Kirby each owned 100,000 shares, or a total of 200,000. This was more than the Central board owned, but it was less than 3 per cent of the 6,447,410 shares outstanding. Victory depended on the decisions of some forty thousand shareholders —the "Aunt Janes," as Young called the small independent corporate owners.

Investment trusts, insurance companies, pension funds did not hold Central. Neither did banks in their investment and trust accounts. Its dividend record had been too erratic. The only big block of stock was that owned by the Chesapeake & Ohio. Young could depend on the favor of the C&O management. He had sold Alleghany's controlling stock in C&O to his friend, Cyrus S. Eaton, and had seen to it that Eaton got ensconced in the command seat. But C&O, under Interstate Commerce Commission order, could not favor Young with its votes. Chase Manhattan Bank (then the Chase National) was trustee of the stock. It possessed voting power under an ICC order. Young had hoped Chase would remain neutral— and not vote the stock. But when Ebbott of the Chase voted against Young's "offer" to assume the Central chair, Young set his mind and financial resourcefulness on those 800,000 shares.

John Brooks told the story in the *New Yorker* magazine of how David Baird, a friend of Young, and a member of the New York Stock Exchange, offered, during a talk at Palm

---

[1] He was retired again from Central in July, 1957. He had served his purpose.

Beach, to try to organize a syndicate to buy the stock: "Young was delighted. But then, after two critical days, during which Baird had nothing conclusive to report, he began to get nervous. Central stock was churning around on the Stock Exchange in anticipation of the proxy fight; it had jumped from twenty to twenty-five. If Young couldn't arrange to have the C&O's block bought quickly, its price might be so high that no one would want to buy it.

"On the third day, Young, still in Palm Beach, received a caller—an old friend of his named Don H. Carter, who was a business representative of Clint W. Murchison, the free-wheeling Texas oil man and investor. In the past, acting through Carter, Murchison had found Young's promotions profitable to the extent of several million dollars. As Young recalls it, Carter came to see him about another business matter, and while they were in the middle of discussing it, the following cryptic bit of dialogue took place:

"Young: 'Don, I think the New York Central represents the greatest speculative opportunity in America—under new management.'

"Carter: 'Bob, what's going to happen to all that Central stock that Chase is holding for C&O?'

"That started the ball rolling. Young, trying not to seem eager, asked Carter if he thought Murchison might be interested in buying the stock. Carter said perhaps, and, after telephoning to Murchison, reported to Young that Murchison did, indeed, seem interested. Young then put in a call for Walter J. Tuohy, president of the C&O and Young's former subordinate there, asked him whether C&O might care to sell its Central stock at a price rather higher than the $20 or so a share the company had paid for it. Maybe, said Tuohy, if the price was 26.

"Young was now in the ticklish position common to brokers in big deals. The market price of Central stock was fluttering around 24, and because of the uncertainties of the proxy fight, it might soar or sink at any moment. If it soared, Murchison would not buy, and if it sank, the C&O would not sell. Either way, the deal would be off. On Monday, the 15th, Central stock had touched 26. Young began negotiating with Murchison by telephone. He had reason to suspect that Tuohy would come down to 25 and he pointed out what a bargain the stock would be at that price. Murchison said the price was all right. He also said he would need a partner and had one ready in the person of Sid W. Richardson, another Texan with a penchant for shortening his given name and enlarging his bank roll. . . . But neither of the Texans liked the idea of putting up all the cash. Young thereupon undertook to raise the cash for them."

What followed is one of the strangest transactions in financial legerdemain. The price came to $20,000,000. Alleghany Corporation, controlled by Young, advanced $7,500,000 on an unsecured note. Kirby, Young's associate, advanced $5,-000,000. And a group of Cleveland banks advanced the rest. This last loan was secured by the stock. Nor was that all. The Texans had a "put,"—an option—to sell the Alleghany Corporation half their stock at the purchase price. Moreover, Richardson had a separate agreement with Kirby, whereby Kirby would take the 200,000 he could not put to Alleghany. Murchison's risk was on 200,000 shares. "The only possible loser," commented the *New Yorker*, "appeared to be Alleghany," which Young dominated by owning 0.7 per cent of its common stock.

This was the grand coup of the proxy battle. White promptly charged skulduggery. He told his lawyers to argue that Young still dominated the C&O. Therefore, if Young got Central, he would be a two-railroad man, which flouted established ICC policy. But the ICC ruled the stock had been properly transferred to the Texans. It could be voted.

The transaction had its embarrassments for Young. He was using other people's money and credit—Alleghany's, that is— as if it were other people's money. When a newspaperman asked Young's office what interest was being paid on the Murchison-Richardson note to Alleghany, the answer came back: "We are not saying at this time." Later, it was disclosed at 4½ per cent. Alleghany was not laden with cash. So, it, in turn, had to borrow to lend the Texans funds to pay the C&O.

Nevertheless, the transaction revealed Young's wizardry. Doubtful shareholders were now convinced that Young had the Midas touch. He could promote. He could achieve his ends. Besides, he now had 1,000,000 shares in hand—16 per cent of the Central stock. In most companies that was control, working control.

The struggle for votes that followed proved that politicians know their business. White knew what would appeal to bona fide investors—to banks, insurance companies, managers of trust funds, university endowment funds. He made no bold pledges. He said he was working hard to reduce costs, improve the Central's properties, that ultimately he expected to be able to pay small but regular dividends. In the 'twenties, that pitch would have paid off. Central then was an investment stock. But in 1954, approximately 45 per cent of the shares were in brokers' names. They were owned by speculators, traders—persons who were far more interested in an upward move in the market and the capture of a capital gain than in tortoiselike progress through gradual increases in earnings and dividends.

Young was the hare. His proxy statement said: "Dear Fellow Shareholder: Put us to work to make your stock more valuable. We have bought stock with a present market value of $25,000,000 in the faith that we can." Young then pointed out the timidity of White—the best he hopes for is a "*possible*

$2 dividend in four or five years or a little less. If this had been our view we would not have acquired our shareholdings."

Young cited his own magic—how the prices of securities of Alleghany Corporation, Nickel Plate, Chesapeake & Ohio, Pere Marquette, Missouri Pacific, and Pittston Company, had advanced between 1938 and 1953. The dates were convenient. For 1938 was a depression year in stocks. Nineteen fifty-three was a bull market peak after the war. *Fortune* magazine editorialized on Young's convenient timing. It also pointed out that in Nickel Plate the big gain occurred after Mr. Young had sold out. But Young's flamboyant display of statistics convinced many shareholders.

Fortune's editorial was so favorable to White, or rather so condemnatory of Young, that the New York Central reprinted and distributed it to stockholders—without permission. *Fortune* sued and won $7,000. White regarded the money well spent, but was later to settle a lawsuit because of it.

White's campaign was one of aloof ridicule. Young was a man of promises unfulfilled. White called attention to Young's boasts and dreams—to "Train X," long on the drawing board but never on the tracks; to C&O's adoption and abandonment of a central ticket service; to Young's purchase of passenger cars in bulk and the subsequent sale of the cars to other roads at a loss; to his investment in the Greenbrier Hotel at White Sulphur Springs, which White said was losing money; to Young's suggestion that the railroads use refrigerator cars cooled mechanically instead of with ice (White said this was fantastically expensive).

White pointed out that in 1942 Alleghany Corporation had owned 1,929,779 shares of C&O stock; that at the end of 1952 it owned only 104,854 shares. So Young controlled C&O with ownership of only 1.3 per cent of the stock, even as he controlled Alleghany with less than 1 per cent. Inference: Young talked owner-management but he would sell out after he got control if it served his purpose. Further, White pointed out that Young and Kirby, as principal officers of Alleghany Corporation, which at the time controlled Investors Diversified Services, Inc., had entered into a transaction with themselves whereby Alleghany exchanged stock of Investors Diversified Services for Alleghany Series A preferred stock which they owned. Out of this deal, said White, Young and Kirby stood to make a profit of more than $7,600,000. This statement was not challenged. It subsequently was the basis for a lawsuit and for a Securities and Exchange Commission recommendation to the Interstate Commerce Commission that Alleghany Corporation be made subject to SEC regulation under the Investment Company Act. That act bars investment company officers from dealing with themselves and affiliates without SEC permission. They must prove arm's-length dealing.

Young answered some of White's statements. He said, for example, that the New York Central and other railroads have "moved in the direction" of central reservation bureaus "but not nearly to the extent which public convenience and economy require." He protested that the Greenbrier Hotel, far from being a white elephant, is a valuable asset because it is a "favorite gathering place for top executives—whose good will can contribute immeasurably to C&O traffic." But his principal method was to accuse.

Alleghany advertised that W. P. Murphy, president of the Standard Railway Equipment Manufacturing Company, had left a will bequeathing railroad executives $2,000,000. Among the beneficiaries were F. E. Williamson, a former president of the New York Central ($100,000), Martin W. Clement, former president of the Pennsylvania Railroad ($100,000), and others. Here was an ingenious innuendo: Murphy was remembering men who had done him favors. White answered that Murphy had also left $34,000,000 to Northwestern University. To that, Young replied: "If Murphy's profits were excessive, what kind of service was it to railroad shareholders? While Mr. White does not defend, he seems to condone."

Young probably benefited from White's answers. Maybe the idea of mechanically refrigerated cars was impractical. Maybe the lightweight low-slung train was closer to a dream than a drawing board. None the less, such ideas had an appeal. They were progress.[2] They were ideas a man who was not a railroader could understand. He did not want doubts and details. He wanted vision and promise. Young supplied those—even promising he would sell New York Central real estate to reduce the debt. When White calmly noted that mortgages encumbered the properties and prevented disposal, it seemed like sniping.

Stockholders were inundated with literature. Each side sent out seven mailings. The management hired Georgesen & Company, largest firm of professional proxy solicitors, to call up shareholders and bring in votes. Central employees also "volunteered." Young said he would not use professional stock solicitors but later hired the firm of Kissel & Company. White supplemented the New York Central public relations staff with Robinson-Hannegan Associates to drum up pro-management sentiment. Young had his own public relations man, Thomas J. Deegan, Jr., who subsequently became a vice president of Central and, still later, resigned to form his own firm with Central as a client.

From the start, Young emphasized that the management was using company funds to pay the expenses of the proxy fight. "The present board is not entitled to have unlimited access to the treasury . . . in an effort to maintain themselves as directors." Young announced he had commenced suit to stop such expenditures.

[2] And the Pennsylvania and the Central have both put in use newer type cars since.

At the same time, Young said Alleghany Corporation, he, Kirby, and other candidates for the board were spending their "own money and energies" in behalf of shareholders "because we have bought over a million shares of Central stock in the full faith that under sound management it can again sell far above its present price and pay far in excess of its present dividends."

In the final swirl of proxy-getting, New York Central employees used telephones and rang doorbells in behalf of the management. Clint W. Murchison, as controlling shareholder in Diebold, Inc., office equipment firm, put its salesmen at the beck and call of Young. Also bankers and brokers, who were actively associated with either side, tried to corral votes. One Oklahoma friend of Murchison had received a list of shareholders in the state with the request to call them up and bring them in on Young's side.

On May 26, a stockholders' special left the Grand Central Station, New York City, for Albany. The train was packed. Young's followers wore buttons—"Young at Heart." When Young arrived he was greeted with cheers and made a Churchillian sign of triumph. White came along a bit later. He had a pipe in his mouth; photographers had to beseech him for a picture. They asked him, too, for the Victory sign. He made it, but, as the *New Yorker* put it, "in a deprecatory, mechanical way."

The rivals walked through the train electioneering. They were only two cars apart at Poughkeepsie. They were certain to meet in the aisles. But the train stopped. White got off and took the second section.

The stockholders' session, held in the drill shed of the Washington Avenue Armory, was more ritual than practical. The counting of proxies would take three weeks. Some shareholders, overwhelmed by attention, had signed proxies of both sides with a sense of indiscriminate power. Only the last-dated proxy would count. But tellers had to plow through the mountains of forms and cancel all proxies which had been superdated.

Flanking White on the platform were Harold S. Vanderbilt, William H. Vanderbilt, James A. Farley, and several other directors—the targets of Young's charges of old-guardism. The two men stockholders wanted most to see, the Texans for whom Young raised the money to produce his own coup, Murchison and Richardson, weren't there.

The show went on, though there could be no results that day. White called the meeting to order. Mrs. Soss protested on a point of order. Speeches were made. Many persons tried to speak at once. Late in the afternoon, Young announced: "Shareowners, I'm happy to tell you you have won." White protested the audacity and the presumptuousness: "By what authority did Mr. Young speak?" But White knew Young was right.

White had been beaten because he was the kind of person he was, the kind of person who could not conduct a campaign to appeal to speculators. Young, on the other hand, had political flair. He made his pitch to the large group of traders and speculators who had bought Central for a market advance, who had not even troubled to have the Central stock transferred. They left the shares in brokers' names. The statistics bear this out.

Stock in brokers' names went for Young by a two-to-one margin—1,372,000 shares to 678,000, including the 200,000 shares owned by Young and Kirby. Even eliminating these shares, the margin in favor of Young was ten to six. White got a majority from stockholders who had registered the stock in their own names. These are persons who might be described as long-term investors, the Aunt Janes, whom Young was "saving." But the margin was insufficient to overcome Young's advantage in street-name stock. White had this moral satisfaction: individual stockholders voted for him nearly two to one—23,033 versus 12,522.

Young did not live up to his campaign promises. At the shareholders' meeting, he ostentatiously announced that he was voting his personal shares for cumulative voting. He did this to win the allegiance of Lewis D. Gilbert and Mrs. Soss. But when Gilbert put this in the form of a proposal on the Central proxy statement for 1955, the board of directors voted unanimously against. "Its adoption might invite some of the previous directorate and their numerous and powerful allies to seek reinstatement with no other purpose than to keep us from achieving our goals, thus justifying their own unhappy predictions of doom."

Young's fear was fanciful. The former Central directors hadn't enough stock to elect one of their number to the board. And they were unlikely to want to sit on Young's board. Further, to serve as a militant, bickering minority would be contrary to their principle of management. As heads of institutions they believed in law, order, harmony and management rule.[3]

Again, on the matter of expenses, Young's post-election performance belied his preëlection knighthood. When he began soliciting proxies, he asked shareholders in big, black type this rhetorical question: "Why Are We Spending Our Money and Energies on Your Behalf?" [4]

Young went on to say that the cost of the proxy solicitation will be "borne by Alleghany Corporation and the fifteen nominees on the basis of their average holdings of New York Central stock." But after the battle was won, he submitted a bill for $1,308,733.71 to New York Central shareholders for approval—a complete repudiation of his seeming promise. Alas, seeming promise it was! He had a legal escape clause.

[3] As the next chapter will prove.
[4] Proxy statement and accompanying letter of April 8, 1954.

In his letter to shareholders was this sentence: "Whether Alleghany and the nominees will seek any reimbursement from the Central will depend on the outcome of a lawsuit."

The lawsuit was to stop the Central management from using Central funds to fight Young. Since, traditionally, corporation managements have always used the corporation treasury to solicit proxies—it is part of the cost of operating the business—Young's suit was unlikely to succeed. Courts have upheld the right of management to spend corporation funds to keep itself in office.

Argued Mr. Young: "If the expenses of only one side are to be so borne, it would seem not only more equitable, but more within the wishes of shareholders, that it be the expenses of the victors. Consequently, your board has been persuaded, and we believe rightly, that it would be a discouraging precedent to owners of other non-owner director companies for us to defray our own expenses when the benefits redound to all Central shareholders, pro rata, just as the expenses would automatically be borne if the company defrayed them." [5]

Some New York Central stockholders were confused. Originally, they voted for Young because he showed a willingness to spend his own money; now they could not make up their minds whether Young's concern was his own pocketbook or some future unknown shareholders for whom he might be setting a discouraging precedent. And this came out at the first annual meeting of New York Central shareholders after Young's election. The *New York Times* account of the meeting instructively delineates the difference between Young's practice and preachment on corporate democracy: "Mr. Young refused to entertain any question put to him that indicated the questioner was not in full agreement with the en-

[5] Proxy statement, April, 1955.

tire Young program. He declared at least six stockholders out of order for remarks or objections directed to the chair."

But the mass of shareholders were for Young. The resolution to reimburse was passed by a vote of 4,885,136 to 384,-812. The margin is not quite so substantial as the arithmetic. The total included about 1,000,000 shares which Young, Kirby, Alleghany, and the Texans owned. But it again proves the impotence and ignorance of the rank-and-file shareholders, the Aunt Janes.

Criticism was not confined to the New York Central family. *Life* magazine suggested that Young was guilty of shoddy ethics and morals in implying he would not seek repayment. *The Washington Post and Times Herald* carried an editorial suggesting that such requests for reimbursement of outlays in proxy battles should be carefully audited: "This whole problem deserves the attention of the average citizen as well as of stockholders. What is to prevent a group of wealthy operators from recklessly spending huge sums of money to gain control of a corporation if they then are to be reimbursed by the corporation and its stockholders? This possibility opens up a new form of piracy. It is naïve to say that the matter should be left to the good judgment of shareholders. It would be possible, of course, for New York Central stockholders, properly warned and organized, to turn down Mr. Young's request. But it would be very difficult. . . ." [6]

Shareholders do what their managements suggest—unless some strong man, like Young, emerges to organize a contest against the management. A group of adventurers, anxious to take over control of a company, would be encouraged to spend freely. The more they gamble, the greater would be their chances of getting votes and control, and, therefore,

[6] *Washington Post and Times Herald,* April 21, 1955.

reimbursement. Half-hearted spending might lead to defeat.[7]

The New York Central fight emphasizes that proxy battles are not a poor man's game. Young, as noted, was enthusiastically voted $1,308,000 by Central shareholders for his and Alleghany's outlays. White, according to Young, spent $876,-000. However, thanks to litigious shareholders who sued Young and to Young who sued White and the old Central board of directors, New York Central did not have to ladle out all this cash. Young, the newly chosen board of Central directors, and Alleghany Corporation settled for $300,000 a suit demanding return of $1,308,000. That is at the rate of 22.9 cents on the dollar. A suit against White and the old directors for misuse of Central funds was settled for $125,000, or 14.3 cents on the dollar.[8]

The settlement by White and Central directors runs counter to the concept that company officials have a right—nay, a duty—to use corporate funds to keep themselves in office. In theory, the directors were selected and elected by stockholders; in theory, they selected and elected a president to run the corporation. So, presumably, in their opinion he is a good manager. Therefore, they ought to fight—with all the corporation's resources—a grab for control, a threat to oust him.

Under such circumstances, why would an ousted board of directors whose members included officials of J. P. Morgan & Company, the Chase Manhattan Bank, numerous major corporations, and White, himself, pay off with their own

---

[7] In the Montgomery Ward campaign, Louis E. Wolfson and his associates spent over $500,000, of which Wolfson, himself, put up more than $170,000. Sewell Avery, the victor, spent $766,000 of Ward's funds to defend his power. Wolfson and his family acquired 59,000 shares of Ward stock at an average price "in the low 70's." He sold in the "high 80's." His profit must have approximated a million. It was not a financial defeat.

[8] Young's suit against the old Central directors was discontinued. He was in an ambiguous position, asking that he be paid for his outlays while White be denied payment.

money a lawsuit if they were convinced they had fulfilled their duty? The question is particularly pertinent, inasmuch as there never has been any doubt about White's ability as a railroad man. Young, himself, asked White to stay on as chief operating officer of the Central. And, after White was out at Central, he became president of the Delaware & Hudson Company, a railroad much smaller and less influential than Central, but better heeled financially and far more profitable.

The answer is to be found in a court decision handed down on July 8, 1955, long after the Central proxy fight, but right in the middle of the litigation over proxy expenses. A group of shareholders of Fairchild Engine and Airplane Corporation had sued to recover from present and former officers and directors payments by the company of expenses of both sides in a bitter and costly proxy fight. The stockholders objected not only to the reimbursement of expenses of the challenging group, which was successful and took office, but also to the use of corporate funds by the defeated management, to keep itself in office. Even though the plaintiffs did not succeed, the case—Rosenfeld *vs.* Fairchild—could make history. The ruling of the New York Court of Appeals, in allowing the payment of expenses, was so close, four judges to three, that it raised doubts about the validity of such payments under slightly modified circumstances. How would this court, New York's highest, decide in another instance? The switch of one jurist could change the law.

The minority of three judges questioned whether expenditures, aside from sending out notices of the meeting, informing shareholders of the issues, and paying proxy solicitors to alert stockholders to their voting rights, were legal. "Purely campaign expenses of a management group do not serve a corporate purpose." [9] And, one of the majority judges indicated in a separate opinion that if the plaintiff had demanded a particularization of expenditures, proper and improper, he might have ruled out some of the management's outlays in its unsuccessful effort to stay in office. In that case, the decision would have been four to three the other way.

Confronted with this Fairchild decision, the lawyers for the old board of directors of Central were in a quandary. If they contested the suit, the attorney for the suing stockholders would demand a bill of particulars, and the court might reverse itself four to three, and disallow some of the outlays. One expenditure would certainly be questioned—the $97,000 for the reprinting and mailing to shareholders of the article from *Fortune* in violation of the copyright. Lawyers for White, *et al.*, raised this point: Agreed that all other expenses were proper, might not a court rule out an expense which admittedly violated the copyright law? Already, legal expenses to defend the suit had come to $100,000; if the suit went on through the courts, perhaps to the U.S. Supreme Court, such expenses might reach another $100,000. Therefore, when the proposal to settle for $125,000 was reached, it seemed sensible to cut the loss and let the principle go. Some of the board

[9] The majority opinion, written by Judge Charles W. Froessel, took the conventional view: "In the event of a proxy contest, if the directors may not freely answer the challenges of outside groups and in good faith defend their actions with respect to corporate policy for the information of the stockholders, they and the corporation may be at the mercy of persons seeking to wrest control for their own purposes, so long as such persons have ample funds to conduct a proxy contest." Central directors, as directors in proxy contests heretofore, had been guided by this legal concept.

The four-to-three Fairchild decision also approved the vote of shareholders to pay the expenses of the successful insurgents. But the decision hinged on the separate opinion of Judge Charles S. Desmond, who felt that the plaintiff had failed to particularize and, therefore, could not prove "unreasonableness." The minority of three reasoned that "the corporation lacks power to defray the expenses of the insurgents in their entirety. The insurgents were not charged with responsibility for operating the company." The minority opinion is potentially so significant that I have reprinted a large part of it in Appendix I.

were opposed to the very end to settling, but they went along with the majority. And so $125,000 went into the Central till.

In all, the proxy battle cost Central shareholders at least $1,500,000 cash. Of this, $1,008,000 went to Alleghany, Young, and others for their outlays. And at least another half million represented costs incurred by White in his unsuccessful effort to stay in power.[10]

Was the change in Central's management worth that price?

Wall Street historians will have to answer. This much we know, Robert R. Young took over his trusteeship for Central shareholders at a good time—when the 1953–54 recession was ending. Business and carloadings expanded vigorously a few months after he became chairman.

He increased the dividend, and at the 1956 stockholders' meeting reiterated his faith in an $8 to $10 eventual dividend. But will he deliver the dividend? Toward the end of 1957, Wall Street expressed grave doubt about Young's chances. Central stock fell from a post-proxy-fight high of 49½ to around 15. And Young was paying dividends in shares of Reading Company stock, which had been bought for investment, in order to conserve cash. And will he treat stockholders less cavalierly than he accused the former management of doing? The 1957 meeting, as noted in Chapter VIII, was as stormy and arbitrary as that of 1955.

What we will never know—because history is only made up of events, not might-have-beens—is what would have happened to Central had White won. Nor will we know how much of Central's earnings improvement in 1955 was due to policies initiated by White earlier. All we know is that White

---

[10] White argues that the $876,000 total used by Young in his suit was too high; it included, for example, the full costs of the annual meeting, which would have had to be held, anyway. However, it does not include the diversion of employee time and effort from routine Central business to the proxy contest.

promised very little to shareholders. He was held down by the immediate problems of the Central—heavy losses on passenger traffic and the burdens of running a railroad in a highly populous area—a so-called terminal facility. The Central, like the Pennsylvania and other eastern railroads, picks up freight from the West at places such as Chicago, St. Louis, or Pittsburgh, then moves the commodity—wheat, cotton, cattle, refrigerators, steel, or anything else—over a comparatively short haul. Or it picks up manufactured articles and delivers them to its western terminals. When traffic was not so congested, when terminals had extra capacity, that was profitable. But in today's hurly-burly, the eastern roads complain that these costs are inadequately paid for—that the long-haul roads make the money on the freight run and the eastern roads lose money on the terminal operations.

Young vaulted over such details. He is not an operating railroad man. He would get a railroad man for that; he chose Alfred E. Perlman, executive vice-president of the Denver, Rio Grande & Western. To Young's credit, he selected a man, after White said no, who had an impeccable reputation as a railroad operator.

Young would deal with larger problems—cutting Central's debt; utilizing its expensive real estate; planning for new equipment, such as lightweight passenger cars, to cut down the passenger deficit. These promises appealed to shareholders, who had no way of evaluating their feasibility, to dissatisfied shareholders, vexed by the erratic dividend record, and to speculators.

Yet promises in proxy contests, like promises in politics, do not always produce victory. In his fight for Montgomery Ward & Company, Louis E. Wolfson set forth an expansive program to add stores, split the stock, raise the dividend, and use surplus cash to call for tenders of stock at $95 a share (at a time when the stock was selling at $80). These pledges were calculated to sell Wolfson to shareholders and call attention to the ultra-conservatism of aged Sewell L. Avery. Wolfson got only 30 per cent of the votes and half these votes were stock he and close associates and friends had acquired.

And it was not because his promises to add stores, split the stock, and boost the dividend were reckless. They were adopted by John A. Barr who shortly after the proxy contest succeeded Avery in an internal corporate revolution. Question: Why, if Wolfson's policies were sufficiently right to be adopted, did he lose? Answer: He lost because Ward shareholders were a different breed from Central shareholders.[11] They were investors. Ward had been a steady dividend-payer. The bulk of its shares was held by investment trusts, banks, insurance companies, trustees, and large individual shareholders. Many of these were Chicagoans. They were not going to have this great midwestern enterprise taken over by an unknown eastern quantity. Avery was a known quantity.

Wolfson might divert assets. He had used funds of Devoe & Raynolds (paints) and New York Shipbuilding to buy Ward stock to help his cause. This was not corporate cricket any more than Young's lending Alleghany's money to Murchison and Richardson. And, whereas speculators in Central did not care about the niceties of money management, Ward holders did. They were for-keeps investors. They wanted a steward for their property who would develop consistent long-term policies to improve the company. They distrusted short-term maneuvers which would boost market quotations.

Avery kept attacking Wolfson's record, that he was a Johnny-come-lately in corporate finance; that he had started

[11] This is not second-guessing. Just before the Montgomery Ward meeting, I pointed out, in my column in the *Philadelphia Bulletin* and other newspapers, that if the Central voting pattern were to prevail, Wolfson was sure to lose. Because, unlike Central, there was not a big street vote to go to the challenger.

out as a junkman. Implication: He would turn corporate milk-
man. The attack worked. Wolfson had promised too much
for Ward's shareholders; whereas White had not promised
enough for Central's.

Stockholders were not interested, in either case, in detailed
records—what the past managements had done, what the new
managements might do. They were given images. White
painted himself as a conservative. Young was the look-far-
ahead man, the great promiser—by his own and by White's
description of him. Avery was the arch-conservative. He said
so. And so did Wolfson of Avery, accenting the image. The
stockholders voted accordingly.

Men vote and candidates win and lose by the images they
construct of one another. In other words, a proxy battle is just
another political campaign. And stockholders, like voters,
choose only as well as their knowledge of the men and the
issues permit, which, considering that most stockholders are
too busy with their own affairs and careers, is usually superficial.
Only when the professionals, the institutions, get into a proxy
fight is there knowledge and understanding in depth. And
proxy battles, as we shall see in the next chapter, is what the
pros do not get into! That is the great gap in stockholder
potency.

CHAPTER XII

The Institutional Investors—
In Management We Trust

STOCKHOLDERS not only deserve what they get, but they get what they want. The annual meeting of Montgomery Ward & Company in April, 1949, was a demonstration of how decorous and self-restrained stockholders are. This goes particularly for the large, sophisticated institutional shareholders, such as investment trusts, insurance companies, trust companies. The bigger they are, the staider they brawl.

This meeting had plenty of advance publicity. Merrill Griswold, then chairman of the giant Massachusetts Investors Trust, which owned 104,000 shares of Montgomery Ward & Company, had publicly expressed his dissatisfaction with Sewell L. Avery as Ward's commander in chief. Too many good men either had quit or been fired by Avery. Among them:

Raymond Folger, whom Avery bid away from W. T. Grant & Company, and who departed from Ward, saying: "It's not because I have another position." Subsequently, he rejoined Grant as president.

Walter Hoving, who took the presidency of Lord & Taylor, New York, and later formed Hoving Corporation.

Frank M. Folsom, who subsequently became vice-president and then president of Radio Corporation of America.

Avery's policies were so at variance with the postwar tempo

that he could not hold directors. George Whitney and Harry P. Davison, of J. P. Morgan & Company, the firm which persuaded Avery to lend his executive talents to Ward's in 1931, resigned from the board. Avery had a conviction—that America was in for a postwar depression à la 1919–20. He refused to expand. He kept a tight control on inventories. His merchandising officers fretted. They were losing sales. Sears, Roebuck & Company, their powerful rival, was gaining, gaining, gaining.

Wellington Fund, another nationally known investment trust, followed Massachusetts Investors Trust's lead. It, too, felt Avery was running for a storm cellar instead of an inflation hedge. So, when the meeting day arrived, Chicago had an influx of out-of-town financial writers. And all the Chicago newspapers were represented. Maybe there would be fireworks.

Alas, for expectations! Massachusetts Investors quietly voted its stock for nominees other than Avery. A. Moyer Kulp, vice-president of Wellington, issued a statement before the meeting saying he was cumulating Wellington's vote for one director, David A. Crawford, president of Pullman Company. Vocal dissonance came solely from W. McNeil Kennedy, an attorney representing the Chicago investment counsel firm of Stein, Roe & Farnham. Kennedy protested against the "exodus of managerial talent, over forty in number, that had marched in and out of Montgomery Ward in the last few years." The Stein, Roe & Farnham stock wasn't voted at all.

After that, the meeting fizzed like an improperly loaded firecracker. Some stockholders rose to praise Avery as the grand old man of Ward's. Of all nominees for director, Avery corraled the greatest number of votes. His own holdings, of course, could have been cumulated to that effect. Anyway, he was morally victorious. Most banks, trust companies, insurance companies, investment trusts, and individual investors, large and small, went along with law, order, and the line of least resistance—Avery. Maybe Ward's was not keeping up with Sears. Maybe Avery's policies were hypercautious in a period of postwar prosperity. Maybe he was high-handed in handling men. Still, he paid dividends regularly. Ward was a comfortable, safe stock. And that, essentially, is what most investors want.

Newspapermen filed out of the Ward meeting thinking that this was a beginning. Other large shareholders in Ward's, whether openly or working behind paneled doors, would take up what MIT, Wellington, and Stein, Roe & Farnham had started. For Avery, then seventy-five, had already become a butt for quips. In May, 1946, *Fortune* quoted an unnamed Chicagoan as saying Avery was "the most extraordinary business genius this town has ever seen—and its greatest living argument for compulsory retirement at age sixty-five."

Not for five years were the newspapermen to be right. Officials of Massachusetts Investors and Wellington Fund had no taste for organizing a group to oppose Avery. They were not willing to assume responsibility for choosing a successor. What if the successor failed? They would be labeled poor pickers. Investing was their job. Not managing companies, not being the power behind management. Indeed, MIT and Wellington ultimately sold all Ward holdings. When the proxy battle finally took place, both sat on the sidelines.

The man who stormed Avery's bastion was not a man born to the Wall Street Luncheon Club, the Bankers Club, the University Club. He was no member of the Chicago meat-packing or railroad moguls. He was an outsider who wanted in.

Louis E. Wolfson did what the trusts, the trust companies, and other large investors hadn't a stomach for. He decided that Montgomery Ward & Company needed a change, that he was the man to change it. He and a group of friends, nicknamed the "hungry angels," started to buy Montgomery Ward stock in 1954. And soon, Wall Street became aware that a proxy battle impended. But note this—for it is the burden of this chapter—Wolfson was not like Massachusetts Investors, Wellington, or other large trust companies and institutions that owned, either directly or for clients, Ward stock. He was not defending, protecting, what he already had. He was not, as a stockholder, an owner, improving his company. He was buying a fight, picking a fight. He was interested in taking over a company for himself. He used the cloak of corporate democracy, just as Robert R. Young did in his successful battle for control of New York Central.

That is the striking fact about proxy fights. They are not engineered, financed, and strategied by simon-pure investors. They are the work of men with a yen for control, for managing. Thus, Wolfson has frequently been called a corporate raider. Avery charged that he was after Ward's huge cash reserve—something over $300,000,000, a sum so large that the company was dubbed the only "bank in the world that issues a mail-order catalogue." Many persons believed that Wolfson would use Ward funds for leapfrog operations. He had gained control of other companies and then used their assets to take over others. Indeed, during the proxy battle, he used funds of Devoe & Raynolds and New York Shipbuilding Corporation, which he controlled, to buy 40,000 and 6,000 shares respectively of Montgomery Ward.[1] And Devoe & Raynolds and New York Ship contributed $60,000 and $10,000 respectively to the proxy campaign.

Such antics, which are traditional (and legal if they work) in the world of finance, do not appeal to conservative inves-

[1] These purchases were widely criticized and cost Wolfson votes. At a press conference, Wolfson said that if he had to do it over again, he would not have made such purchases because of the talk it caused. His defense was that he and other officers of Devoe & Raynolds and New York Ship looked on Montgomery Ward stock as a good purchase. On March 20, 1956, the *Philadelphia Bulletin* reported that both companies had disposed of their Ward stock. Devoe realized $289,000 from capital gain and dividends, New York Ship $9,021, after deducting their proxy campaign contributions.

tors—to insurance companies, bankers, investment trust managers. And so when the vote was finally tabulated, the very investors who were disturbed by Avery's inability to hold executive talent chose him rather than Wolfson.

The struggle bared Avery's incapacity. At the stockholders' meeting, he constantly reached back into the past and repeated himself over and over again. You could see and hear the retrogression of a once-outstanding mind. (*See* Appendix II.) As an aftermath, he had to quit, along with the man he had made president, Edmund A. Krider.

Long before this, large investors had been getting out of Ward stock because of loss of faith in the management. MIT and Wellington, as noted, had sold. Those that held on did so because the intrinsic value was there—excellent book value. Some investors counted on an enhancement in value once Avery was out. "He can't live forever," was one brutal comment. At the end of 1948, investment trusts held 399,600 shares of Montgomery Ward stock. By the end of 1954, that was down to only 193,300 shares, a 50 per cent drop. In contrast, investment trust holdings of Sears, Roebuck fell from 1,380,000 to 1,200,000,[2] or only 14 per cent. The trusts were deserting Avery. They were doing so quietly, discreetly, so as not to break their own market. They were not acting as sophisticated protectors of the "little man," as one writer hopefully thought they might, thus: "Investment companies may serve the useful role of representatives of the great number of inarticulate and ineffective individual investors in industrial corporations. . . . Throughout the course of the existence of such industrial corporations, various problems are presented to stockholders [requiring] knowledge of financial and management practices not possessed by the average stockholder. Investment companies by virtue of their research facilities and specialized personnel are not only in a position to adequately appraise these

[2] Data supplied by Vickers & Company, New York.

situations but also have the financial means to make their support or opposition effective. These investment companies can perform the function of sophisticated investors. . . . They can appraise the activities of the management critically and expertly, and in that manner not only serve their interests but the interests of other public stockholders." [3]

The institutional investor functions primarily as an investor, not as a militant or crusading shareholder. No Gilberts there! Any assistance rendered the small shareholder is a by-product, the result of a common interest. Institutional investors as well as individual stockholders, large and small, desire good management, good earnings, good dividends, and steady growth. But, like all stockholders, they are competitors. This competition, this divergence of interest, was bluntly indicated by the vice-president of a large insurance company who wrote in reply to a questionnaire:

"We believe in investing in Management. If the Management is sound, we believe in supporting Management. If the Management should prove not to be capable, we try to be out of the situation before it becomes evident publicly." Thus, in the Wall Street game of investing, you try to pass on to some unsuspecting buyer a security which you suspect will decline—and you do it before other holders have similar suspicions. [4]

[3] I apologize to the author for having misplaced his name. I thought the quotation came from an SEC report, but a check at the SEC through Orval L. DuBois, secretary, was unrewarding.

[4] In *The General Theory of Employment, Interest, and Money* (Book IV, ch. 12, p. 155), John Maynard Keynes likened professional investing to "a game of Snap, of Old Maid, of Musical Chairs—a pastime in which he is victor who says Snap neither too soon nor too late, who passes the Old Maid to his neighbor before the game is over, who secures a chair for himself when the music stops. These games can be played with zest and enjoyment, though all the players know that it is the Old Maid which is circulating, or that when the music stops some of the players will find themselves unseated.

"Or, to change the metaphor slightly, professional investment may be likened to those newspaper competitions in which the competitors have to pick out the six prettiest faces from a hundred photographs, the prize being awarded to the competitor whose choice most nearly corresponds to the

In many purely management matters—in which it might seem as if the large investor and the small investor would have identical interests—the attitudes are not necessarily the same at all. Consider the case of executive compensation—salaries, stock options, bonuses, pensions, which often are submitted to shareholders for approval. It is not entirely clear on which side of the table the managers of large investment assets sit. They, themselves, are executives. They, themselves, often are interested in liberal pension plans, stock bonuses, etc., etc., for themselves. If they criticize, as too liberal, compensation of companies in which they invest, they will, in a sense, be placing a limit on their own compensation. So, they may not be too critical of generous plans of other companies. This dulls their critical faculties. Most institutional investors have a simple investment rule: In management we trust. The senior vice-president of one of New York's largest banks, put it this way: "No security is purchased or held very long unless we have confidence in the integrity and ability of the management. Therefore, when we establish a basis for this confidence, we are inclined to give management substantial freedom of action in carrying out its functions. We consider such functions as the determination of compensation, amount of pensions and other similar matters to properly fall within the area and jurisdiction of management. In our view the test as to whether there is a basis of confidence is the accomplishment of management, and so long as performance warrants and the proposals are in our judgment reasonable we are willing to express

---

average preferences of the competitors as a whole, so that each competitor has to pick, not those faces which he himself finds prettiest, but those which he thinks likeliest to catch the fancy of the other competitors, all of whom are looking at the problem from the same point of view. It is not a case of choosing those which, to the best of one's judgment, are really the prettiest, nor even those which average opinion genuinely thinks the prettiest. We have reached the third degree where we devote our intelligences to anticipating what average opinion will be. And there are some, I believe, who practice the fourth, fifth and higher degrees."

our confidence by voting in favor of the proposals of such management."

This in-management-we-trust view is seconded by the head of one of America's large mutual funds: "As you well know, institutions, such as this trust, make a thorough investigation of all aspects of a company's situation before purchasing stock. One of the most vital factors investigated is the character and capability of the management. Therefore, it is a rare occasion indeed when controversies or great differences of opinion as to management policies arise between institutions such as the trust and managements. Furthermore, it is undesirable that quarrels of this type become open and public inasmuch as the position of the rank and file of shareholders, as reflected in market quotations for the stock, is usually harmed thereby."

These were carefully considered statements made in reply to a questionnaire I sent to institutional investors—insurance companies, investment trusts, and banks—on their policies as stockholders in companies.[5] The terse reply of a large insurance company to the nine questions is revealingly typical of the institutional investor's uncrusading attitude:

> 1. Is the rôle of the large institutional investor limited to voting for or against management and stockholder proposals on proxy statements?
> *Yes.*
> 2. Should an institution offer proposals in proxy state-

[5] Institutions good enough to respond to the questionnaire in sufficient detail to make their replies useful were: American Insurance Group; Bank of America, San Francisco; Bankers Trust Company, New York; Boston Fund; Calvin Bullock; Chase Manhattan Bank, New York; Chemical Corn Exchange Bank, New York; Commonwealth Investment Company, San Francisco; Delaware Fund; First National Bank of Chicago; Girard Trust Corn Exchange Bank, Philadelphia; Glens Falls Insurance (group); Graham-Newman Corporation; Insurance Company of North America; Massachusetts Investors Trust; National Securities and Research Corporation; State Street Investment Corporation; Wellington Fund.

ments on matters of policy, such as cumulative voting, limitation on salaries, pensions, stock options?

No.

3. Should the institution take the lead or openly participate in a fight to organize stockholder action to unseat an unsatisfactory management or to defeat a management proposal?

Only in case of fraud.

4. Do you favor cumulative voting to strengthen the position of minority stockholders vis-à-vis management? Have you other suggestions to strengthen the position of shareholders?

No.

5. In the past year (12 months) have you voted against any management proposal? If so, can you indicate which companies, the nature of the proposals, and your reasons for voting against them?

No.

6. In the past year have you initiated any proposals of your own in management proxy statements? Can you indicate the companies involved and the nature of the proposals?

No.

7. In the past year have you taken any affirmative measures (other than Question 5) to organize stockholder action vs. management?

No.

8. Have management policies motivated you to sell a company's stock when perhaps other considerations might have disposed you to keep it? Can you furnish an example?

No.

9. In view of the growing importance of institutional investors, is it desirable for them to act purely as investors—that is, vote for or against management proposals and sell

stock if dissatisfied? Or should they assume leadership and furnish the small investor with sophisticated guidance?
Our opinion is stockholders should act as investors.

Institutional investors are not aloof from management or management problems. Just the opposite. They maintain "close and friendly contacts" with companies in which they are heavily invested. But this is for their own self-protection and guidance, not for other stockholders in general. They employ security analysts to follow and learn, in advance if possible, about earnings trends, research and development progress, expansion plans, and the character and strength of competition. The president of an insurance company wrote:

"In the vast majority of cases, we find managements of corporations very anxious to discuss affairs with us and to obtain suggestions that might improve their operations in any way. If the suggestion is a good one, they are happy to adopt it; if it is not a good one, they are ready and willing to explain the reasons for their opposition."

This company related the following unusual incident:

"We were substantial holders of the common stock in a grocery chain. We wrote a letter to the president asking certain general questions. We did not receive an acknowledgment or reply until more than three weeks had passed, and when the reply came it was completely unsatisfactory and in very general form and was furnished by the secretary of the company. Feeling that the general nature of the reply was possibly caused by the form of our inquiry, we wrote a very detailed letter of four pages, containing specific questions and statements for answer and comment. Some weeks passed before we had any reply to this, and the reply came ultimately only by pressure which we exerted through the firm's bankers. When it did come, the answers were anything but full and were entirely unsatisfactory. Since neither the president nor the secretary saw fit to give us the information we felt we were entitled to, our Finance Committee decided that either the firm had extremely poor stockholder relations or that possibly something was being covered up. In any event, as a result of management policies (or lack of them), we disposed of our rather substantial holdings."

Large corporations have come to recognize the power of the market place. So, usually when institutional investors ask for information they get it—and cordially. The institutional investor has "ins" with management, directly or through its bankers. Oftentimes, managements will seek the views of large shareholders beforehand on major proposals, such as a new stock issue, a stock option plan or a bonus which would increase costs. When institutional investors have doubts about proposals, they will inquire directly—by letter or personal contact. They will stay out of proxy fights, avoid publicity. The trust officer of a bank explained why his institution avoided proxy fights, thus:

"Who would bear the cost of such a struggle? The owners of the investment would not want to assume the burden. The bank, in order to protect some of its clients, could not impose the cost on its own stockholders. Besides, holdings in any one security represent so small a fraction of the bank's total portfolio that a fight would take a disproportionate amount of time, effort, and expense. So we're disposed to sell when we don't like what a company's doing."

One banker made the buck-passing suggestion that the trust department of a bank "might very well be fully justified in confining its activities to the rôle of investor. However, a mutual fund, life insurance company, or other institutional investor might very well assume leadership and furnish a small investor with sophisticated guidance." Executives of mutual funds and insurance companies would undoubtedly reply that they are no more justified in using stockholders' funds to help out investors in general than is a bank in using its stockholders' funds to protect stocks held in trust funds. In short, institutional investors lust for peace not jousts.[6] They are not Sir Galahads.

Therefore, institutional investors are lukewarm on cumulative voting. The head of a leading investment trust wrote: "It's unsatisfactory—it opens the possibility for two or more dissenting groups to have places on boards of directors, with the result that the management effort is not unified."

An insurance company executive supplemented this: "Theoretically, yes, I'm for cumulative voting. Practically, no. Very often it results in undesirable individuals gaining a nuisance position in an organization. They are often only concerned with their own selfish interests and their actions greatly disrupt a smoothly functioning business operation." The institutional point of view is fairly standardized: Harmony on boards of directors is more important than the critical stimulus of argumentation.[7]

Yet, it would be naïve to conclude that institutional inves-

[6] Graham-Newman Corporation believes that institutional investors ought to assume leadership in proxy struggles, as it, itself, has done. But it is hardly a conformist type of investment trust. It goes in for "special situations," often buys into companies which have been rundown and then attempts to revivify or take over the management. It openly criticized, for example, the management of American Hawaiian Steamship Company in a letter to shareholders. Officers of Graham-Newman actually became officers in the Philadelphia & Reading Corporation, formerly Philadelphia & Reading Coal and Iron.

[7] The division of the board of directors of Fairbanks, Morse & Company, nationally known manufacturer of motors, pumps, diesel locomotives, is a case in point. The attempt of Leopold D. Silberstein, head of Penn-Texas Corporation, to buy control ended in litigation and a negotiated settlement, under which Robert H. Morse, Jr., president, selected five directors, Silberstein five directors, and the eleventh director was named by Morse and was acceptable to Silberstein. Morse, under the Federal Court order, will be president and general manager for five years. However, this was not resolved by men with harmonious and similar objectives. It was a compromise, dictated by mutual frustration and by stalemate. Question: Will the board members collaborate peacefully, or is this merely an uneasy truce, during which Morse and Silberstein watch one another like wrestlers seeking the other's ultimate fall? Institutional investors deliberately shy away from managerial wrangles.

tors are no help whatsoever to small shareholders. Obviously, when representatives of banks, insurance companies, or investment trusts check up on management, and make suggestions, they improve the position of all shareholders. Further, the institutional investors act as an informed conscience. In submitting stock option, bonus and pension plans to shareholders, company officials know that the expert analysts of institutional investors will scrutinize them. This awareness may curb avarice. A corporate conscience is not solely an internal creation. It is helped along by a realization that actions, even though not openly opposed, may be criticized or disapproved. Word gets around the clubs, banking houses, that "So-and-so sure helped himself. . . ."

Thus, the institutional investor, by applying professional skill to investing, helps to improve the managerial breed. And so it helps out all stockholders, all investors. But it does not do this as a champion. It will not lead proxy fights. It will not try to organize opposition to company plans. It works behind the scenes—without publicity. And when it feels the management is on a completely wrong tangent, then quickly, quietly, and unqueasily it sells out—leaving other shareholders to be the Old Maids.

Institutional investors will argue that this, in itself, is an important function. A decline in the price of a stock often persuades a stubborn management to mend its ways. Or some large stockholder, or an outsider, seeing that stock can be bought at a reasonable price, moves in. That is how a Louis Wolfson, a Robert R. Young, a Russell McPhail, or a Ben Heineman provides a service. It is not the institutional investor that produces the change. He does not use his insight or purse to improve the company. He leaves that to the newcomer, the raider, a greatly misapplied term. The raiders of yesterday are the textbook heroes of today just as today's raiders will be storied characters of tomorrow.

Commodore Cornelius Vanderbilt's methods of capturing control of the New York Central in the 1860's would never pass the sixteen-ounce-gloves test of the 1950's. Robert R. Young's methods are prissy in comparison. The Commodore had got control of the New York & Hudson Railroad, on which the Central depended in winter for the transfer of passengers and freight from Albany to New York when the Hudson River was frozen over and boat lines could not operate. According to Stewart H. Holbrook, in his rewarding book, *The Age of the Moguls*, "The Commodore felt his Hudson should get all the business, summer and winter. . . . So, one bitter day in winter, the Hudson train stopped short at East Albany, almost two miles from the Albany depot, its usual terminal."

Passengers and freight were stranded by two miles of snow, sleet, rain, and Commodore Vanderbilt's will. "Almost immediately the stock of Central began to slide. When it had fallen to what Commodore Vanderbilt considered a reasonable price, he bought eighteen million dollars' worth of it and became president." He later combined the Central and the New York & Hudson into a single system, calling it the New York Central & Hudson River Railroad. In a different way, John D. Rockefeller, Sr., was a raider—he developed the great Standard Oil trust by squeezing his competitors through price-cutting and secret railroad rebates and then buying them in at "reasonable" prices. Daniel Drew and Jay Gould, whose names have not been tinted in pastels by history or famous heirs, were notorious raiders in their day. Drew, Gould, and Jim Fisk, the show girl's delight, collaborated on the Erie, battling Commodore Vanderbilt. Later Gould took over the Missouri Pacific, Union Pacific, and other roads, using the *New York World*, which he bought in its pre-Pulitzer era, to influence the stock market and vilify his enemies.[8]

In modern times, the raider usually goes in after the stock

[8] Jay Gould sold the *World* to Joseph Pulitzer in 1883.

is depressed—after the institutional investors have washed their portfolios clean of it. But the stockholder who stays with the company cannot be certain whether the new management is better than the old. He does not have the benefit of the institutional investor in the proxy fight—if the institutional investor is out of the stock.

If this is a criticism of the institutional investor, for being narrow-minded in approach, it is also a monolatrous compliment. The institutional investor does not get involved in side issues or side problems. Some investment companies have a rule: No officer may serve as director of any company, because it might influence investment judgment. The institutional investor tries to serve only one master: his own shareholder or client. In this rôle and attitude, he does what the small shareholder, himself, would do: Serve himself and well. In investing, the rule is not to expect others to do what you would not do, yourself: Dragon-slaying is for those who get something out of slaying dragons.

CHAPTER XIII

Management *über* Alles—
The Ford Stock Sale

IF THE PRECEDING CHAPTER failed to convince you of the over-riding homage paid by institutional investors to Management *über Alles*, perhaps this chapter—the story of the legal device behind the public offering of 10,200,000 shares of Ford Motor Company—will.

In mid-January, 1956, an underwriting syndicate, headed by such gilded names as Blyth & Company; First Boston Corporation; Goldman, Sachs & Company; Kuhn, Loeb & Company; Lehman Brothers; Merrill Lynch, Pierce, Fenner & Beane; White, Weld & Company; [1] offered stock to a palpitating public at $64.50 a share.

A grand coup! Before you could say Merrill Lynch, etc., the Ford Motor Company had 300,000 shareholders, more than Westinghouse Electric, RCA, Columbia Broadcasting, Union Carbide, du Pont, or Socony-Mobil Oil. It became the fifth most widely held corporation in America. Only American Telephone & Telegraph, General Motors, Standard Oil (N.J.), and General Electric had more owners. No such widespread distribution of a common stock had ever before been attained so quickly anywhere. It was a tribute to the marketing ability of

[1] Nearly everybody but Morgan Stanley & Company, which is closely associated with General Motors Corporation.

Wall Street underwriters and the touching desire of so many Americans to be owners of Ford.[2]

But this ownership had—and has—a difference. If stockholders in American Telephone & Telegraph become dissatisfied with the management of President Frederick R. Kappel, they can vote to throw him out. Likewise, General Motors shareholders can vote Harlow H. Curtice out of office. Standard Oil and General Electric shareholders possess similar power, if not disposition, to depose presidents.

Not Ford shareholders. They could never—well, hardly ever—dislodge Henry Ford II or his successors from office. That is because the public shareholders bought—were sold—Class A shares. And these Class A shares, though they have voting rights, have circumscribed voting power. They are second-class shares.

The members of the Ford family are first-class shareholders. They own Class B shares, which, far from being junior in status, endow the Fords with a right of management that is durable if not divine. This stock possesses a voting power with a reverse ratio. As Ford family stock in the company diminishes, the voting power of its stock increases. The legal dignitary who magicked this ingenious device earned his fee, if not the plaudits of persons who believe in equity at the corporate ballot box.

On the surface, the voting plan seems reasonable, even generous. Through gifts and bequests from Henry Ford, founder of the business, and his son, Edsel, the Ford Foundation received 88.4 percent of the total equity in the company. Understandably, Henry, the first, and Edsel wanted their immediate heirs to control the destiny of the corporation; they did not

[2] This anxiety for ownership was undoubtedly tinctured by a yen for speculative profits—a yen which was not satisfied. Ford stock rose to about $70 a share on the over-the-counter market, quickly fell back to the offering price, and then when the selling syndicate stopped supporting the market, dropped below $64.50. *Sic transit . . .*

want a foundation appointing directors and officers. So, Foundation shares were voteless. So long as the Fords, a few officials, and the Foundation owned all the stock, this was no public affair and it met the corporate mores of the times.

But then the trustees of the Foundation concluded it was not sensible to be completely dependent on the fortunes of a single company in an upsy-downsy industry, such as the automobile industry. Investment prudence demanded diversification. And besides, as U.S. District Judge Charles E. Wyzanski, Jr., a Foundation trustee, expressed it, such a large single investment "might psychologically promote too close a connection between a great charity and one business enterprise." [3]

Once the decision to diversify was reached, the Foundation, the Ford Motor Company, the Ford family, Wall Street underwriters, and the New York Stock Exchange faced a problem. The New York Stock Exchange has a rule that only voting stock may be listed on the Exchange. And the Fords, the Foundation trustees, and the Exchange, itself, felt an Exchange listing was essential. The company was recapitalized to this purpose. The Ford family agreed to vest 60 percent of the voting power in the stock the Foundation would sell to the public, regardless of the number of shares sold—6,000,000 shares as originally planned, 10,200,000 shares which were sold, or even ultimately 46,348,620 shares if the Foundation disposed of all its stock.

So it appeared as if the family actually handed over voting control to the public, as if the new investors could, if they saw fit, oust the Fords. Arithmetically, no doubt, they could. Practically, as we shall see presently, that is more improbable than Baron Munchausen's tales.

This superficial sacrifice did not go unrewarded. In the recapitalization, all the non-voting shares in the company, including 190,347 shares owned by the Ford family, were exchanged for

[3] In a letter to me, replying to comments in my column on the transaction.

new stock at the rate of fifteen new shares for each old share. But the 172,645 shares of voting stock held exclusively by family members were exchanged at the rate of twenty-one shares for one. So, for giving up the exclusive right to vote, the Ford family got a bonus of 1,035,870 shares in recapitalization. The family equity in the company was increased from 10.38 per cent to 12.12 per cent, and all its shares were accorded Class B voting power.[4]

Nobody can say precisely just how much a New York Stock Exchange listing is worth in cash to a particular company, an individual investor, or to a foundation with stock to sell. The Exchange is proud of being the nation's biggest and most active market place in securities. It boasts about its method for policing dealings on the floor, to see that investors—buyers and sellers of stocks and bonds—get a fair break from their brokers. This reputation for fair dealing is so well established and the breadth of the market so well accepted, that some investors will deal only in securities traded on the Big Board, as the New York Stock Exchange is known in Wall Street. Often stocks will go up on the bare announcement of intention to list. And the Exchange has compiled figures to show that it costs companies with New York Stock Exchange listing 56 per cent less to float stock than companies whose stocks are not listed.[5]

---

[4] The formal statement of the Foundation explained this thus: "This increased equity reflects, in addition to other terms of the plan, the relinquishment of the exclusive right to vote in the affairs of management. In transferring 60 per cent of the voting rights to the new common stock, holders of old 'B' shares accept an immediate drop in their voting rights from 100 per cent to 40 per cent for all family interests."

[5] Economic Research Memorandum of June, 1957. In gross terms, Big Board statisticians figure that the cost of raising $100 in new capital by selling common stock was $2.60 for companies with a Big Board listing against $5.97 for companies whose stocks were not listed on the Exchange. To be sure, Big Board companies are the biggest. So gross difference in cost of all issues is not conclusive. However, other evidence was adduced. The cost of selling three stock issues of New York Stock Exchange companies with assets of less than $25,000,000 came to 2.85 per cent versus 7.84 per cent for

The advisers to the Fords and the Foundation obviously regarded a listing as a thing of value. An actual price, deliberately or inadvertently, was decided on when the Fords "traded" a voting privilege, which was a necessary enabling action to secure a listing, for 1,035,870 shares of additional stock. At $64.50, the offering price, this listing privilege became worth about $65,000,000. To the Foundation, the right to say, "The company has applied for listing of the common stock on the New York Stock Exchange," was doubly helpful:

First, in the immediate sale of 10,200,000 shares to the public; second, in the future sale of some or all of its remaining 36,148,620 shares.

Investors will pay more for a listed stock and, inferentially, for a stock with voting power. The Class B voting stock of

twenty-seven issues of companies of approximately the same size off the Big Board; for companies with assets ranging from $25,000,000 to $49,999,999, the comparative costs were 3.05 per cent for nine issues and 5 per cent for twelve issues of off-Big Board companies; for companies with assets from $50,000,000 up to $100,000,000, the percentages were 3.31 per cent for eleven issues and 6.08 per cent for ten issues. There were too few examples for valid comparisons for companies with assets above a hundred million.

On the basis of number of shareholders—indicating the degree of public acceptance of the corporation—the comparative costs of common stock flotations were:

No. of Shareholders	Big Board Companies		All Other Companies	
	No. of Issues	% Cost	No. of Issues	% Cost
Under 2,500	4	3.40%	14	8.82%
2,500-4,999	10	3.63	14	4.90
5,000-9,999	10	2.66	4	3.68
10,000-24,999	14	2.67	6	3.00

The comparison by size of issue was as follows:

Amount of Issue	Big Board Companies		All Other Companies	
	No. of Issues	% Cost	No. of Issues	% Cost
Up to $4,999,999	19	3.36%	43	6.17%
$5,000,000 to $9,999,999	13	2.31	7	5.06
Over $10,000,000	Too Few Examples			

M. A. Hanna & Company customarily sells about 2 per cent higher than the Class A non-voting in the over-the-counter market. Indeed, when M. A. Hanna decided to put out non-voting stock, Keith Funston, president of the New York Stock Exchange, urged George M. Humphrey, then head of the company and later Secretary of the Treasury, not to do so. A non-voting stock, Funston reminded Humphrey, would not be listable on the New York Stock Exchange and a company, such as Hanna, might some day want listing on the Big Board.

From the outset, the Ford family and the Foundation decided that a publicly held Ford stock ought to be listed on the Big Board along with GM, Chrysler, American Motors, and Studebaker-Packard. For Ford to be on a lesser exchange would be—er, er, well, demeaning. To the "un-marketwise," it might suggest that the company was not worthy of listing. Besides, the company's management wanted as many shareholders as it could possibly muster for merchandising reasons. Every Ford stockholder is a potential preferrer of a Ford car. The more stockholders, the more prospective sales. And a Big Board listing would make it easier to obtain lots of stockholders.

Listing of Ford on the New York Stock Exchange was a blow to Edward T. McCormick, who left a Securities and Exchange commissionership to become president of the New York Curb Exchange and who changed the name of the Curb to the American Stock Exchange for dignity. McCormick had expected to get Ford on his board. The American Stock Exchange lists non-voting shares. He knew the Big Board did not. And he did not anticipate that the Fords would relinquish voting control. In this judgment he was right. But he did not reckon with the flexibility of New York Stock Exchange rules.

Keith Funston, president of the New York Stock Exchange, wanted Ford on his exchange. The stock was sure to be actively traded. That would mean commissions for New York Stock Exchange member firms. There would be listing fees.

Initially, the Big Board received more than $70,000. And each year there is an annual fee of $6,850. Finally, as one of the largest companies in the world—rich in reputation as well as finances—Ford would impart prestige to the Exchange, even as an Exchange listing imparted prestige to Ford. So elasticizing a rule in a self-serving cause was sound financial doctrine for Funston and the New York Stock Exchange.

The rule requiring all common stocks to have voting power was formulated after the investment banking firm of Dillon, Read & Company bought Dodge Brothers in 1925 and then turned around and retrieved its outlay by selling securities to a public which was just as anxious to buy Dodge stock then as a later generation was to buy Ford stock. Dillon, Read neglected, in selling securities to the public, to attach any voting privilege to the stock. The firm retained all voting control itself. Wall Street, at the time, did not mind. But Professor William Z. Ripley, of Harvard, who throughout his life fought against insider privilege in corporations, did. He protested in his book, *Wall Street and Main Street*, that the Dodge plan "bears every appearance of a bald and outrageous theft of the last tittle of responsibility for management from the actual owners."

His writings caused Wall Streeters—and particularly members of the New York Stock Exchange—to reëxamine the customs and procedures of the day. Professor Ripley's memorial is this statement in the Big Board's instruction to companies, called the "Company Manual": "Since 1926, the Exchange has refused to authorize listing of non-voting stock, or of any non-voting stock, however designated, which by its terms is in effect a common stock." As a general rule, the Exchange will not list the securities of a company in which a class of stock possesses voting power disproportionate to its equity. However, no specific standard for determining "appropriate apportionment of voting power" is set forth. (*See also* Chapter XIV.)

This is useful in the clubby atmosphere of Wall Street, where one man's principle is another man's convenience. And it was convenient for powerful persons, many of whom participated in the negotiations between the Ford Motor Company and the Foundation, many of whom were trustees of the Foundation, many of whom were associated with powerful institutions, to have Ford stock listed on the New York Stock Exchange. Among the trustees of the Foundation were John J. McCloy, head of the Chase Manhattan Bank and former U.S. High Commissioner for Germany; Charles E. Wilson, former head of General Electric Company, who served as chairman of a special finance committee of Ford Foundation trustees to arrange the plan; such well-known publishers as John Cowles, of the Cowles publications, and Mark F. Ethridge, of the *Louisville Courier-Journal*; Donald K. David, former head of the Harvard School of Business Administration; Judge Wyzanski.

George J. Leness, partner in Merrill Lynch, Pierce, Fenner & Beane, and Alexander M. White, partner in the investment firm of White, Weld & Company, advised the trustees. Sidney J. Weinberg, partner in Goldman, Sachs & Company, served as financial adviser to the Ford family, and Frederick M. Eaton, as legal counsel. The finance committee of the Foundation retained Eli Whitney Debevoise as legal counsel.

Such names radiate rectitude. And their actions were certainly righteous. There was full disclosure. The public was told everything about the voting provisions. The prospectus presented a tabulation showing how the shares of stock of the Ford family could rise from their 1.114 votes per share to 14.846 votes per share.[6] The tabulation also indicated that the Ford family could retain its 40 per cent vote with only 5.1 per cent of the total equity; a 30 per cent vote with only 2.8 per cent of

[6] This was not in the original prospectus; but newspaper articles calling attention to the deficiency either prompted the company to spell out the vote or the Securities and Exchange Commission to ask for amplification.

the equity. Question: Is that not disproportionate voting power—the right to a 40 per cent vote in a three-billion-dollar enterprise with only 5.1 per cent of the equity?

In essence, the Ford plan is not materially different from the Dodge Brothers plan. The voting power offered the public shareholders is sham power. And the participants in the transaction, including Keith Funston, of the Exchange, must have been aware of it. At the time of the sale, the Ford family owned 6,480,750 shares of Class B stock, or 12.1 percent of the total shares outstanding. Each of these shares, as noted above, had 1.114 votes, which gave the Fords 40 per cent of the outstanding votes. The 10,200,000 shares sold to the public plus the 623,100 shares owned by officers and employees (10,832,100 shares in all) each had one vote per share. The Foundation's 36,148,620 shares were not entitled to any vote. However, if the Foundation disposed of additional stock, that stock, when disposed of, was entitled to one vote per share.

Disposition of shares by the Foundation would not reduce Ford voting power. It would reduce the proportionate voting power of each public shareholder. If, for example, the Ford Foundation were to sell an additional 10,000,000 shares, each share of Ford family stock would automatically be entitled to 2.14 votes per share. Thus, the family would retain its 40 per cent vote. The proportionate vote of the common shares would be diluted by the sale of additional stock. There'd be 20,832,100 shares sharing the same 60 per cent vote instead of 10,832,100.

Furthermore, if the Ford family were to sell two million of its high-powered Class B shares, those shares, under the terms of the plan, would then be converted into ordinary one-vote-per-share common stock. Then there would be only 4,480,750 shares of Ford family stock. And these would then automatically rise to a higher voting power—3.4 votes per share—to provide the family with its preordained 40 per cent of the vote.

The Ford family could sell 3,780,750 Class B shares, reducing its holdings to 2,700,000 shares or 5.1 per cent of the total outstanding stock, and still retain 40 per cent of the vote. Think of what that means. If a group of stockholders disliked the Ford management for any reason, if they wanted to oust the executives, they would have to amass more than 85 per cent of the outstanding common shares. Eighty-five per cent from almost 300,000 shareholders widely scattered in the United States![7]

Nor is that the entire story. The Fords could reduce their holdings to all but 1,500,000 shares, or 2.8 per cent of the total equity, and they would still have effective voting control. Their Class B stock would get enough votes per share—in one extreme case 14.846 votes—to provide the family with 30 per cent of the vote. A group of dissident shareholders would have to collect nearly 72 per cent of the outstanding shares to take over the company. Since the Fords would control the proxy machinery, since shareholders ordinarily pursue the path of least resistance, and since Ford officers and employees also own common stock and presumably would side with the management, the chance of a successful stockholder revolt at Ford has been reduced to near zero. The voting plan perpetuates Ford family control for several generations, regardless of the quality of its management.[8]

Why, then, if this public voting power in Ford is nugacious, if it can never achieve the real purpose of voting, which is to elect officers freely (or, in corporate affairs, to dislodge an incumbent management), why did Wall Street accept it? Wall Streeters stood to gain much. First, the underwriting commission on 10,200,000 shares amounted to more than $15,000,000;

---

[7] As of July, 1957, there were 292,000.

[8] To retain their high-power voting stock, the Fords must hold a minimum of 1,500,000 shares. If their holdings drop to 1,499,000 shares, then the B stock is automatically reduced to only one vote per share. However, since the Fords start with 6,480,750 shares, that means they can dispose of more than three-quarters of their holdings—to meet inheritance taxes, to make gifts, etc.—without endangering their prerogative to control.

and the Stock Exchange was interested in fees per se. These are items, of course. But they would have been thrust aside if Wall Street, as an institution, as a collective in the distribution of securities, had been militantly mindful of voting rights, of so-called corporate democracy. The fact is that institutional Wall Street does not too much care. Its social horizons are bounded by tall buildings, a river, a churchyard, and, lamentably in this case, a dollar sign.

The ousting of a management is a last resort, something that institutional investors want no part of. They would rather sell the stock than get embroiled in a proxy battle. And when a company the size of Ford—with a reputable and historic background—brings out a stock, the absence of true voting power can be easily overlooked. Thus, as of March 31, 1956, twenty-six investment trusts held 211,000 shares. They felt like Miss C. V. Nader, of Cleveland, who, after reading several of my columns on the Ford voting setup, wrote:

"I cannot understand all your clamor about the voting rights of Ford stock. The Ford family has done a pretty bang-up job over the years in running that concern without the help or vote of outside stockholders."

Miss Nader is entirely right. Henry Ford II and his brothers have proved their managerial skill. They have gathered about them a group of executives who took a company which was floundering under the direction of Henry Ford, the first, in his older years and his son, Edsel, and edged it up to No. 2 spot in motordom—yapping at General Motors' heels. On the record, the Fords are eminently entitled to a vote of stockholder confidence. Henry Ford II has proved his capacity to manage. And being in the manager's seat, he could count—as do the officials of General Motors, American Telephone & Telegraph, General Electric, RCA, and thousands of other corporation executives and directors—on being returned to power. By deeds, not by lawyers.

But the Fords chose otherwise. They preferred the protection of a legal device—to insure their control against a raider. A raider could never take a chance at Ford. If managerial sclerosis set in, if the stock went down, shareholders would be held off by a fully disclosed legal ingenuity. The Fords obtained that protection because Wall Street and institutions give lip service to voting rights. They preach the right to "throw the rascals out," but don't practice it. They cast their vote, when something is wrong, not in the ballot box, but in the market place. Institutional Wall Street believes in Management *über Alles* until it has reason not to believe in management, and then it does not care. The institutions figure that when managerial sclerosis sets in, they will diagnose it first and get out. So they do not rise up in protest against a voting power which is paper power, sham power—which was devised in consultation with the New York Stock Exchange to permit listing but not ousting. That is the materialistic meaning—the pragmatism—of the Ford flotation.

CHAPTER XIV

The Stock Exchange in Sir Galahad's Clothing

ON MARCH 22, 1866—before the days of typewriters—the following form letter (printed) went out to the Secretary of the Delaware, Lackawanna & Western Railroad:

> SIR,
>
> The Stock Exchange of New York desire to collect Reports and Documents connected with Finance and Rail-roads, and to this end have appointed a Committee.
>
> I therefore beg to request you will direct, that from time to time, as they may be issued, the Reports of your Company be sent to the Secretary of the New-York Stock Exchange, George H. Brodhead, Esq., and if not occasioning you too much trouble, you will greatly oblige by furnishing, also, the Reports and Statements from a period as far back as they have been preserved.
>
> I am, respectfully,
G. L. GERRARD,
Chairman of Committee

That was seventy-four years after a group of twenty-four brokers first began trading under a Wall Street buttonwood on May 17, 1792. It marked the dawning on the members of the Exchange that they had a responsibility to know something about the companies in whose stocks and bonds they were dealing.

Thenceforward, the Stock Exchange pursued a persistent, though not always consistent, policy (1) of getting more information for shareholders, (2) of improving the quality and comparability of the information, and (3) of trying to see that stockholders' rights as stockholders were protected against improper and dubious practices of investment bankers, brokers, and managers of corporations, themselves. In its pursuit of rectitude the Exchange often met rebuffs.

The policy was self-preservation. The members of the New York Stock Exchange were often investors and speculators on their own account. They would like to have some insight into the companies in which they were staking their own money. If they relied on members of boards of directors, they never could be sure that they would be getting straight dope. Did J. P. Morgan tell Kuhn, Loeb? And did Kuhn, Loeb tell Joe Doakes & Company? Men in low places wanted to be as informed as those in high places—and as fast. They wanted equality of informational opportunity. Brokers also had a fiduciary responsibility. Often they acted as advisers to customers. And how could they advise sensibly and honestly, how could they answer simple questions on dividend prospects, unless they had some official information on earnings?

Finally, informational standards were good for business, for prestige. By demanding that companies report their earnings and make statements of their assets and liabilities, the New York Stock Exchange could put a stamp of disclosure on the stocks traded. "Listed on the New York Stock Exchange" ultimately became a valued hallmark for that reason. And the threat of delisting gave the Exchange power. Shareholders cherished a Big Board market. So did company officials.

Stewart Holbrook calls the era just after the Civil War when Gerrard sent out his letter the "era of brass knuckles." Information was worth money. Candor was what you did not trust. Daniel Drew had only recently introduced the phrase "watered stock" by thirsting his cattle, feeding them salt, and then leading them to water just before they walked onto butchers' weighing scales. He was the master of Erie Railroad for years, and his manipulation of the stock inspired this bit of Wall Street free verse, always quoted when Drew's name is mentioned:

> When Uncle Dan'l says "Up"
> Erie goes up,
> When Uncle Dan'l says "Down"
> Erie goes down,
> When Uncle Dan'l says "Wiggle-waggle"
> Erie bobs both ways.[1]

By 1866, Commodore Cornelius Vanderbilt had decided there was more money in railroads than in steamboating—he had acquired the New York & Harlem and the New York & Hudson roads, and was getting set to take over Central. Jay Gould, Jim Fisk, Drew's on-and-off cronies in conniving, were other titans of finance, along with Jay Cooke, who had won fame as a patriot—selling government bonds to finance the Civil War. Cooke had used full-page advertisements, brass bands, rabblerousing speakers, and flags, flags, flags, and flags to raise fighting dollars for the boys in blue. He was a forerunner of Charles E. Mitchell, chairman and super-salesman of the National City Bank of New York in the 'twenties. John D. Rockefeller had yet to establish his hegemony over oil. Andrew Carnegie had just begun to forge his Carnegie Steel Corporation, which in 1900 J. P. Morgan was to use as a nucleus for his steel trust—U.S. Steel. Morgan, himself, was still to become the "rationalizer" of American finance.

The New York Stock Exchange's voice was wee and lonely. So wee that the secretary of the Delaware, Lackawanna & Western Railroad answered the Stock Exchange request for reports in these curt words, written on the back of Gerrard's own letter:

[1] Once a broker saw a slip of paper drop from Drew's pocket. He picked it up; saw it was a duplicate order to buy thousands of shares of Erie. He bought, in anticipation of a rise. But Drew was selling! The duplicate order was a ruse.

The Delaware, Lackawanna & Western R. R. Co. make no reports, and publish no statements, and have not done anything of the kind for the last five years.

Not until 1895 was the Exchange bold enough to suggest forcefully to listed companies that they file regular annual reports. And not until 1900 was the Exchange sure enough of its own prestige to make annual earnings reports and balance sheets a prerequisite to listing. In 1932, the Exchange removed the stock of Brockway Motor because the company issued no annual report. In July, 1933, the Exchange felt powerful enough—helped along by the depression climate—to threaten to delist a truly large corporation for improper reporting. This was the famous case of the New York Exchange vs. Allied Chemical & Dye Corporation, in which the Exchange officials had not only to risk the ire of Allied officials and shareholders but also the wrath of members.

The members of the Exchange, the brokers, were and are a heterogeneous group of men with miscellaneous loyalties to commercial bankers, investment bankers, and corporations and individuals who give them business. In the 'twenties, the Exchange was often called a "private club," ruled by a board of governors closely tied to the big private banking firms, such as the House of Morgan; Kuhn, Loeb & Company; Dillon, Read & Company; Lee, Higginson, and to the large Wall Street commercial banks, such as National City, Chase National, Guaranty Trust Company.

It was common knowledge in those days that standards for listing the stock of a company with a well-placed board of directors were more lenient than for a company which did not have the right connections. And Allied had its friends among brokers and bankers—men of influence. Nevertheless, over a stretch of time—incident by incident—the New York Stock Exchange exerted its influence on corporate ethics. Some of the historic incidents which led to the formulation of rules [2] which improved the lot of shareholders are here reviewed:

ALLIED CHEMICAL & DYE

In the early 1930's, Allied Chemical & Dye was dominated by Orlando F. Weber, its president, a secretive man who feared that "foreign interests" or "business adversaries" might discover something about Allied to its competitive disadvantage. Weber worshiped accounts [3] and kept the corporate records of Allied in a series of black notebooks, marked by symbols, in a steel cabinet behind his desk. He was justifiably proud of Allied's performance during the depression. The company was comfortably in the black, though its earnings had fallen below its $6 dividend, and Wall Street never doubted that Allied's dividend was safe. The company's wad

[2] This chapter is concerned with the rules and regulations of the New York Stock Exchange which have helped to improve corporate behavior in relation to shareholders; it does not go into the rules which the Exchange has adopted to safeguard purchasers of stock against the insolvency or misconduct of its own members. In this latter category would be the rule requiring members to have a minimum capital of $50,000; the rule insisting on periodic examinations of the financial status of members; the rule governing the conduct of specialists; the rule which requires a member to report any unsecured loan of $2,500 or more. This last is known as the "Richard Whitney rule." Just before Richard Whitney & Company failed, Whitney borrowed from other members of the Exchange on his own recognition. Some members, not in the inner circle, were honored to lend him money. Thereafter they could call him "Dick." Such unsecured loans, if they had been generally known, might have been a tipoff of his firm's insolvency. Now, both the borrower and the lender are expected to report on unsecured loans. There is also the August Belmont Rule which forbids a sole proprietorship to deal with outside customers. When August Belmont died in 1924 there was no partner to carry on the business, and the customers who had securities or funds with August Belmont & Company had to await the settlement of his estate.

[3] As a hobby, he developed a set of accounts—a balance sheet and income statement—for the United States. He was deeply interested in protectionist economics. Friedrich List, the German economist and philosophical antagonist of Adam Smith, was a Weber hero. Weber liked to distribute List's *The National System of Political Economy*.

of investments, carried at $94,600,000 in the balance sheet, was big enough to float a major industrial enterprise. It gave Weber an impregnable sense of security, an independence of bankers. He was his and Allied's master. Yet the securities were not immune to the fluctuations of the stock market. They declined in value. And Weber, despite his love of bookkeeping, carried them at cost, an accounting heresy which concealed from competitors, foreigners and, inevitably, Allied's own shareholders the real condition of the company. Allied was strong but not so strong as its reports indicated. When the New York Exchange suggested that this manner of accounting was unorthodox and deceptive, Weber insisted that Allied had a listing agreement with the Exchange which admitted no change except by mutual consent. The Exchange responded that "requirements and practices should keep pace with the changes in business customs and conditions." Among the stocks in Allied's cache were its own common and preferred shares. Dividends received on these shares were treated as regular income. Since Allied was not earning its full dividend, this inflated profits. The Exchange declared the absence of details in its reports to shareholders made it possible for Weber "to vary the reported income up or down, at pleasure. . . . We do not say that this great power has been abused. We do say that it ought not to exist." The Exchange announced that Allied stock would be stricken from the list. Grudgingly, at the last minute, Weber assented to reforms. Today, Allied Chemical's accounts are complete—fully up to Stock Exchange and SEC standards.

The victory could never have been gained in the 1890's or the 1920's. But in 1933, the times called for disclosure. The 1929 crash led into the depression of 1930–33, the closing of the banks, and the Senate investigation of Wall Street and the New York Stock Exchange. The investigation disclosed how respected Wall Street bankers used funds to finance

speculative pools with themselves as participants and beneficiaries; how Albert H. Wiggin, the highly respected chairman of the Chase National Bank, sold Chase stock short
while, in his capacity as head of the bank, he authorized the
use of bank funds to support the price of the stock; how officers of American Commercial Alcohol (today American Distilling Company) made a phony report to secure listing of
additional stock on the New York Stock Exchange, and de-
prived their own shareholders of preëmptive rights to purchase stock—of which more later. And there were many, many
more shameful disclosures.

Never again would the New York Stock Exchange be a
private club ruled by an inner clique. It was now a public institution, whose public character would soon be formalized
by Congressional legislation. Ethical standards which the
Stock Exchange tried to obtain by persuasion were soon to be
imposed by law. Of that more later, too. Let's first go into
the "Erie Rule," and how Daniel Drew outfoxed Commodore Vanderbilt, and how some eighty-seven years later that
affected Peabody Coal Company, second largest bituminous
coal producer in the United States.

The Erie Rule and Peabody Coal

In 1869, the Exchange adopted a rule requiring corporations to report any increases in outstanding stock immediately. This was to prevent overissuance and the flooding of
Wall Street with stock no one knew existed. This is the Erie
Rule, for reasons to be made obvious. The year before, Commodore Cornelius Vanderbilt had decided to add the Erie,
then controlled by Daniel Drew, to his railroad empire. So
confident was Vanderbilt that he publicly announced he was
buying Erie, despite the recognized wiliness of Drew and his
associates, Jay Gould and Jim Fisk.

The public, backing Vanderbilt, bought Erie. Up and up it went. Then, suddenly, as if from nowhere, fifty thousand shares were offered to Vanderbilt's brokers. They bought, certain that these were short sales, certain that someone, maybe Drew, was selling into a bag. Promptly Drew's brokers delivered for cash crisp stock certificates, newly printed. Another fifty thousand shares were offered. Again, Vanderbilt's brokers bought, but not so confidently. Again, stock certificates, crisp off the press, were tendered in settlement. Drew had taken the precaution, when Vanderbilt was so indiscreet as to bellow his plans, to call a meeting of Erie directors, authorize an issue of Erie bonds convertible into common stock, and then buy the bonds himself at a price of 72½ per cent of par. He then converted the bonds into stock and let the Commodore have it!—at prices of $80 and up, netting himself and his fellow insiders a handsome profit. Wrote Drew, always the cattle dealer at heart, "Erie stock went down like a dead heifer." [4]

The Erie Rule was applied with ex post facto finesse to Peabody Coal Company in 1955 after directors voted a 780 per cent increase in its shares, from 831,835 to 7,323,999, without Stock Exchange authorization. The company planned to use the additional shares of stock to acquire the Sinclair Group of coal properties. It notified its own shareholders but did not ask for a vote. The Exchange insisted that a vote was necessary, because this was not a routine transaction. Peabody went ahead anyway. It discharged the Continental Illinois Bank & Trust Company, of Chicago, as the registrar of its stock. The Continental had an agreement with the Exchange not to release new shares without Exchange approval. Then

---

[4] Subsequently, Vanderbilt tried to make a private deal with Drew to take Erie stock off his hands. But Gould and Fisk followed Drew to Vanderbilt's New York lair. There, a peace was made which relieved Vanderbilt of his Erie stock, at Erie's expense, of course. The settlement ousted Drew from control, and Gould and Fisk took over.

Peabody named as registrar a small bank which had no agreement with the Exchange. At that point, the Stock Exchange delisted Peabody stock. Nine months later the company swallowed its derelictions and sought relisting. It asked shareholders to approve the issuance of additional shares the year before and satisfied the New York Exchange that a large majority of the original shareholders approved the Sinclair transaction. Then it reëngaged the Continental Illinois as registrar.

THE DODGE DODGE AND THE DILLON, READ RULE

The Stock Exchange's outstanding defense of shareholders' rights was a reaction to the stench which filled Wall Street after the sale by Dillon, Read & Company of Dodge Brothers debentures and preferred and common stocks in 1925. To clear the air, the Exchange decided that it would give "careful thought to the matter of voting control" in the future listing of securities.

Dillon, Read had engineered the coup of the period. Dodge Brothers had been extremely successful as an automobile company. The Dodge name rivaled Ford. The banking house bought the Dodge properties from the Dodge family and offered debentures and preferred and common shares to an anxious public—keeping control and realizing such a handsome profit, that the Michigan Securities Commission wrote at the time: "None of the monies [raised by the sale of securities] are to go to the company. It is all to go to the promoters of the deal. The only excuse offered as justification for this sort of financing is that it is based upon the earning power of the company. The public . . . is asked to bear the entire burden of financing . . . despite the fact that it will have no voice whatever in the conduct of the affairs of the company, which is controlled absolutely by the promoters and brokers through 500,000 Class B shares. Nor do the promoters and

186

brokers risk any of their own funds. The stock is held as a pure gift." As a result, as noted in the preceding chapter, the Exchange adopted its rule against the listing of common shares of companies with non-voting common stock.

After the Dodge dodge, the Exchange worked diligently and successfully to persuade R. J. Reynolds Tobacco Company, Liggett & Myers, and American Tobacco to do away with non-voting shares. And with important deviations, as in Ford and W. R. Grace & Company,[5] it has been faithful to the principle that "shareholders should have the opportunity to vote on matters which substantially affect their interests." [6] This, of course, would refer to mergers, increases in capital, and the election of directors.

As a natural follow-up of its refusal to list non-voting shares, the Exchange later refused to list shares in a voting trust, except under court-approved reorganization plans. A voting trust occurs when shares are deposited under a legal plan authorizing the trustees to vote for the shareholder on all matters pertaining to the company's affairs for a set period of years. Thus, the shareholder has no vote. A voting trust yields a blank check to management. The voting trustees, except in court reorganizations, are appointed by management.

[5] The W. R. Grace & Company preferred stock, owned by members of the Grace family, has one vote per share, in contrast to one-tenth of a vote per share for A and B preferred stocks, and one-fortieth vote per share for the common stock. There is a "family" affinity between the Ford and Grace voting plans. Charles E. Wilson, who was a director and a consultant to W. R. Grace & Company at the time Grace was listed on the Big Board, was a member of the board of trustees of the Ford Foundation and chairman of the finance committee of the trustees which worked out plans for the Ford stock sale. The levered vote in the Grace plan undoubtedly set the pattern for the Ford plan.

A deviation also occurs in the listing of shares of foreign corporations. The laws of countries in which the companies are chartered are controlling, and the Exchange cannot readily obtain equality of voting power for U.S. shareholders. However, few Americans who put their money in foreign companies ever expect to exercise their voting franchise.

[6] Observation of Keith Funston, *in re* Peabody Coal.

So, for the duration of the trust, the shareholder abdicates his right to say no.

In the 1900's, the mechanism of the Stock Exchange was used to prolong voting trusts; for example, Southern Railway. In 1902, a voting trusteeship, which included J. P. Morgan and George F. Baker, for many years president of the First National Bank of New York and a Morgan ally, expired. The old trust certificates representing Southern Railway shares were removed from Stock Exchange trading and new voting trust certificates were listed. But no effort was made to list Southern Railway shares, themselves. So holders who declined to extend the trust lost the market for their shares. The Exchange became an instrument of coercion, of stockholder disfranchisement. Not so today.

THE IVAR KREUGER RULE

The suicide of Ivar Kreuger in March, 1932, and the subsequent bankruptcy of Kreuger & Toll, bared both the inadequacies of the Stock Exchange's system for keeping tabs on corporate accounts and the inadequacy of Wall Street's self-developed machinery for protecting investors.

Kreuger was the mystery man from Sweden, who spellbound financiers, dealt with kings, and dazzled American investors. In return for the exclusive right to sell matches, he made loans to—took bonds of—France, Yugoslavia, Rumania, Poland, Latvia, Hungary, and other cash-needy countries that could not readily raise funds in the international bond market except at exorbitant interest rates.

Under the debenture agreement between Kreuger & Toll and its American bankers, headed by the banking house of Lee, Higginson & Company, Kreuger had the right to switch collateral provided the collateral at all times was equal to 120 per cent of the face value of outstanding debentures. There

188

was no requirement that the market value of the collateral had to be at 120 per cent of par.

Once the Kreuger & Toll debentures were sold in America, Kreuger proceeded to substitute low quality bonds—Yugoslavian bonds, as a specific example—for French bonds. Kreuger & Toll went kaput, completely unexpectedly. The company's reports, often imaginative contrivances of Kreuger, were always reassuring. Debenture holders were left holding inferior assets. Kreuger & Toll's American stockholders were wiped out.

Subsequently, the Exchange instituted the Ivar Kreuger Rule: Changes of collateral covering bonds must be announced immediately. Congress went much farther than that later in the Trust Indenture Act of 1939. Trustees were required to act as trustees—to protect the interests of the bondholders for whom they were trustees and not, as had been formerly the case, to favor the interests of the issuer, the corporation, on whom they depended for fees and business. Today a bank or a trustee would be forced, under the law, to disqualify itself in case of a conflict of interests. It could not, for example, be trustee for two bond issues of the same company in which the claims of one group of bondholders would be adverse to the other group of bondholders. If collateral were being switched, it would be expected to defend its trust, not be a mechanical trustee.

SAMUEL UNTERMYER'S PROPHECY

In February, 1914, the United States Senate conducted hearings on regulation of the New York Stock Exchange. Nothing came of it immediately. World War I, for one thing, intervened. But the first witness, Samuel Untermyer, who had been chief counsel for the House Banking and Currency

Committee investigation of the "Money Trust" in 1912,[7] made this years-ahead-of-his time statement:

"It will not be long before . . . corporate officers will be prevented from withholding information and speculating on advance knowledge. . . . The time will come . . . when those [members of the Exchange] who are bitterly assailing and slandering the champions of this legislation will find that it has marked the dawn of a new era of usefulness for them and the exchange." A brilliant prophecy on two counts.

First, Untermyer foresaw the ultimate legislation—legislation which did not come until after the 1929 crash. Second, he realized that legislation, instead of throttling members of the New York Stock Exchange, would actually give them a new sense of freedom, honor, and service to the community. But the members of the Exchange battled legislation in 1914 even as in 1933 and 1934. They did not want to be told how to run their own business. And yet, many of the policies and practices which have been adopted by the Securities and Exchange Commission—which now have the force of law—were actually initiated cautiously and hopefully by the New York Stock Exchange through persuasion and cajolery, through appeals to man's higher ethics.

The Exchange undertook, long before the SEC, to introduce order and uniformity in corporate accounts. Meetings were frequently held with representatives of accounting firms to standardize reports. In January, 1932, J. M. B. Hoxsey, executive assistant to the Committee on the Stock List, recommended to listed companies items which should be in annual reports and how they should be handled to provide

[7] Often referred to as the Pujo Investigation, after Congressman Arsene P. Pujo, of Louisiana, who was chairman of the House Committee on Banking and Currency. The inquiry pointed out the interlocking directorates of private banks, commercial banks, insurance companies, and corporations. It had an influence on later legislation—the Clayton Anti-trust Act and the Federal Reserve Act, which set up a regional banking system designed to remove the domination of bank credit and money from New York.

"full disclosure." A year later the Committee on the Stock List adopted a formal rule requiring independent audits of reports of virtually all listed companies other than railroads; also, it asked to be put on notice if a company changes its auditors or if there is any official relationship between members or employees of the accounting firm and the company.

The Exchange has tried to help stockholders by fighting "impublicity"—by helping investors to know. In his *Wall Street and Main Street*, Professor William Z. Ripley cited the following *reductio ad absurdum*. A banking house published a circular saying that the "best avenue of approach to an estimate of the real net returns of the Loose-Wiles Company [now Sunshine Biscuit] is through a comparison with National Biscuit." Sunshine reports were inadequate; therefore, to find out what the company was earning, analyze the more complete Nabisco report! The Exchange did not yet have the prestige to impose universal standards, and Sunshine stock was in a voting trust.

Sometimes the Exchange was embarrassed by duplicity it could not control. In 1933, American Commercial Alcohol created additional shares to be used to acquire "valuable processes and properties" which it already owned. These shares were duly listed on the Exchange and then were turned over to a group of stock market operators—a pool—managed by Thomas E. Bragg, who had been a member of the Stock Exchange firm of W. E. Hutton & Company. American Commercial Alcohol needed money and Bragg undertook to raise it by selling the stock. Incidentally, the operation was through W. E. Hutton & Company, "B. E. Smith No. 296 Account." Smith was a member of the Stock Exchange, and a prominent pool operator.

Ferdinand Pecora, counsel for the Senate investigating committee, asked Russell R. Brown, chairman of American

Commercial Alcohol, "If you had to do the same thing over again, would you do it precisely the same way?"

"No. But if financial conditions, or the same conditions, existed, whereby the company was, at that time, in bad financial shape, we might have to go ahead and use unusual and abnormal methods. But under ordinary conditions, I should not do that, no, sir."

In those days, men were many-hatted. Brown was not only the head of American Commercial Alcohol, he was a participant in the syndicate that put the price of the stock up. There was then no Federal law requiring full disclosure of purchases and sales of a stock by insiders.[8] Nor was there a statute declaring that profits realized by an insider who trades in a company's stock belong to and are recoverable by the company.

There was no law separating commercial banks from security affiliates. Thus the National City Bank could help finance operations of its own National City Company, which not only underwrote and sold securities but engaged in pool operations, in which officers and directors of National City themselves participated. This was also true of banks in Detroit, Chicago, and other cities. The Banking Act of 1933 made it unlawful for banks to have security affiliates.[9]

No doubt, the prosperity of the late 'twenties fuzzed up ethics. An officer of a company which is making plenty of profits and paying good dividends persuades himself that he

[8] An "insider" is defined by the Securities Exchange Act as an officer or director of a company, or anyone else who owns more than 10 per cent of its stock.

[9] Not only did commercial banks retire from security underwriting as a result of this law, but major private banking houses had to choose between staying in underwriting or banking. J. P. Morgan & Company stayed in banking; the firm of Morgan Stanley & Company took over its securities business. Brown Brothers, Harriman & Company stayed in banking and Harriman, Ripley took over its securities business. Kuhn, Loeb & Company, Dillon, Read & Company, Lehman Brothers, Lee, Higginson, and Goldman, Sachs & Company, prominent private banking firms and investment bankers, chose to cling to investment banking, as did Drexel & Company, the Philadelphia branch of J. P. Morgan & Company.

is doing all right by his stockholders and that it is only fair for him to help himself. As head of National City, Mitchell received more than a million dollars a year in salary and bonus. The Mitchell bonus was determined by an unsigned vote of all the officers who worked under him. The officers in a signed ballot indicated how they would distribute the rest of the fund, each omitting himself from consideration. At the Chase, a similar plan was used to reimburse Albert H. Wiggin and the other officers. Weren't the officers, in effect, voting themselves melons? (Similar self-benefaction has taken place in the 'fifties, as corporation executives tenderly vote themselves bonuses, stock options, and post-retirement consulting contracts,[10] which will be considered in the next chapter.)

[10] Further examples of the "prosperity morals" of the 'twenties: A. Newton Plummer, a publicity man, gave New York City newspapermen "calls" on stock or outright cash for putting bullish items in their newspapers. Newspapermen mentioned were on the *Times*, *Herald-Tribune*, and *Wall Street Journal*, and there were others. The Stock Exchange subsequently passed a regulation saying that any gift to a newspaperman may not be made without the knowledge of his employer. The "derelict" newspapermen could have easily persuaded themselves that they were doing no wrong in seeing that news of their "friends" got into the paper.

There was actually an American peerage in Wall Street, made up of men and women on the J. P. Morgan preferred list. When Morgan had a hot security to sell, one which would go up immediately above its offering price, the firm set aside shares for its "friends." Among these were: Joseph Nutt, treasurer of the Republican National Committee; Charles Francis Adams, Secretary of the Navy; Edmund Machold, speaker of the New York State Assembly and State Chairman of the Republican Party; Silas H. Strawn, President of the United States Chamber of Commerce and President of the American Bar Association; William Woodin, president of the American Car & Foundry and later Secretary of the Treasury under Franklin D. Roosevelt; F. H. Ecker, president of the Metropolitan Life Insurance Company; Mitchell, of the National City Bank; Wiggin, of the Chase, and numerous other bankers; Charles A. Lindbergh, son-in-law of Dwight Morrow, a Morgan partner; Bernard M. Baruch; Newton D. Baker, former Secretary of War under President Woodrow Wilson; former President Calvin Coolidge, and John W. Davis, who ran against Coolidge for President in 1924.

Morgan, of course, was not alone. The National City Company, the Chase Securities Company, Dillon, Read, and other firms all had their preferred customers. Drexel & Company had a peerage separate from Morgan, which naturally included W. W. Atterbury, then president of the Pennsylvania Railroad, and numerous presidents and officers of leading Philadelphia banks and companies.

The depression adversity also became an excuse for moral laxity. Men who controlled investment trusts used them as dumping grounds for their own depreciated securities and real estate at undepreciated prices. Richard Whitney, Exchange president, appropriated securities of the Exchange's own Gratuity Fund, to meet his obligations. The Exchange, because it was made up of members who were on all sides of every fence—they did business with bankers, corporations, investment bankers, insurance companies—was not in a position to make hard and fast rules. It could use its influence—and did—toward obtaining greater disclosure of corporation earnings; [11] toward raising standards of corporate morality in relation to shareholders. The Exchange showed great courage in 1929 in declining to list the shares of investment trusts unless they conformed to certain high standards in reporting—standards which the Securities and Exchange Commission ultimately set forth following the Investment Company Act of 1940. But the Exchange needed an outside stanchion, a prop; and that it got from the statute.

[11] Reports of General Electric Company, originally listed in May, 1892, as a result of a merger of Thomson-Huston Electric Company and Edison General Electric Company, furnish a running historical account of the Stock Exchange's success in obtaining fuller disclosure. The first application contained no consolidated balance sheet of the two companies and no earnings figures. In 1900, however, the company had a consolidated balance sheet and a profit and loss statement for the preceding seven months; no annual earnings, however. The profit-and-loss statement was in the old horizontal style of accounting—costs on the left hand, sales and income on the right. The company's 1929 application presents the income account in modern dress—sales at the top, then costs, then income from other sources. The income account covers three years. In 1956, an application to list debentures was fortified by the prospectus filed with the Securities and Exchange Commission; prospectuses are acceptable to the Exchange in lieu of its standard listing form. This suggests how the work of the New York Stock Exchange and the Securities and Exchange Commission have coalesced.

Interestingly, the Stock Exchange does not ask corporations for per share income in their listing statements. It prefers total net income. Theory: If the per share data are handed over on a silver platter, lazy persons will not trouble to analyze how the common earnings are derived. Are they after preferred dividends? Were there non-recurring profits? Etc., etc.!

The New York Stock Exchange, once the "private club," has become a public institution. It works hand in hand with the Securities and Exchange Commission to uplift standards of corporate comportment. And it is a rare member of a Stock Exchange firm who would not wholeheartedly accept Untermyer's statement that because of, and not in spite of, the legislation, a new "era of usefulness" has dawned. Untermyer didn't live to see that phase of his prophecy realized. He died in 1940, when the securities legislation was still being hammered out—case by case and battle by battle—into today's model of financial and corporate comportment.

CHAPTER XV

And Congress Said:
"Let There Be Light"

A period of self-searching
Every now and then
Is as good for corporations
As it is for men.
    ——Morgan Stanley & Company

MORGAN STANLEY & COMPANY did not exactly versify that statement. But this sedate, highly respected, powerful investment banking offshoot of J. P. Morgan & Company most certainly "inspired" that doggerel in a 1938 memorandum on the Securities Act of 1933 and validated Samuel Untermyer's prophecy that Wall Street, instead of abhorring regulation, would find it useful.

The Morgan Stanley memo said: "A period of self-searching every now and then is as beneficial for corporations as it is for individuals. Those in underwriting houses who specialize in the preparation of prospectuses can recount . . . situations long overlooked or ignored which have been pulled into the foreground for daylight scrutiny by officers and boards of directors. . . . In many cases, long-delayed remedial or corrective action is taken even before the registration is filed."

Right there is the sum, substance, and the spirit of the se-

curities laws in operation: Scrutiny which leads to self-scrutiny. What a change forty years has made! Bernard M. Baruch tells in his autobiography [1] of the president of a large
corporation who defined his business as "addition, division
and silence." He tells also about a meeting of George Perkins,
a Morgan partner, with James Stillman, then president of
the National City Bank of New York (now the First National
City) after Stillman's return from Europe.

> PERKINS: "I see you're back."
> STILLMAN: Silence.
> PERKINS: "Oh, you need not confirm it."

Today corporation executives and securities underwriters
and dealers must do more than confirm what others observe.
For Congress said, "Let there be light," and the Securities
and Exchange Commission sees—through its staff of lawyers,
accountants, and securities analysts—that there is light. Men,
who once had been the law unto themselves, now find other
men looking behind their statements and asking questions
backed by the power of subpoena. Nothing so quickens the
conscience as examining yourself in other men's eyes. Conscience makes us better men, not cowards, as Shakespeare
had it. This is what members of the SEC staff refer to as the
"prophylactic power of the Securities Acts."

The SEC does not pass on the merits of securities. It is a
crime for anyone selling a stock or bond to suggest that the
SEC does. But the SEC does examine and judge the adequacy
of information and establishes standards for financial accounting. Inevitably, its power to accept or reject, to say yes
or no, emboldens corporation lawyers and accountants in
dealings with stubborn, secretive officials: "That won't get by
the SEC" are six words of singular potency.

The original Truth-in-Securities Law, the 1933 Act, set the

[1] *My Own Story*, Henry Holt & Co., 1957.

tone of full disclosure—the truth, the whole truth, and nothing but the truth, even if the truth might discourage investors. Thus, the 1956 prospectus of the Freedom Insurance Company, of California, confided that this is a "new enterprise with no operating experience," and added the damaging confession that an earlier effort to register the stock was held up by the SEC for inadequate information. Again, in 1955, the Farmington Funding Corporation, formed to operate oil refineries and pipelines, related in its prospectus that if all the shares are sold, the "public will have paid $3,750,000 for 33.9% of the oustanding shares, while officers, directors, promoters and others will own 66.1% . . . for which they will have contributed $198,512 cash and certain assets. . . ." The investor, the future stockholder, is forewarned—if he reads the prospectus—on just how much he is getting for his cash and how much the insiders are getting for theirs. That's a standard requirement in all prospectuses—to state what the underwriting commissions are and what the entrepreneurs bring to the enterprise. No secret rebates or commissions! Often company officials will alter a "deal"—their own "take" —when they see what the prospectus sets forth: "It makes us look too bad!" That is the law's prophylactic power. When the 1956 report of Bellanca Corporation to the SEC failed to reveal (1) important transfers of property from one subsidiary to another, (2) sales of assets, and (3) loans to Sidney L. Albert, its president, the SEC ordered that trading in the stock be suspended—lest insiders, who knew the true condition of the company, dispose of shares to innocent buyers. The penalty was drastic and a forewarning to other evaders.

The SEC's accounting staff often makes suggestions which "tone up" officers and directors. In a registration statement, Continental Air Lines reported earnings of $1.49 per share for 1956. The accounting suited the Civil Aeronautics Board. But the SEC suggested a change in accord with its standard, and earnings were reduced to $1.22 a share.

To practice before the SEC, accounting firms must be independent. Firms have been barred because they were beholden to companies they were auditing. Perhaps members of the accounting firm owned stock in the company; perhaps they had relatives who were officers or directors, or perhaps the company was the firm's principal account, and therefore held a financial life-and-death sentence over the auditing firm.

Accounting firms are held responsible for departures from accepted accounting principles. In May, 1957, Touche, Niven, Bailey & Smart was suspended from practice before the SEC for fifteen days for permitting a company to understate reserves for uncollectible accounts. Yet the deficiency had occurred years before. Another firm, Haskins & Sells, was suspended for ten days in 1952 for certifying a balance sheet in which patents and licenses were, in the SEC's judgment, clearly overstated in relation to the "commercial experience" in using them. This not only alerts accountants to their responsibilities to shareholders but stiffens their backbone in dealing with intransigent corporation officials. Allied Chemical & Dye could not dictate to accountants today as in 1933. Since all auditors who practice before the SEC are subject to the same rigid standards, corporations do not shop for a firm with loose ethics and flexible principles.

The SEC also has made clear that full-disclosure means no withholding of information. There is the famous case brought in 1945 by the SEC against the Bankers Securities Corporation, an investment-holding company, and Albert M. Greenfield & Company, an associated Philadelphia real estate firm. Both companies were interested in hotels and office buildings in Philadelphia, many of whose bonds had defaulted on interest payments. Agents for Bankers Securities and Albert M. Greenfield & Company approached owners of the defaulted bonds and purchased them—at market prices. But the SEC argued in a civil suit that the buyers had failed to reveal that earnings had improved, that interest arrears might be paid up, and that market prices, which were influenced by insider buying and selling, may not have reflected this improvement. Allegations of wrongdoing were denied, and the case was dropped when an agreement was made to rescind purchases.

This practice of insider buying of inactive securities was fairly common in the postwar inflation. Another real estate enterprise, Baker Properties, Inc., of Minneapolis, took advantage of depressed market prices to buy through Lakeside Holding Company, owned by Morris T. Baker, president, either for cash or twenty-year-installment notes, Baker Properties common stock, which was likely to appreciate—and did appreciate—in the rising market for office buildings, hotels, stores, and garages. The SEC insisted that the trades were made without "adequate disclosure." The company agreed to undo the transactions "as a matter of policy" but was unwilling to publicly "concede that there was any failure at any time to make sufficient disclosure." None the less, the SEC made its point: Insiders must act, in effect, as trustees in dealing with security holders whose properties, whose assets, they are managing.

Full disclosure is backed by law—and criminal penalties [2]—penalties, which unfortunately have to be invoked. (As Damon Runyon so sagely remarked, where human beings are concerned the odds are frequently nine to five against). Thus, in mid-1957, Walter Tellier, head of Tellier & Company, a high-

---

[2] Curiously, the Securities Act of 1933 and the Trust Indenture Act of 1939 provide penalties of a $5,000 fine or five years in jail. However the Securities Exchange Act of 1934, the Public Utility Holding Company Act of 1935, the Investment Company Act of 1940, and the Investment Advisers Act of 1940, provide for a maximum jail term of two years but raised the maximum fine to $10,000. In addition, the Securities Exchange Act stipulates that stock exchanges may be fined up to $500,000, and the Public Utility Holding Company Act permits a holding company fine up to $200,000.

pressure specialist in low-pressure securities. was appealing a 4½-year fraud sentence. His salesmanship was not characterized by understatement. And, as another instance, in 1955, J. Arthur Warner, head of J. Arthur Warner & Company, an over-the-counter firm with offices in twelve cities in the East, including New York, Philadelphia, Boston and Providence, pleaded guilty, rather than go to trial, for overzealousness in trading inexperienced customers in and out of securities for the firm's not the customer's, reward. Favorite trick: To get a customer to buy stocks just before dividend payments, then when the dividends arrived to tell the customer that this extra income came from the firm's expert timing of purchases. Some customers were too naïve to know that dividends had been included in the original purchase price. Warner was put on probation for two years and fined $5,000.

Over the years, the number of criminal actions has declined. In 1940 (fiscal year) fifty-nine cases—the all-time high —were referred to the Department of Justice for prosecution. The highest number of persons ever indicted in a single year was 368 in 1936. The highest number convicted was 199 in 1939. In 1956, only seventeen cases were referred to the Department of Justice and twenty-one indictments were obtained. There were no convictions. The fall-off is attributable, in part, to the success with which the SEC has contained swindlers and swindling. However, the rise in stock prices during the 1940's and 1950's engendered avarice. Naïve people with savings became increasingly receptive to tall promises of high profit. "Boiler rooms"—not to be confused with "bucket shops"—boomed. (*See* Appendix IV.)

In drafting the securities laws, Congress determined that corporation officials not only must disclose what they are doing with other people's money but also with their own money. The Securities Exchange Act of 1934 declares that insiders—defined as officers, directors and holders of more than 10 per cent of a company's stock—must make monthly reports on their purchases and sales of the company's securities. And these reports are made public by the SEC. Moreover, any profit realized by insiders "within any period of six months" is recoverable by the company.

The SEC does not sue to recover the money. That is up to the company itself, or a stockholder. But the SEC makes sure that alert shareholders find out about insider profits. This is through the SEC's proxy rules. If a company, subject to SEC supervision, solicits proxies, its letter to shareholders must detail the remuneration of officers, including salaries, bonuses, pension benefits, stock options and other income, and, here is the catch, indebtedness due the company. Thus, the 1956 proxy statement of Kerr-McGee Oil Industries, Inc., disclosed that Senator Robert S. Kerr (Dem. Okla.) chairman of the board, owed $65,260 as of June 30, and that "no interest has been paid or charged." Other officers also owed money to the company at variable rates of interest. Some officers of some companies, when faced with the necessity of debt disclosure, have paid off their loans—which has the effect of raising corporate mores. Officers of corporations ought no more to borrow from their own companies than union leaders from their unions.[3] The officers are lending to themselves. That is short-

[3] Senator John L. McClellan (Dem. Ark.), chairman of the Select Committee on Improper Practices in the Labor or Management Field, observed that James R. Hoffa, then vice-president of the International Brotherhood of Teamsters, had misused his trust as an union official by borrowing union funds for personal ventures. Moreover, the AFL-CIO Codes of Ethical Practices emphasize the fiduciary responsibility of union leaders in handling funds of members, and offer this observation: "Because the funds of a labor union are both held in trust for the benefit of its members and are held to further legitimate trade union purposes, practices which may be acceptable in business organizations should be limited if not completely eliminated among labor organizations." To my way of thinking, the standards of conduct of corporation officials in relation to the funds of shareholders should be no less impeccable than those of union officials. The more so, since corporation officials are not subject to the political restraints, including the electioneering, characteristic of most democratic unions.

arm's-length borrowing. The Investment Company Act specifically prohibits officers of an investment company from borrowing money or from engaging in transactions with the company they manage, or with any affiliate of the company, without specific SEC permission. This is to guard against self-dealing. Thus, Congress already has passed judgment on the propriety of corporate borrowing by insiders.

Some companies have managed to avoid direct disclosure to shareholders by not soliciting proxies. The insiders—officers and directors—have sufficient stock for a quorum at annual meetings. In the interest of active stockholder participation in corporate affairs, the New York Stock Exchange has ruled that all companies wanting to list shares must agree to solicit proxies. Moreover, the Exchange has carried on an active campaign to persuade companies already listed and which do not solicit to do so. Sun Oil Company, controlled by the Pew family, has not solicited proxies from 1943 to 1957. Letters inviting shareholders to annual meetings have made clear that no proxy was asked for. Other companies which have not solicited proxies are H. J. Heinz Company, Richfield Oil, City Stores, A. O. Smith Corporation, Cuneo Press, Johnson & Johnson, Cannon Mills, and Getty Oil. Such companies do disclose remuneration in their reports to the SEC and these reports are on file at the SEC's public reference room in Washington; also duplicate reports are sent to the reference rooms of all exchanges on which a company's stock is listed. In addition, the reports of all companies not listed on the New York Stock Exchange and American Stock Exchange are filed in the SEC's regional office in New York; and reports of companies listed on the New York and American stock exchanges are available in Chicago. These sources of information are a great convenience to lawyers, accountants and professionals in the security business. But the ordinary shareholder oftentimes does not trouble to read the reports sent him, let alone go to a library to look up detailed data. He needs the proxy letter to learn what goes on.

SEC staffers specifically inquire if officers and directors have realized any profits within six months through trading in the company's stock. If they have, that is a recoverable asset of the corporation and a debt of the official. This requires insiders to review—analyze—their purchases and sales. If they have made money trading, they must so declare in the proxy letter. This is indebtedness by statute and an open invitation to a lawsuit. Rather than make this damning disclosure, many company officials simply pay over their profit to the company. Among these in recent years was Leopold D. Silberstein, chairman of Penn-Texas Corporation, whose over-the-counter brokerage firm of Uno Equities traded extensively in Penn-Texas stock. Many officials of companies stay away from trading in their own stocks as a prophylactic measure. Quite a contrast from the 'twenties when company officials traded in their stocks as a sideline!

Full disclosure extends to shareholder inter-communication, which Emerson and Latcham, among other enthusiasts, consider the cornerstone of corporate democracy.[4] If Joe Doakes has a proposal to make to other shareholders and mails it to the president of the company, the president dare not file it in the wastebasket. The SEC has decreed that Joe has the right to communicate it to Jane Doe, Tom Smith, Harry Brown, his fellow shareholders. And, on the company's own stationery! This is known as the Shareholder Proposal Rule. In a peripheral fashion, it, too, activates the executive conscience. The very fact that a shareholder can communicate to other shareholders resolutions such as these:

> Resolved, that the by-laws be altered to place a ceiling on the company's pension payments to officers at $25,000 a year; or

[4] *Shareholder Democracy*, previously noted.

> Resolved, that the by-laws be altered to provide for members of the board of directors who are not officers of the company; or

> Resolved, that the company's summary of the annual meeting of shareholders present stockholder as well as management views of controversial issues.

alerts the management to the rights of shareholders and forces officers to determine what impression the proposals will make on shareholders. Thus, shareholders cease to be a "stack of proxies."

In 1954, Lewis Gilbert submitted to American Machine & Foundry Company a proposal to limit executive pensions to $25,000 a year. The proposal went to shareholders in the company's proxy statement. At the annual meeting, a woman asked for the floor and said that she thought a ceiling on pensions was a good idea. Maybe $25,000 was too low, but how about $50,000? When Gilbert resubmitted his proposal for the 1955 proxy statement, George A. Hills, counsel to the company and a director, telephoned him, recalled the woman's suggestion and suggested they split the difference—at $37,500. Gilbert agreed, and withdrew his proposal for a $25,000 ceiling. That same year, Gilbert also withdrew proposals requesting both American Can Company and American Telephone & Telegraph to amplify their summaries of the annual meetings. Officials of both companies agreed—after conferences with Gilbert—to incorporate some of his recommendations. (For SEC rules governing stockholder proposals, *see* Appendix III.) As noted in Chapter XII, institutional investors—investment trusts, banks, insurance companies, pension funds, etc. —do not resort to the roundabout route of a proxy proposal to "get an audience" with management. That is for the small shareholder. But it has its effect.

Full disclosure "cleans up" proxy contests. Struggles for corporation control no longer go to the best mudslinger. In the Libby, McNeil & Libby contest, in 1956, the challenging group sent out proxy solicitations without SEC clearance. The solicitations contained "Have you stopped beating your wife?" questions about the management. The SEC obtained a court order to enjoin the group from further solicitation; also, all proxies received were declared null and void. In the Montgomery, Ward & Company contest, the SEC refused the company permission to distribute articles about Louis E. Wolfson, by Leslie Gould, financial editor of the *New York Journal American*—on the ground that the management could not sustain all of the statements in the articles. It was not enough for the SEC that a reputable writer made charges. The company had to be able to prove them.[5] The SEC also demands that participants in proxy fights reveal their holdings of stock and their personal backgrounds, even to disclosing bouts with the criminal courts. If promoters selling securities have to "tell all" to get the use of other people's money, so must persons who want control of a business, which also is other people's money.

The SEC has also been able to develop a prototype of an ideal corporate charter. However, it applies only to companies subject to the Public Utility Holding Company Act. All electric and gas companies under SEC jurisdiction have to issue clearly defined securities. A bond must be a bond; a preferred stock a preferred stock, and a common stock a common stock. No gimmicks. Income bonds—bonds whose interest is payable only when earned—have not been permitted. If preferred dividends are omitted for four successive quarters, the SEC-supervised charters stipulate that preferred shareholders then get the right to elect a majority of the board of directors. And

[5] This led Gould to accuse the SEC of censorship. To me, the accusation is poorly founded. The SEC did not censor what Gould wrote. It did not ask to see his copy before it was published. It merely restrained Montgomery Ward from using material the company, itself, could not sustain with indisputable evidence. Reprints must meet the same standards as the material contestants send as their own.

common stocks must have a vote. Non-voting or levered voting stocks, which grant disproportionate power to insiders, were forbidden. Had the Ford Motor Company been a public utility, subject to the SEC, its ingenious voting plan could not have got by. Further, the SEC has opposed staggered boards of directors (*see* Chapter VIII), which hobble shareholders in proxy fights. The "ins" can stay in even if they lose the election. It has favored cumulative voting to assist minority shareholders to get representation on boards of directors. And, it has required reorganized utility companies to have "outside" directors, so that companies will not be officer dominated and insulated against external judgments. Again, this fits the theme of alerting the corporate conscience. Outsiders—men whom the officers presumably respect—are looking in, and on. The SEC also has opposed the issuance of warrants to purchase common shares. Why? Because they constitute a prospective dilution of earning power. Warrant holders convert into common stock when it is strategic either to collect increased dividends or to dump stock on the market at high prices. In either case, it usually happens when it is least advantageous for the small, unwary shareholder. It is significant that the National Association of Securities Administrators, the "trade association" for State Securities Commissioners, has twice looked upon warrants or stock purchase options "with great disfavor" and "a basis for denial of applications to sell securities except in unusual circumstances." [6] Non-utility corporations are not bound by these SEC standards. Nevertheless, the standards are there for all to see. And when promoters set up companies which depart from this pattern, stock purchasers should examine with care. This constitutes prophylaxis by inference, by example.

More positively—under the Securities Act of 1933 and the

[6] Resolutions at the twenty-ninth annual convention in 1946 and nine years later at the thirty-eighth annual convention.

Securities and Exchange Act of 1934—the SEC has implanted certain minimum standards of behavior. Corporations subject to the acts—and these are the biggest corporations, the corporations smaller corporations emulate—must have earnings reports and balance sheets certified by independent auditors, something the New York Stock Exchange had tried for many years to accomplish by persuasion. The SEC put real teeth in the short-selling rule and barred insiders from selling short their own stock. It ruled out the "Communist ballot" in proxy solicitations to shareholders. The company must provide "yes" and "no" boxes for voting on all proposals and only matters on which shareholders have been notified in advance may be voted on at meetings. So goes bye-bye a favorite corporate stratagem of pre-SEC days: Send out blank-check proxies and vote on any questions the officers see fit, even including mergers or sales of property or the company itself. Yes, stockholders often gave "blank checks" approving deals the officers, themselves, profited by.

Like all man-made customs and procedures, SEC rules had to be hammered out by trial, error, practice, and experience. They evolved. The SEC had to decide what properly belonged in a registration statement; what constituted fair, accurate and adequate reporting to shareholders; what legitimately should be revealed to shareholders in proxy statements. Initially, this was not easy. In 1934, when the Securities and Exchange Commission was first established (with three Democrats and two Republicans), the regulatees eyed the regulators apprehensively, like youngsters whose stepmother catches them in the jampot. For this was a New Deal Democratic administration, poaching on a Republican preserve—Wall Street and Big Business. Everything was new to everybody. The commissioners were new, the members of the staff were new, the legislation was new, and an organization had to be created from a diagram, an organization chart.

Presidents of companies who had been plenipotentiary emperors on their own islands of corporate power had to reckon with a third force in their relations with shareholders. Investment banking firms, in floating securities, discovered that they had to satisfy the SEC as well as the company officials in the information to be disclosed. Stock Exchange officials suddenly realized that all their rules governing members were subject to outside scrutiny. Everyone was tense and uncertain in this brash new world of federal regulation of securities.

The names of the early SEC commissioners became nationally-known as the result of their pioneering effort: Joseph P. Kennedy, first chairman, who had been a successful Wall Street operator, and who later was made Ambassador to England; James M. Landis, one of the framers of the securities laws, who later returned to Harvard Law School as dean and still later became chairman of the Civil Aeronautics Board; William O. Douglas, who became a Supreme Court Justice; Robert E. Healy, known as the Great Dissenter,[7] who served twelve years, the longest tenure of any commissioner, and who was the original expert on the Public Utility Holding Company Act; Jerome Frank, who became a judge of the U.S. Circuit Court of Appeals; Leon Henderson, the phrase-making, cigar-smoking price controller in the forepart of World War II; and Ferdinand Pecora, who conducted the investigation of the stock-market crash which led to the establishment of the SEC.

Now that is ancient, hard-fought history. By the time President Eisenhower took office in 1953, the early distrust and skepticism—the fear and hatred, you could honestly say—had been dissipated. Self-searching has become an integral part of Wall Street and corporate practice. The trickery which en-

---

[7] Once Judge Healy (as he was always called—he had been a member of the Supreme Court of Vermont) passed out his dissent to his fellow commissioners even before they had had a chance to read the opinion the staff had submitted on approval!

abled Daniel Drew to dump Erie shares on Commodore Vanderbilt is improbable today. And if it occurred, it would be fraud per se and subject to criminal prosecution. The SEC has put all investors, all analysts, willing to read, on an equal footing in terms of knowledge. Full disclosure means full disclosure for all, not the few, and at the same time. No more of that, "Does J. P. Morgan tell Kuhn, Loeb?" secrecy.

As of mid-1957, the SEC had a staff of approximately eight hundred to carry on its work. About five hundred persons were stationed in Washington and three hundred in regional offices, the largest of which is New York, with about one hundred employees. In 1941, the SEC had as high as 1,700 on its payroll. As the work of the SEC became codified, solidified, and standardized, staff requirements diminished. Corporation lawyers, accountants, and officials came to know the rules, regulations, and procedures. SEC analysts and accountants did not have to worry about each *i* being dotted. There was less crossing and crisscrossing of correspondence. More filings were right the first time. It became possible to cut red tape—simplify.

In 1954, Congress approved amendments recommended by the SEC making it possible for investment dealers to circularize an abridged prospectus to acquaint investors with new security flotations even before the SEC has approved the final registration. Wall Street had argued for this for many years, asserting it would actually help security buyers. Many of them might read a short form; only the security analysts, the professionals, have time for the long form. Finally, the SEC came around with a proposed bill to Congress. The SEC had come to understand Wall Street even as Wall Street had come to understand the SEC.

When President Eisenhower took office, it was thought that the new SEC chairman, Ralph H. Demmler, who had come to Washington from an influential Pittsburgh law firm, would make wholesale changes. He did not; he could not. SEC forms, traditions, and customs had already been structured. Alterations are made, it is true—but cautiously. Thus, the "short" prospectus was adopted; and the commission did away with its policy of requiring preëmptive rights for shareholders under the Public Utility Holding Company Act. New commissioners raised the question: Are preëmptive rights clearly beneficial to shareholders? The staff could not demonstrate this. After all, it is cheaper for a corporation to sell stocks or bonds in the open market than to offer them to shareholders at a discount—through rights. And shareholders who want to maintain their proportionate share in the company—which preëmption makes possible—can do so by subscribing to the new issue. Thus, rule changes are argued out within the SEC.

Demmler proposed for reconsideration by the full commission the rule that all public utility issues be sold by competitive bidding. He suggested that issues which had been approved by state public utility commissions be exempt. After a public hearing the proposal was abandoned. Also, the SEC rule requiring "junior registration statements" for small issues —issues of less than $300,000—was reëxamined under Demmler. The argument offered was this: Congress specifically exempted small issues from the Securities Act of 1933. Well, if small issues are exempt, why should an offering circular be required? The filing of such a circular, a junior prospectus, is tantamount to a rescission of the exemption. After informal reconsideration, batting it around with the staff, the proposal was allowed to die—without a public hearing. An offering circular protects investors against wild claims and misstatements. It makes the promoters and corporation officials look at themselves as others see them. It quickens their conscience. Again, the prophylaxis motif.

Unhappily, full disclosure is not universal disclosure. SEC

standards extend to only about three thousand companies. They do not penetrate by law to such massive and nationally known enterprises as Humble Oil (assets of $1,400,000,000), Creole Petroleum (assets of $1,100,000,000), the Bank of America (assets of $10,000,000,000), Great Atlantic & Pacific Tea Company ($500,000,000), Weyerhaeuser Timber Company ($500,000,000), Travelers Insurance Company ($2,800,-000,000), Aetna Life Insurance Company ($3,070,000,000), the Chase Manhattan Bank ($7,700,000,000), and many, many more, including Singer Manufacturing, Time, Inc., Duke Power, M. A. Hanna Company. (*See* Appendix V.) Yet all of the above have thousands of shareholders—the Bank of America, 200,000; Travelers Insurance, 30,000; Humble Oil, 8,400. Those shareholders are SEC stepchildren. Why?

Because the stocks of these companies are not *listed* on a stock exchange.

Yet stocks of many of these companies are actively traded on stock exchanges. Humble Oil, Singer Manufacturing, and A&P are on the American Stock Exchange. But, not being formally listed, registered, they are treated as over-the-counter securities, and over-the-counter companies do not have to make regular reports to the SEC, do not have to comply with SEC rules of disclosure in proxy statements. Officers, directors and 10 per cent shareholders of such companies escape "insider" profit penalties. They can buy and sell their own shares freely, using inside information. Apparently, when Congress said, "Let there be light," Congress saw fit to keep two classes of companies in the shade:

One, banks and trust companies. The legislators were persuaded that banks are supervised by the Federal Reserve Board, Comptroller of the Currency, Federal Deposit Insurance Corporation, and the State Banking Departments. Ergo: Supervisory sufficiency. However, this is a special kind of supervision. Bank examiners look to the protection of depositors. Banks do not have to disclose the type of earnings and balance sheet information which studious stockholders require; they do not have to send shareholders—and customarily do not—proxy statements indicating the remuneration of principal officers. Nor do they have to provide, in their proxies, "yes" and "no" ballot boxes. Finally, their officers escape the insider trading rules.

Two, companies whose stocks are traded in the over-the-counter market, whose shares are not listed on an exchange. Congressional theory: These are small companies, which ought not be burdened with the cost of hiring high-priced legal and accounting talent to comply with SEC rules and regulations.[8] Hence, by the simple process of not listing stocks on exchanges, Humble Oil, Weyerhaeuser, Travelers, A&P, etc., squeeze under the small-business parasol. Yet such companies are far larger than many on the New York Stock Exchange, with its minimum listing requirements of $7,000,000 of assets, a million dollars a year in earnings, and 1,500 shareholders. Other exchanges have less rigid standards.

To correct this disparity between listed and unlisted companies, Senator Joseph Allen Frear, Jr. (Dem. Del.), introduced a bill in 1949 to subject companies with three hundred shareholders and $3,000,000 of assets to SEC regulations. Both banks and insurance companies were exempt from his bill, insurance companies because they could argue that their accounts were supervised by state insurance departments. The Frear bill consistently got pushed aside by more pressing legislation. In 1957, Senator J. William Fulbright (Dem. Ark.)

[8] There is a minor exception. Unlisted companies which have registered at least $2,000,000 of securities with the SEC are required to file annual and semi-annual reports under Section 15 (d) of the Securities Exchange Act. This does not bind them to regulations covering proxy solicitation or insider trading.

made another effort.[9] He introduced a substitute for the Frear bill which would bring about 650 unlisted companies into the SEC sun by requiring unlisted companies with one thousand shareholders and $10,000,000 of assets to meet SEC standards, with banks and insurance companies excluded.

Such legislation is long overdue, and I would include banks and insurance companies along with the larger unlisted companies. And why not? All shareholders, whether in listed or unlisted companies, whether in small or large companies, are entitled to the benefits of legalized disclosure. In truth, since companies whose shares are listed—registered—on an exchange regularly divulge more information than unlisted companies, it could be argued that Congress has discriminated against those who get the least and need the most light. In short, Congress should widen the sunroom in adding to its House of Full Disclosure.

This house, twenty-five years old, is already an integral part of America's social and economic landscape. It is structured by the securities laws and bolstered by administrative actions,

[9] At the suggestion of the SEC, the Fulbright bill exempts insiders in unlisted companies from the six-month trading rule. The rationale is that often over-the-counter brokers, who make active markets in the stock of small companies, are directors of such companies. If they had to disgorge short-term trading profits, they would stop making a market and marketability would be impaired. In my view, this is a poor exemption. In the first place, the Securities and Exchange Act was designed to prevent the use of inside knowledge for stock market gain. Insiders in unlisted companies have fully as much opportunity for such profits as insiders in listed companies. In the second place, it is spurious logic to suggest that an over-the-counter stock with an active market would suddenly cease to have an active market if an over-the-counter firm, which is represented on the company's board of directors, stops trading in the stock. If it is profitable for firm A to make a market, surely firm B, C or D would wish to fill the vacancy. And, in the third place, this is such an old argument. . . . It was trotted out twenty-five years ago when the Securities Exchange Act was being debated in Congress. Wall Streeters protested that officers and directors often step in and buy when the market is declining. Conversely, they sell when the market is rapidly rising and stock for sale is scarce. Hence, officers and directors are a stabilizing influence in the market. None the less, the listed markets have survived the insider restriction all these years!

precedents, rules and procedures. Here are a set of standards, a code of conduct, backed by court orders and the power of punitive persuasion. And that is an essential difference, a point of departure, from the 1920's.

Then, for exemplars of behavior, Wall Streeters and corporation officials looked to the bankers and the New York Stock Exchange—to J. P. Morgan & Company, Richard Whitney, the National City Bank, etc. These paragons of power constituted the Wall Street, the corporate, conscience; they were the ethical arbiters of the 'twenties. Yet, sometimes these paragons nodded, slipped, engaged in actions and transactions which cast doubt on their rectitude. J. P. Morgan had its "preferred list," by which it dispensed quick stock market largesse to its friends and business associates; Richard Whitney, as president of the New York Stock Exchange and as a broker, misappropriated other people's securities and went to jail; the National City Bank, along with all the other banks, had its "sticky" bonds and stocks to sell, and abided by the first law of nature, self-preservation. Morals were—let's use a kind word—slack. As one instance, among many, of fallen ethics, an officer of the National City Bank went to an officer of the National City Company, the bank's security affiliate, and arranged for a $10,200 unsecured advance—accommodation—for a friend, who just happened to be an official of the Port of New York Authority, whose bonds National City distributed. This was an illegal loan for the bank. It was paid in cash, not by check. It was a diversion of stockholders' money. It went into default. And it made extremely bad headlines—for Wall Street—when Ferdinand Pecora dragged it out in testimony at the Senate Banking and Currency hearings. That "loan" never was intended for printer's ink.

Now that Congress has said, "Let there be light," men in places of trust and power keep their consciences cocked. They constantly ask themselves: How will that look in the headlines? How will my friends, my competitors, my associates react to this? Well have Congress and the SEC wrought: Scrutiny which leads to self-scrutiny. Prophylaxis.

Diogenes, the Greek cynic, traveled about Athens in broad daylight, thrusting a lamp in the faces of passers-by in his search for an honest man. He felt that extra light—even with the sun shining—would bare the shadows, the lines, which tell the truth. So be it. Light—lamplight, sunlight, or SEC light—best serves those who use it.

And the light of full disclosure is a special light. It is a torch, a trust, a responsibility, conferred by Congress on those who can use it intelligently—the analysts in banks, insurance companies, investment trusts. These are today's "investment insiders." Their strategic position thrusts on them an ethical obligation: Self-imposed guardianship of the strong for the weak; the protection of the read-and-run, haven't-got-time stockholder by the pro. This is an ill-defined, amorphous responsibility, whose nature, significance and potential are analyzed in the final chapter.

CHAPTER XVI

The Corporation Versus
the U.S.A.: Afterword

"CHARITY has no business to sit at boards of directors." In those crisp words, a British court in 1883 determined that a railroad, in liquidation, could not grant severance pay to workers who had lost jobs. A corporation is a business enterprise, reasoned the court. Its funds are to be used for the benefit of shareholders—either to build up the enterprise or for dividends. They must not be frittered away in charitable impulse. And that was the law not only in Britain but in the United States well into the twentieth century. But no longer.

In 1953, a New Jersey court decided that the A. P. Smith Manufacturing Company could contribute $1,500 to Princeton University—with no strings attached. The giver did not have to establish that the gift would help stockholders by advancing the affairs of the corporation. The court considered it proper for directors to use corporate assets for educational welfare, for national welfare.

This satisfies social mores. Corporate giving is a mid-twentieth-century commonplace. General Motors, Standard Oil (N.J.), United States Steel, General Electric, Scott Paper and hundreds of other companies make gifts to educational institutions, the Community Chest, Red Cross, hospitals, etc. Charity has become an accepted business expense—in the corporation's self-interest (although in some states, charitable contributions by public utility companies are not permitted to be included in the rate base).

This change in the attitude of the courts, in the attitude of officers and directors of corporations toward charity, marks an erosion in stockholder status. Twenty years ago, A. A. Berle, Jr., was embroiled in an argument with the late Professor E. Merrick Dodd, of the Harvard Law School. Berle insisted that officers and directors held corporate powers "in trust for shareholders." Professor Dodd declared such powers were in trust for the entire community. Berle now concedes that "the argument has been settled (at least for the time being) squarely in favor of Professor Dodd's contention." [1]

The shareholder gets the last bite on the apple core. (*See* Chapter IX.) Executives, in administering the affairs of the company, look to the perpetuation of the enterprise. They are more immediately concerned with maintaining "sound relations" with customers, suppliers, workers and the government and community than with shareholders whom they dangle on proxy strings. And so it becomes insistently important for those to whom investing is a business—the institutional investor, the professionals—to see that officers and directors do not, in their zeal to perpetuate the corporation as an institution, slight the shareholders financially, and, more significantly, morally.

Today the corporation has an identity distinct from its owners. I can offer no stronger evidence than Peter Drucker's book, *Concept of the Corporation.* Drucker served as a consultant to General Motors for several years; he talked to GM executives, visited GM plants, analyzed the company's organizational structure, studied its relations with unions, customers, and suppliers, and examined the manner in which de-

[1] *The Twentieth Century Capitalist Revolution*, by A. A. Berle, Jr., Harcourt, Brace & Co., 1954, p. 169.

cisions were made. For his book, he used GM as the very model of a modern major corporation.

Yet, the word "dividend" is not in the index. Nor, for that matter, is the word "stockholder." But you will find "worker," "labor unions," "taxation," "public relations," "consumer." You find a reference to "profit, division of," and behold, it relates to the division of "gains from increased efficiency between wages and profits." Worry about the shareholder? Hardly. The persnickety problem is how much to let the union have; how much to keep for the corporation.

This is no criticism of Drucker. He was defining, analyzing, characterizing the corporation as it is, as he found it. He was dealing with priorities, realities. Drucker derides "the old crude fiction" which "regards the corporation as the sum of the property rights of the individual shareholders. . . . In this conventional formula, the corporation is transitory . . . the shareholder is regarded as permanent and actual. In the social reality, the corporation is permanent, the shareholder is transitory."

Where does that leave shareholders Joe Doakes, Jane Smith and Tom and Henry Brown? Frank W. Abrams, former chairman of Standard Oil (N.J.), says corporations can "achieve their greatest social usefulness . . . when management succeeds in finding harmonious balance among the claims of the stockholders, employees, customers, and public at large. But management's responsibility, in the broadest sense . . . [is to be] a good citizen." [2]

A good citizen! The corporation now has a new identity apart from profit-making, apart from its charter, by-laws, and legal trappings, apart from its shareholders. It is Good Citizen, Inc.! And the corporation executive comports himself to

[2] Cited in J. D. Glover's *The Attack on Big Business*, an excellent analysis of the folklore and reality of criticism of the modern corporation, published by the Graduate School of Business Administration, Harvard University, 1954.

reflect that corporate citizenship. He wears his church clothes every day, not just on Sundays. In his paneled office, in his travels about the country, in his community relations, he represents, not himself, but The Corporation. He represents not the stockholders, but The Corporation.

The shareholder is the residuary beneficiary of Good Citizen, Inc., and this gives rise to two-toned morality—one set of morals with which executives, corporations, greet the outside world, and another set of morals with which they treat shareholders. After all, the shareholders are transitory.

But the corporation's unions are permanent; their suppliers are permanent, and the customers are permanent, they hope. Customers can correct corporate inattention by ceasing to be customers. The unions can strike. The suppliers, if they feel they are getting a dirty deal, can look for other customers. The corporation, to retain the good will of these "permanent relatives"—the unions, customers and suppliers—comports itself as a fair, upright, honest company. I recall a conversation I had with Henry Ford II just after the company granted Walter Reuther's United Auto Workers union Supplemental Unemployment Benefits, misnamed guaranteed annual wage. The theory was current among labor experts that as soon as the auto industry suffered any curtailment in sales and production, Detroit would "export unemployment." Auto manufacturers buy as well as produce parts themselves. In slack times, they would slash orders for parts from suppliers so as to concentrate employment in their own plants and thereby minimize contributions to SUB. I asked Ford about that and his reply was very simple. I can only paraphrase it at this date: "We depend on suppliers in good times, in bad times and at all times. If we treated them unfairly in bad times they'd treat us poorly in good times. We'd lose out in the long run."

Stockholders in the large, well-managed, successful corporation are like poor relatives: They are seldom in a position to correct management, nor do they have any compulsive reason to—unless they are dedicated men like Lewis D. Gilbert, or contenders for power like Robert R. Young. For stockholders, dividends are sufficient. And so, managements can be fine citizens—upright leaders in the community—and find nothing incongruous in treating their shareholders like poor relations, like supplicants who lack the power to wrench consideration (unlike, for example, labor leaders, who don't beg but demand!). In this regard, American Telephone & Telegraph Company is unique. Not because the officers and directors are drawn from a group of men whose ethical strain is different—after all, AT&T directors are frequently the heads of corporations who treat their own shareholders like, well, like shareholders—but because AT&T, as previously noted, is one corporation which, from the nature of its business, constantly goes to its shareholders for additional capital. Its shareholders are suppliers of money in the same sense that the rubber companies are suppliers of tires to General Motors, Chrysler, etc., or that can companies are suppliers of containers to Campbell Soup and H. J. Heinz.

Although corporation executives are often criticized—muckraked by union officials and left-wingers—they also have the power of benevolence to dispel said criticism, to symbolize themselves as paragons of thoughtfulness and Good Citizenship. This is the power of the corporate purse. When United States Steel Corporation, General Motors, Procter & Gamble, or Ford dispense scholarships, fellowships and wads of cash to universities, the presidents and professors at those universities are likely to be well disposed toward corporation policies, especially since the fount of largesse is continuous. When corporation executives take to fund-raising for the Red Cross, Cancer, Community Chest and Boy Scout drives, and disburse corporate as well as personal funds in these national and community endeavors, an awareness of the social conscience of the corporation is readily engendered. Benevolence is disarming and self-serving. Criticism is dulled and gratitude whetted by the lively expectation of further favors to come.

And this, the concluding section of *The American Stockholder*, tries to look behind this façade of Good Citizenship and examine the social consequences of the erosion of shareholder power—how the incapacity to correct and restrain corporation executives has become a grant of excess freedom. Executives have become an overprivileged class in a democratic society. Their power to overpay themselves, with legal sanction, could, if unchecked, erode the very structure on which they and their corporations depend for survival. The Good Citizen, whom so many young men and women want to emulate, could become the Bad Example. Spread over time, self-gorgement by executives could become epidemic and proliferate into social decadence. Cartoonists would pull "Mr. Moneybags" out of their prewar portfolios. Corporate power could become synomymous with grab-bag morality.

America, at this juncture in its industrial power and diplomatic leadership of the Western world, needs a moral force to curb this tendency of the good citizens to destroy their own good fortunes. Such a force is analyzed in this chapter, which is divided into four sections—The Irrationale of Executive Compensation; The Tax-Sheltered Elite; Executive Pay at the Cross-Purpose, and, finally, The Moral Obligation of the Institutional Investors.

IRRATIONALE OF EXECUTIVE COMPENSATION

Does it make sense that American Telephone & Telegraph Company, with 785,000 employees, should have paid its chief executive, Cleo F. Craig, $257,200 in 1956, while Bethlehem Steel Company, with 150,000 workers, paid Eugene Grace $809,000; E. I. du Pont de Nemours, with 89,000 workers, paid

Crawford Greenewalt $600,886; and Gulf Oil Corporation, with 58,000 employees, paid W. K. Whiteford, its president, $300,061?

And is it economically explicable why James M. Symes, president of the Pennsylvania Railroad and a 100,000 employee payroll, should have drawn only $127,981, while Neil H. McElroy, with 17,700 employees took $319,000 from Procter & Gamble, while Morse G. Dial, tapped Union Carbide Corporation (79,000 employees) for $300,000 and Frank Stanton, president, and William S. Paley, chairman, drew $312,335 and $316,526 respectively from Columbia Broadcasting (16,000 employees)?

Business Week magazine, in analyzing 1956 executive compensation, as reported to the SEC, noted that there were twenty-three jobs which paid more than $300,000 in cash. General Motors, du Pont, and Ford accounted for four each among the nation's top money collectors; Bethlehem Steel, three; Columbia Broadcasting, two, and Union Carbide, Republic Steel, Distillers Corporation-Seagrams, Procter & Gamble, Gulf Oil, and United Merchants & Manufacturers, giant textile firm, one each. (*See* Appendix VI.) Now note this: No public utilities were among the top pay-outers, no railroads, no airlines. And, if SEC data covered banks and insurance companies, they would not have been included either.

Top salaries in banking would range between $150,000 and $200,000; John J. McCloy, chairman of the Chase Manhattan, and Howard C. Sheperd, of the First National City Bank of New York, have reported to shareholders pay of $175,000. It was not always thus. In the 'twenties, Charles E. Mitchell, of the National City, got above a million dollars for heading up the bank and its security affiliate, the National City Company, since divorced. A. H. Wiggin, of the Chase, also got pay in the upper reaches. Again, the security affiliate—not the bank—was the big contributor. In insurance, Carrol M. Shanks, of the Prudential, seems to be top man—$250,000; Frederick W. Ecker, president of the somewhat larger Metropolitan, drew $160,000. Salaries of other life insurance executives cluster around $100,000. But casualty companies pay somewhat more. The Insurance Company of North America paid John A. Diemand, president, $140,000, and it has a stock option plan too.

The argument is made that the telephone, public utility, railroad, banking, insurance, and airline industries are semimonopolistic in nature. Outside competition is remote (try telling that to a railroad man who has lost his high-price freight to truckers and his passenger business to the plane, automobile and bus!) and job tenure in the top echelons is secure. On the other hand, the automobile industry, entertainment, textiles, distilling, tobacco, soap all are characterized by high earnings, high risk, and much advertising. Executives are constantly confronted with profit-and-loss decisions—styling, new products, slogans. The jobs are killing—seven days a week, twenty-four hours a day. So, compensation is roughly proportional to sales and profits.[3] Often there are bonus plans. On the other hand, banking, railroading, public utility-ing, etc., are more placid, less demanding.

I am suspicious of this argument. It implies a forbearance, a self-restraint which is not an outstanding attribute of men who get to the top. When they do not exercise their strong "gift of grab," I suspect it is the nature of the job, not the nature of the man. After all, the stockholders are not a restraining influence on the president of a railroad any more than on the president of a television company; American Telephone & Telegraph or First National City Bank officials could

[3] "Annual Report on Executive Compensation," by Arch Patton, of the management consulting firm of McKinsey & Company, *Harvard Business Review*, September-October, 1957, associates high pay with high sales and profits.

readily talk themselves into a bigger take—merely on the basis of what other executives get. But they do not. Why?

All of these industries are quasi-public. All are subject to outside regulation—banks by the Comptroller of the Currency, state superintendents of banking, Federal Reserve Board, etc. When examiners look into the operations, they often make comments to directors about the reasonableness of executive salaries in relation to earnings. An onus is put on directors to question extreme payments. Life insurance companies must file their salary schedules with state superintendents—and they, too, are subject to questioning. The railroads report to the Interstate Commerce Commission; American Telephone & Telegraph Company submits to state commissions as well as the Federal Communications Commission. Public utilities constantly go before state regulatory bodies to justify rate increases. High pay to high executives would damn their designs. Air transport companies are subject to Civil Aeronautics Board supervision.

A career man in any utility, AT&T, Commonwealth Edison Company of Chicago, or the Philadelphia Electric Company, etc. is indoctrinated from apprenticeship in the importance of seemliness, of correctness, in all dealings with the public and with utility commissioners. He knows that every detail of the company's operations will be measured, examined, pried into at rate hearings—and be publicized. He curbs his appetite for money in order to satisfy his appetite for success in his own company. He takes his pay in other forms [4]—notably in the position he holds in his community and in a high, assured pension. In addition, of course, there are the normal emoluments which go with being a chief executive—a liberal expense account, company automobiles, etc. It is a bearable

---

[4] Inhibitions did not afflict the holding company impresarios in the 'twenties before the death sentence. But then they seldom appeared before public utility commissions; they were not operating men; they were financiers.

life, even though it is not on the same financial level as that of the presidency of General Motors, du Pont, or Radio Corporation of America. When John J. McCloy of the Chase Bank or Frederick R. Kappel, of AT&T, call on Harlow Curtice of General Motors ($695,000 in 1956), Curtice does not expect them to kneel.

Prior to the New Deal, the compensation of corporate executives was a deep secret. When the "numbers" first were made public by Congress, executives resented the intrusion on their privacy. Now, however, it has become something of a game—who is tops? Many executives relish the publicity as much as the high school student the notation in the graduating class program "highest honors." SEC reports on remuneration constitute an informal ranking of executives. The "highest paid executive in America," "highest paid executive in the chemical industry," "highest paid person in entertainment" meets the exhibitionistic urge inherent in most of us. A few corporation officials, eschew this numbers game. Thomas B. McCabe, of Scott Paper, draws no salary. Louis E. Wolfson, of Merritt-Chapman & Scott, limits his (see Chapter VIII), and so does Juan Trippe, of Pan American World Airways. But these are exceptions, whose satisfactions take other forms.

The late Judge George Thomas Washington and V. Henry Rothschild II made this pertinent observation: "Corporations whose managements are not subject to control by large stockholders or by financial interests tend to give higher rewards to management than companies in which those controls are present." [5] Judge Washington had made a study in 1941

[5] *Compensating the Corporate Executive*, Ronald Press, 1951, page 419. Incidentally, the du Pont family, which controls General Motors Corporation, is an exception to this generalization. The du Ponts apparently believe in high compensation. Three officers at General Motors received over $500,000. And du Pont's own president, as noted, received $600,000.

which supports the theory that those who are beholden to nobody become generously disposed toward themselves.

Uninhibited corporation executives festoon themselves with post-retirement consulting contracts—so that they get paid five to ten years beyond the sixty-five-year age limit. The company commits itself to pay for today's services out of tomorrow's production and dividends. Such special benefactions are amplified by stock options, which give executives a call on the stock—in case the business prospers. All that and pension plans too!

This self-serving is so prevalent that I apologize for mentioning specific plans and companies. They are not singled out as unusual, but only for illustration. Allegheny Ludlum Steel executive contracts provide for retirement pay at age sixty-five to "perform consulting services as requested and not to render service to any competitor and, in the case of death, the aggregate amount of such compensation is payable to the estate of the individual without reduction." This is a transparency. An estate cannot consult. This is deferred compensation—for tax purposes. Allegheny Ludlum also wool-lines executive futures with stock options plus a pension plan. The standard justification for such devices is: "If we don't pay our key men, other companies will take them away." Yet, it is noteworthy that these contracts are changeable at the will of the officers and directors who make them. When Allegheny Ludlum introduced a stock option plan in 1954, both the president and executive vice-president terminated, with the consent of directors, their old contract in order to be "in a position to participate in the employees' stock option plans on a more favorable basis." Here is a case—and it must be emphasized that it is illustrative—in which a contract, presumably binding on both officers and company, was altered to improve the status of the two principal officers, whose annual cash income at the time was $123,000 and $80,000 respectively, and which in 1956 had risen to $150,000 and $110,000.

Or, consider the stock options extended to the officers of General Dynamics Corporation, the company that struck it rich by splicing together Consolidated Vultee Aircraft Corporation, Stromberg-Carlson Company, and the original Electric Boat Company, maker of the nuclear-powered submarine, *Nautilus.* The late president, John Jay Hopkins, in 1956, received $151,000 in salary, and was granted an option on thirty thousand shares. Nor was that all. He exercised earlier options to buy forty-five thousand shares at $14.05 at the time the price was $40.71. Indicated paper profit: $1,190,000. Executive Vice-President Frank Pace, Jr., who had been Secretary of the Army under President Truman, did even better. His 1956 pay came to $97,000, his estimated retirement benefits would amount to $32,593 and he was able to purchase 31,500 shares at $14.05 at the time the market was $49.75. Indicated profit: Over a million dollars. Pace has since ascended to the presidency.

Such gains are not unusual. The *Wall Street Journal,* in February, 1955, under the appropriately alliterative heading, "Option Opulence," noted that Frank Stanton, president of Columbia Broadcasting, had an indicated paper profit of $4,-500,000 on options. Option plans have become so popular that the Pennsylvania and New York Central Railroads are using them. And legislation has been introduced in Congress to permit national banks to issue options. Bankers say they cannot attract aggressive young men to the institutions—or retain them—because of greater inducements elsewhere. The National Association of Security Administrators "buys" this with a caveat: "Sometimes the retention of executives of proven worth may be assured by the granting of options, but it is submitted that usually less objectionable means are available for accomplishing this objective." [6]

Hershey Chocolate Corporation, a tidy concern with annual sales of about $150,000,000 and annual profits ranging from $7,000,000 to $12,000,000 paid its late president, P. A. Staples, only $75,000 in straight cash. In 1956, J. J. Gallagher, general sales manager, who succeeded to the presidency, got $40,000. Possible explanation: Seventy per cent of Hershey stock is in trust for the Milton Hershey School. A Hershey executive cannot deal himself what he thinks he is worth without "checking in" with the "large shareholder."

Sometimes, it is said a good man is hired away from a company because of pay, because of stock options. But it is always well to search behind the "given" reason. It might be that the departee was in a job in which his path was blocked. The new opportunity might offer an open field to an island of power, on which he, as president, can determine his own emoluments through an agreeable board of directors and we'll-let-you-alone-just-give-us-our-dividend shareholders. For this is the twentieth century way of "battening down" one's future. The well-trod avenue to an "old age competence" is control of other people's money, of a corporation, and compensating yourself in the manner your industrial peers consider proper.

In this, it seems to me, social morals are infringed. The very men who benefit from this system can damage it, perhaps destroy it through greed. An outside conscience—with power to persuade—is required. Disclosure is not enough. Exhibitionism, "I'm tops," whets cupidity instead of sensitivity to public opinion. I can foresee a Congressional investigation of executive remuneration—an investigation which, in its way, will rival that of Senator McClellan's investigation of racketeering in labor unions. Congressmen will ask pointed questions: Who decided on this plan of compensation? Who

[6] Resolution noted in Chapter XV.

recommended it to the board of directors? Did the board of directors study it carefully? Was any voice raised in opposition? It could make unpleasant headlines—even as the headlines about the take of bankers during the Senate investigation of the depression 'thirties.

Shortly after the foregoing was written, Estes Kefauver (Dem., Tenn.), as chairman of a Senate Judiciary Subcommittee investigating causes of inflation, asked steel company executives if the high salaries they paid themselves were not a "challenge, a goad, a red flag to labor unions and individual workers to seek and receive all they can." Kefauver took due note that Bethlehem Steel's chairman, Eugene Grace (since retired) was the highest paid corporation official in America. He left the inference that when steel executives argue that steel prices were raised to offset wage increases, they, the executives, were to blame.

THE TAX-SHELTERED ELITE

Executive compensation today affronts society on two counts. First, executives have made themselves into a preferred group, a tax-protected elite. The ordinary worker—the mechanic, the schoolteacher, the salesman, the newspaperman, the bricklayer—cannot escape the impact of the tax laws, except by dishonesty, by outright evasion. But the businessman has been able, with the help of lawyers and accountants, to contrive a shelter. By deferring his compensation— by charging his services to latter-day stockholders and consumers—he gets pay for past services when his income-tax bracket drops. He does this by making a contract with his company. But, as we shall see, this is tantamount to making a contract with himself. In contrast, a physician, a lawyer, or an author cannot easily defer his payments for services rendered into retirement years. And if he does, under a strict contract with his patient, client, or publisher, he has to do so through arm's-length bargaining. So why should the executive—by using a self-made consulting contract—be able to shelter himself in his retirement years with what amounts to a tax subsidy from government?

In the same dubious category are stock options. If the ordinary Joe Blow wants to build up a capital-gains fortune, he has to take a risk. He buys stocks or real estate with his own or borrowed money. If prices drop, he takes a loss. Because of the danger of loss, of the risk, Congress excepted such gains from the regular income tax schedule. Now our canny executives use the exception to apply to their "regular pay." They grant themselves options to buy shares at 95 per cent of the market value; they make sure that they do not sell the stock within two years from the granting of the option; they also make sure that once they have bought the stock they hold it for more than six months.[7] Then whatever profit accrues is subject to the capital gains rate of 25 per cent rather than progressive taxation, which rises to 52 per cent, 76 per cent and even 91 per cent.

Executives justify such tax devices by saying that they cannot get along on a straight salary. Taxes eat up too much. Consequently, it has become customary in many corporate proxy statements to show shareholders just how tax-ridden executives are. As an example: The Campbell Soup Company reports to shareholders that the cash remuneration of Pres-

[7] Example: An option is granted to buy stock on January 1, 1957, at 95 per cent of the market value at that time, which we will say is $50. That means the price to the executive is $47.50. A year and a half later, on July 1, 1958, the stock is selling for $100. So he exercises the option at a paper profit of $52.50 per share. To get the benefit of the 25 per cent tax rate, he must hold the stock for six months, or until January, 1959. That is his risk. But he has a 52-½ point cushion against loss. Downy, if you can get it! Options at 85 per cent of the market value are also allowable; but then part of the profit is treated as ordinary income and subject to the high progressive income taxes; it does not get capital gains status.

231

ident William B. Murphy was $225,000 in 1956. His estimated "net" after deduction of estimated income taxes was shown as $70,068. This estimated "net" allows for standard deductions and for no dependents other than wife. Such estimates are purely hypothetical—with only an accidental semblance to reality. Here, it seems to me, the Securities and Exchange Commission deviates from its principle of full disclosure. Either the executive should reveal his actual income after taxes—allowing for all deductions—or the corporation should not be permitted to use salary minification in a proxy statement. It is not as if the cash were fallow. The executive can make charitable contributions—sometimes as high as 30 per cent of his income. These contributions give him influence and prestige—with his university, with hospitals, with institutions. He can set up his own charitable trust, and employ a relative or friend to handle the investments or dispense the largesse. The money becomes a source of power. Further, he can use the income for entrepreneurial ventures of his own, such as running a farm (which ex-General Motors' Charles E. Wilson has done) or a business. Money is money and can be used to make more money. And if there are operating gains, they accrue, less taxes, to the executive; if there are operating losses, then they are deductible from salary.

In a society in which the graduated income tax is law, the Good Citizen, the corporate executive, sets a poor example by violating the democracy written into the income tax laws—that is, taxation according to capacity to pay. That there is full disclosure is neither a mitigation nor an amelioration. A practice of getting all this is gettable, of "beating the revenooer," ill becomes an industrial elite. The Corporate Good Citizen holds the moral structure together by the morals, the standards, he himself sets. He gets much out of the system. He can ill afford to tear it down by his own cupidity.

EXECUTIVE PAY AT THE CROSS-PURPOSE

This wool-lining of executive futures is against the national interest. This is the second count. President Eisenhower tried for months to find a replacement for Charles E. Wilson as Secretary of Defense. The post was offered to a number of industrialists. Several bankers refused to take the position of Deputy Secretary of the Treasury vacated by W. Randolph Burgess. The directorship of the International Coöperation Administration was hard to fill. Why?

Private industry has too much to offer. To take the $25,000 job as Secretary of Defense—one of the strategic positions in the United States and the world—Wilson gave up a better than $500,000-a-year post at General Motors. He took a pay cut of more than 95 per cent, and had to sell his General Motors stock. Neil McElroy succeeded Wilson at only a 90 per cent voluntary pay cut. At Procter & Gamble he got over $300,000. I'm not lamenting for Wilson and McElroy. I expect they'll get along. But the U.S. may not, which is my deep concern.

What a contrast with Soviet Russia! There, the bigger the political job, the greater the compensation, the greater the prestige, the greater the emoluments. The Soviet system rewards the commissars well, along with scientists, college professors, engineers, inventors, technicians, teachers, writers, ballerinas, newspapermen. The islands of strategic power in the Soviet system are political, educational and artistic. The control of production resides with the politician. And the politician takes good care of the politician, even as the industrialist rewards himself in our system. Maybe we can learn, in this regard, from Russia, where it is clearly accepted that the chief is above subordinates. In contrast, over here it is the exceptional top industrialist who does not fare better financially than the President of the United States.

For shouldering the burdens of world leadership, we pay the President $100,000 a year in salary and an expense allowance of $50,000—both taxable—and a non-taxable allowance for traveling and official entertainment of $40,000. Compare that with $800,00 and $600,000 and $300,000 presidencies in industry. The Vice-President of the United States receives $35,000 a year plus $10,000 in expenses, all taxable, but no rent-free home, an appurtenance of the Presidency. At Bendix Aviation, a vice-president will get $87,000; at Coca-Cola, $93,750; at General Motors $577,000; at Ford $240,000. Our corporate pay scale operates at cross-purpose to our government. We take care of the managerial class in industry, but stint the managers of the system, the government itself.

An undersecretary in the Cabinet gets $22,000; an assistant secretary $20,000. A justice of the Supreme Court does better at $35,000. But a judgeship takes a man out of politics. The chairman of the Atomic Energy Commission, the Federal Home Loan Bank Board, the Federal Power Commission, and the SEC all receive $20,500. A senator who gets muck-deep in politics every six years, and a member of the House of Representatives who has to campaign for his job every two years, receive $22,500 a year in salary, plus some expense allowances; and in filing income tax returns, they are allowed to deduct $3,000 a year for living expenses in Washington. Surely, on occasion, when they see SEC reports of executive compensation, government men must ask themselves, "Why do we do it?"

General Alfred P. Gruenther, one of the nation's foremost military strategists and former commander-in-chief of the NATO forces, quit the army to become head of the Red Cross at a salary of $30,000 a year plus a residence in Washington. He was only fifty-seven. Edward T. McCormick, an SEC commissioner, yielded to the $40,000 presidency of the New York Curb Exchange, which name he changed for dignity to the American Stock Exchange. At the time, he was paid $15,000 a year. Donald C. Cook, an SEC chairman, resigned after four years, to join American Gas and Electric Service Corporation. His 1957 salary is $49,000. If he had stayed with the SEC, his salary would have risen from $15,-000 to $20,000. Ralph H. Demmler, President Eisenhower's first SEC nominee, stayed less than two years, though appointed for five, to return to his law firm. A. Jackson Goodwin, Jr., another Eisenhower appointee, resigned "for personal reasons" after only a year and a half. He joined the Lee Higginson Corporation. A whole group of admirals and generals went to industry—Admiral Ben Moreell to Jones & Laughlin; General Lucius D. Clay to Continental Can; Walter Bedell Smith to American Machine and Foundry. General Brehon B. Somervell, who was in charge of procurement in World War II, became executive head at Koppers. The Atomic Energy Commission has "staffed" investment firms and corporate research departments with top men. The government has become a preparatory school to enter business or a finishing school for those who have been in business and want to return. Industry even scoops down into the lower echelons. Department of Defense staff men are drawn off into law firms, legal departments of corporations, research staffs, or administrative jobs assisting top executives. The report of the Defense Advisory Committee, headed by Ralph J. Cordiner, president of General Electric Company, cites numerous instances of government losing out to industry—because of salary considerations. It also notes that the Department of Defense cannot match the starting pay of large corporations in the competition for young college graduates. President Eisenhower acknowledged this by saying that a young executive who goes from business into government "practically ruins his business career and his future." Such a distortion in economic incentive only businessmen, themselves, can correct. Sure, you can get a Wilson, a McElroy, a George M. Humphrey, a Sinclair Weeks to take a Cabinet post for a while. They are men who have put aside something to live on; and they have the psychic satisfaction of a Secretary's flag to fly on their automobiles, airplanes to travel around in, chauffered limousines, and invitations to the White House and from all of America's social lion hunters. But that's a helluva way to run a country—through psychic satisfaction that only a comparatively few can afford.

Corporations also draw professors of science and engineering from our leading universities. These men are part of our educational framework. What irony! Corporations, as Good Citizens, Inc., make huge gifts to help educational institutions and then induce away, with high salaries, the very men needed to maintain excellence in education! Youngsters, with an M.A. or Ph.D. degree can command $5,000 to $7,500 at du Pont, General Electric, or U.S. Steel and entertain hopes of advancing to one hundred grand a year with stock options. So, why should they put up with a $3,000 instructor's pay in the hope ultimately of getting an $8,000 or $15,000 professor's salary?

In a young country, in a country of infant industries, great rewards for long hours and intensive labor commend themselves. The inventor who starves himself in a garret to produce a better mousetrap deserves riches in royalties. But in the mid-twentieth century giant corporations pay regular, sure salaries to executives and to scientists. Is such high incentive pay necessary? Especially since the government has undertaken, under the Employment Act of 1946, to provide a high level of job stability? That, in itself, is some insurance against violent ups and downs in income. Our system of rewards, through stock options and deferred compensation not only creates an opulence which the corporation executive has to prove he still deserves, but also threatens the management of our system—the government itself.

Raising government salaries will not solve the problem. As long as the corporate executive can tax-batten his income, the government cannot compete. The only recourse is to force conscientious executives to revalue their own services—to examine what high pay is doing to government, to the political management of the system on which they depend. In a country such as ours, we need competent members of the Cabinet, military men, administrators. We need men who are as brilliantly trained and respected as their Soviet counterparts, where rewards are directed to obtain the best men at the top of the national structure and not, as in ours, where they tend to siphon the best into industry. A *New Yorker* cartoon is not entirely irrelevant: Husband and wife both reading papers. Wife says to husband: "My, it's a big week for everybody! The Russians have the Intercontinental Ballistic Missile, and we have the Edsel." We have developed great industrialists, great products, and great corporations. These industrialists and corporations have helped the United States to win two great wars. It is important that the good citizens, of Good Citizens, Inc., do not make the jobs they have to offer so alluring that we lose the peace for want of brilliant, efficient, perspicacious men in government, science, and education.

THE MORAL OBLIGATION OF THE INSTITUTIONAL INVESTORS

When I first undertook this book, I had an idea to get across. I thought how wonderful it would be if some independent, objective organization undertook to appraise—rate—the managements of various companies each year! This organization would sit on Mount Olympus, examine the reports, policies and progress of United States Steel, Bethlehem, Republic and other companies in the steel industry; it would do the same for food, can, auto and electric power and light companies. It would send out trained personnel to interview executives of corporations. It would form judgments about the long-term plans of the company, its niche in its industry, its service to the nation at large. It would take the broadest possible view—a social view. It would be both a critic and an advocate, concerned with improving the managerial breed. Its standards would be so impeccably exacting that its favorable judgment would be tantamout to a Cellini stamp on gold, its negative comments worse than a low Dun and Bradstreet rating. In a proxy contest, its approval would swing the election.

Then, I discovered that this was not an inactive idea. Jackson Martindell, a former investment counsel and stock market operator, had started rating managements through his American Institute of Management before 1950. As I studied some of his ratings, I became perplexed. Fruehauf Trailer, which has had an erratic earnings record, family troubles, and has helped officers to purchase stock with company credit, a questionable use of corporate assets in my opinion, was given a high rating along with General Motors, American Telephone & Telegraph, du Pont, Eastman Kodak, General Electric, and National Biscuit. Alfons Landa, a Washington attorney, was a director of both Fruehauf and the American Institute of Management. I pondered: Could an organization which had directors of corporations on its board be impartial in appraisals?

I developed further misgivings about my idea. The AIM issued special reports on the Pennsylvania Railroad, the Ford Motor Company, and General Motors. It found the Pennsylvania Railroad wanting because its shuttle train service between Princeton Junction and Princeton, where Martindell lives, unsatisfactory. It criticized the Ford Motor Company for nepotism, notwithstanding the fact that Henry Ford II and his brothers have resurrected the company from the antedated tactics of Henry Ford, the first. It said General Motors Corporation was too big, and ought to be broken up, in spite of its own judgment that GM was excellently managed.

At that point, I concluded that Olympian judgment was possible only on Mount Olympus. There will almost always be two sides to any judgment of management. Examine the reports of investment trusts—the professionals in investing: The same month, one trust buys Sears, Roebuck, another trust, equally professional, sells. If, in a proxy fight, the Olympian Appraisal Institute issued a judgment in favor of one side, society would create an opposing Olympus to espouse the other side. The American system requires pros (no pun) and cons, a Republican Party and a Democratic Party, a force and a counterforce. As soon as one High Court of Management Appraisal became accepted, another equally High Court would be established as a competitor. That there is none in competition with Martindell is, in itself, a commentary on the American Institute of Management.[8]

It became obvious as the book progressed and as I got a deeper hold on my subject that effective appraisal of management—appraisal with the force of moral restraint—could come from one source, and one source only, the professional investor, the institutional investor, the pro who is in there investing day in and day out. Full disclosure helps the pro. Full disclosure quickens the executive, the corporate conscience. But only the professionals can influence the executive—through indignation and disapproval—to see himself as others see him, to recognize the full impact of his actions on America's social, political, and economic institutions—for good and for bad. The professional investors—the presidents of the insurance companies, banks and trust companies, investment trusts, pension funds, and some few well-to-do individual in-

[8] A fine article, "Mr. Martindell's Curious Institute," by Daniel Seligman, *Fortune*, November, 1956, goes into the background of AIM.

vestors, such as the Rockefellers and Whitneys—are members of the same clubs, the same upper stratum of wealth, the same economic dominance. And to them attaches an important fringe group who also have influence—investment bankers, brokers, investment advisers, partners in many-name law firms, and heads of accounting firms. The opinions of this group would carry the social force of equals judging equals, the economic force of experts judging other experts. The members of this group have not only the intellectual capacity and knowledge to use full disclosure but also the positional prestige and power to engender a higher morality in corporate conduct, a morality above and beyond the call of the SEC. Wall Street—the entire complex of Wall Street—the banks, insurance companies, investment banking firms, brokerage houses, investment trusts, pension funds—can exact from the managers of corporations, from the issuers of securities, a single standard of morality—and a very high standard—in self-defense and for the well being of the country. They can take the attitude, "As you do unto others, so you might do unto me." They can display moral courage and protest when the Good Citizens do something sly, unworthy, and prejudicial to the investment community or the national ethic. Yet, where were the leaders of Wall Street when the New York Stock Exchange admitted Ford Motor Company stock to listing with its divine-right-of-the-Fords voting plan? They were participating in the sales commission. Where were the investment trusts, the pension funds, the trust companies? They said nothing. Where were the banks? They knew it was a deviation, a disregard of propriety and of the Exchange's own standards. But this was Ford. If some lesser company with a less American name had attempted such a plan it would never have got across.

All too often, Wall Street tries to serve two masters. Robert Vanderpoel, one of this country's outstanding financial columnists—he was on the *Chicago Sun-Times* when he died— told me how the trust department of a Chicago bank intended to vote Montgomery Ward stock held in investment accounts against Sewell Avery. But when the commercial vice-presidents heard of the plan, no dice. Lose Ward's, Avery's, deposit? Hardly! This was a clear case of misdirected trusteeship.

The financial press is intimately bound up in this Wall Street complex—and it, too, has a responsibility for lifting the moral tone of industry and of finance above the dollar sign. This is a responsibility, I regret to acknowledge, which it has not always discharged with distinction. *Time* magazine has observed that the "most serious flaw in business reporting is the deep-rooted aversion of most business editors to controversy, gloom or criticism—in tacit cahoots with the managerial mentality that believes that the private lives of corporations should be immune from the irreverent scrutiny to which the press routinely subjects politics, government, and the boudoir antics of showfolk." [9] Austin Wehrwein, then financial editor of the *Chicago Sun-Times*, was quoted: "Business too often takes the attitude that the press must coöperate or be guilty of an anti-business attitude."

Sometimes, though I think less and less frequently, newspapers, themselves, are to blame. A formal request to "keep it out of the paper" will occasionally be respected even though the news might affect stockholders, customers, and employees, such as a merger of a bank or the introduction of a new-model car.[10] This encourages the corporation executive to

[9] *Time*, August 12, 1957, page 44.
[10] In June, 1954, General Motors Corporation ordered all its advertising out of the *Wall Street Journal*, after John D. Williams, then automobile editor, wrote a story describing the industry's new models. Attached were rough drawings of the leading cars. GM argued the information was obtained from its suppliers, was private property and confidential. Ford and Chrysler remained discreetly aloof from the controversy, no doubt smiling at the nineteenth century display of outraged power by GM. Ultimately, GM re-

think he is the consulting publisher. When one reporter or one newspaper in a city submits to the pleasure of the men in the news, the men in the news expect to be accommodated by all reporters. And BOM's—business office musts—continue in some cities to lacerate the souls of financial and managing editors. *Time* notes that the financial departments of newspapers all too frequently have been custodianized by tired rewrite men or copyreaders—men who have served their time and are given "pension spots." They are not trained to understand balance sheets, income accounts, and the methods of modern business.

In contrast, British newspapers have trained economists for "city editors." (Financial editors are called city editors in Britain because they cover the City of London, the old city, which is the financial district.) When a new security issue is brought out by a British company, the city editors will analyze it—compare the price-earnings ratio, the dividend, the growth with other companies in the industry. And they will pop out with the answer investors want: Is the stock worth buying? Not many financial editors in the United States are equipped for such critical judgment. And those that are seldom show it in print.

Here we come to a practicality of American journalism: Space. There are in the United States, as we have noted, somewhat fewer than nine million shareholders. Stocks are owned by about 10 per cent of the families. Thus, in the average city, especially in one- or two-newspaper cities, about 10 per cent of the readers would scan the financial and business pages. In the larger, industrialized and banking centers,

turned to advertising in the *Wall Street Journal*. Its attempt to use its advertising purse to influence news policy received a very bad press. I wrote at the time: "GM's withdrawal of advertising touches the sensitive nerve of newspapermen who like to think that news policy is not influenced by the business office. Whenever a big advertiser waves the advertising dollar, backs arch in news rooms."

the percentage would tend to be higher than in smaller cities. And New York, which is the financial heart of the United States and the western world (British writers please ignore!), is *sui generis,* a city unto itself. There are seven daily newspapers; they cater to different income-bracket readers. Both the *Times* and the *Herald-Tribune,* in the morning field, have developed a class circulation. They do not spread-eagle the full range of readership as do papers in most other cities. A larger proportion of *Times* and *Tribune* readers, for example, would be interested in business and finance than would those of the tabloid *Daily News* or *Mirror* in New York, or those of the *Bulletin* in Philadelphia or the *Courier-Journal* in Louisville. They can and do devote more space to finance, business, and stock quotations. Through their Washington bureaus or the wire services, they give fair coverage to activities of the Securities and Exchange Commission and print, as do many papers in other cities, the purchases and sales of stocks by insiders in corporations. They sometimes find space for analysis of business trends, the money market, and corporation practices and policies. And, of course, the *Wall Street Journal,* as the paper of business and finance, and the *Journal of Commerce,* which accents commerce, insurance and shipping, provide specialized as well as general coverage. There are other cities in which above-average concentration of business page readers justifies granting financial editors space and scope, such as San Francisco, Chicago, Boston, Kansas City, San Diego, Atlanta and Philadelphia. The list is indicative, not inclusive. But, as a rule, the coverage is not up to New York's.

You can argue—and I like to—that the readers of the financial page deserve more because they are influential. They are the executives of corporations, the advertising managers, etc. And people tend to advertise in the newspapers or magazines they read. Therefore, "financial" deserves a space allotment in greater proportion to its actual readership. None the less, when the chips are down, financial has to compete with sports, comics, women's pages, and general news. And the very shortage of space is a restraint. The financial editor, torn between printing news and printing a critical opinion of a new stock issue, will almost invariably print the news. A dividend increase by General Motors, an issue of rights by American Telephone is of far greater interest to the paper's readers than a well-reasoned study of the licentiousness of a stock option plan of the XYZ Corporation. I say this with depth of feeling. My syndicated column, "The Business Outlook," is interpretive and critical. But stock prices come first! Then, earnings reports and news from the SEC. What good is full disclosure if it is not disclosed?

Specialized magazines also make a contribution. *Fortune* frequently goes beneath the surface of corporation activities; sometimes it delves into salaries and compensation. So does the *Harvard Business Review*. *Business Week* unearths stories which escape the average financial editor. Here, again, quality pays off. These magazines operate on higher pay scales than most newspapers. A newspaperman, scraping along on $150 a week, will look in awe at a tycoon who is on first-name terms with his publisher. Can he rudely question him about the fairness of the company's proposed compensation plan?

The financial press, itself, is directly associated with the financial community. Which is understandable. This is the community it serves. The *Wall Street Journal*, *Barron's* magazine, which so often has penetrating analyses of corporations, the stock market, and business trends, the *Financial World*, *Forbes*, the *Commercial and Financial Chronicle*, and the *Journal of Commerce*, to mention ones that come immediately to mind, reflect the views of the institutional investors, because the institutional investors, in a very real sense constitute the higher thought of the investment community. These publications do not customarily go in for social criticism.

That is not their purpose. Most social criticism of Wall Street comes from outside Wall Street—from writers on national affairs. And it even happens that financial writers on daily newspapers, who ought to be objective, become apologists for Wall Street. They are drawn into the inner circle of thought and attitudes: Management, if successful, can do no wrong. And this is a pity. And for it, I blame the institutional investors.

Financial writers would be bolder and more useful to stockholders and the Wall Street community, if the institutional investors—the heads of trust departments of banks, the investment specialists in insurance companies, the presidents and investment vice-presidents of investment trusts, the partners in investment banking firms, and partners in accounting firms—were more outspoken; if they were willing to be quoted; if they accepted the ethical leadership which their strategic positions confer on them. They are on the inside looking in. By this I do not mean that they should become Lewis Gilberts—or even corporate raiders, fighting for control of corporations. Neither is their line. But I do mean that the institutions should be more than bystanders in corporate affairs. They have the professional know-how to take advantage of full disclosure.

They ought to examine salary, pension, deferred compensation, and stock option plans critically. They ought to raise questions about the propriety of a corporation president getting five times the cash income of the President of the United States. They ought to express openly their attitudes toward corporate compensation schemes which enable executives to elude the tax collector: What effect is it having on the morality of the nation generally?

Institutional investors protest—and with justice—that they are not stockholders with a capital S. They buy management primarily, and properties secondarily. Yet, this very emphasis—on management—underlines the responsibility of institutional investors. They are trustees for all shareholders. They establish the moral tone in Wall Street. Sure, they can sell securities to indicate dissatisfaction with a company or a management. And they should. Their job is not to pick fights or to oust managements, though that sometimes happens. Merrill Lynch, Pierce, Fenner & Beane, investment bankers for Safeway Stores, did not hesitate when that company's earnings began to fidget in the wrong direction, to suggest privately to Lingan A. Warren, president, that he was superfluous.[11] Robert A. Magowan, a senior partner in Merrill Lynch and son-in-law of Charles Merrill, took over. Merrill Lynch, of course, could not have taken this stand had Magowan not been willing, and, as events have proved, able to manage the company. That is what balked Massachusetts Investors Trust and Wellington Fund when they became dissatisfied with Sewell Avery at Montgomery Ward. They had no candidates for Avery's job. But MIT and Wellington did speak up. They departed from the traditional institutional policy of silence— the silence which so often indicates assent. They get a high mark for that!

Frequently when newspapermen inquire—ask for help or guidance—in analyzing the operations of a large corporation, or the flaws in a new issue, institutional investors clam up. It is not clubby to criticize. Here is the great failure of the institutional investors, the failure to dissociate from corporations, from executives, the failure to sit in moral judgment. The institutions are the buyers and sellers of securities. They are on the other side of the table from the managers of corporations, the executives. They can command attention and informa-

[11] Warren did not leave Safeway an impoverished man. He took with him a consulting contract calling for pay between $50,000 and $150,000 a year, depending on profits, from 1956 through 1960; then, for the next three years, the pay would range from $33,334 to $100,000, again depending on profits. After that, he would be entitled to $2,000 a month for life, and, at his death, if his wife survived, she would be entitled to $1,000 a month for life. He also held on to a stock option.

tion. They are not like college professors or a self-appointed Institute of Management on the outside. They are men corporation executives will listen to. Peers respond to peers. And they ought to be objective critics—and outspoken—in their own interest. For, only by improving the morals of the men from whom they buy securities will they discharge their duties to investors who have trusted their funds to them.

During the depression 'thirties, when unemployment was widespread, when hungry people stood outside restaurant windows eying those eating inside, diners felt uncomfortable. It was unbecoming to display well-offness. Many wealthy men took their chauffeurs out of livery, did away with limousines. Conspicuous consumption was bad taste. But postwar prosperity has brought conspicuous consumption back. Conspicuous compensation has become an index of success. And this could well be an index not so much of prosperity as of a moral breakdown, of an inability of the elite, the economic leaders, to contain themselves. All the more reason for institutional investors to ask questions of their clubmates, their economic peers, about their compensation. If justified, the self-rewarders will be able to justify their rewards. If unjustified, the self-rewarders will feel sufficiently uncomfortable to reconsider their own take. Institutional investors are equipped for this critical function, for this moral suasion. They are not in the thick of corporate competition. They can look at pay scales, at executive behavior, at corporate Good Citizenship objectively. And they have a common interest with corporation executives. They want corporations to perdure; they want them to make money; they want to improve the breed of management—not only of the companies in which they have invested, but also of the companies in which they might invest. The more well-managed corporations there are, the wider will be their own investment choices and opportunities.

Most shareholders—most of the nearly nine million—are

247

like spectators at a ball game. They can boo the umpires; boo the players; or applaud. But they do not have much effect on the play.

The institutional investors do. They can influence the rules of the game; the comportment of the players. But they cannot do it by silence; by being simple investors, first, last, and always. They have to have a sense of trusteeship. They must make their professional judgment felt—by comments at clubs, at financial analyst meetings, by observations to newspaper and magazine writers, as well as by the sale of stocks in the market place. They ought to protest greed, overcompensation, amorality and immorality. They ought to demand behavior above suspicion.

They are the permanent shareholders: as permanent as the corporations they invest in. And their terrain is the entire social structure of the United States. "What's good for General Motors," said Secretary of Defense Wilson, "is good for the country." But it is also possible that compensation can be so good for General Motors management that it is bad for the management and morals of the country.

Executives are too close to themselves to see a conflict of interest. On the other hand, institutional investors who look dispassionately at stocks and bonds, prices and profits, can also look dispassionately, objectively and critically at corporations. When policies are right, the institutional function is to keep them right; when policies are wrong, to make them right —in the institution's and the general stockholder's interest. That is a moral obligation institutions shoulder when they become investment trustees.

—30—

APPENDIX I

Rosenfeld vs. Fairchild Engine & Airplane Corporation

To the victors belong the spoils—and reimbursement for expenses. This has been the precedent in proxy contests. It is still the precedent, and yet . . .

A new theory of law may be developing.

Heretofore, in proxy fights, managements have used corporate funds to fight off insurgents, and courts have said okay. If the insurgents win, it has been somewhat different. They have used their own money, but then have turned around and asked stockholder approval for reimbursement on the ground that they altered the policy of the corporation. Since they have already won the political fealty of shareholders, they automatically get approval, as in the New York Central fight.

This precedent, however, was nearly upset, four to three, in July, 1955, by a New York Court of Appeals decision. Its closeness may foreshadow major changes in the reimbursement of contestants in proxy struggles, and, therefore, changes in the conduct of the contests.

The suit was brought by minority shareholders against both old and new directors of the Fairchild Engine & Airplane Corporation to recover for the company costs of the proxy fight. The decision could easily have shifted four-to-three against reimbursement, for the court divided three ways:

1. Three judges sustained the lower courts in permitting

the corporation to pay $133,966 for the expenses of the old directors, including $28,000 that was disbursed after they were out of office and, therefore, had to be ratified by the new board, and $127,556 constituting the proxy expense of the successful insurgents.

2. Three judges rejected that decision in its entirety in a minority opinion by Judge John Van Voorhis, which is the reason for this Appendix.

3. And Judge Charles S. Desmond concurred with the first three judges in approving the verdicts of the lower courts, but implied, in a separate opinion, that if the suing shareholders had demanded an accounting, he might well have ruled out some of the expenditures that stockholders and directors ratified.

Is it possible the courts, in the future, will restrict the use of corporate funds to mere notification of shareholders? Is it possible that both sides in a proxy fight will be looked upon as contenders for power—for control of the corporate till and machinery—and, therefore, should not be reimbursed for campaign expenses?

And will this put corporation executives who do not have large private fortunes at the mercy of outsiders, raiders, who do have large personal funds at their disposal?

These problems, so basic in proxy fights, are all raised by the minority opinion, and, therefore, I am presenting major excerpts from it:

. . . This is a stockholder's derivative action to require directors to restore to a corporation [campaign expenses in a proxy contest] incurred by an incumbent faction and by an insurgent faction of stockholders. The insurgents prevailed at the annual meeting, and payments of their own campaign expenses . . . were ratified by majority vote. It was a large majority, but the stockholders were not unanimous.

. . . We are called upon to decide whether it was a corporate purpose (1) to make the expenditures which were disbursed by the incumbent or management group in defense of their acts . . . and (2) to defray expenditures made by the insurgent group. . . . The Appellate Division held that stockholder authorization or ratification was not necessary to reasonable expenditures by the management group, the purpose of which was to inform the stockholders concerning the affairs of the corporation, and that, although these incumbents spent or incurred obligations of $133,966 (the previous expenses of annual meetings of this corporation ranging between $7,000 and $28,000), plaintiff must fail for having omitted to distinguish item by item between which of these expenditures were warranted and which were not; and the Appellate Division held that the insurgents also should be reimbursed, but subject to the qualification that "The expenses of those who were seeking to displace the management should not be reimbursed by the corporation except upon approval by the stockholders. . . ."

No resolution was passed by the stockholders approving payment to the management group. It has been recognized that not all of the $133,966 . . . paid or incurred by the management group was . . . merely for information of stockholders. This outlay included payment for all of the activities of a strenuous campaign to persuade and cajole in a hardfought contest for control of this corporation. It included, for example, expenses for entertainment, chartered airplanes and limousines, public relations counsel and proxy solicitors. However, legitimate such measures may be on behalf of stockholders themselves in such a controversy, most of them do not pertain to a corporate function but are part of the apparatus of aggressive factions in corporate contests. In Lawyers' Advertising Co. versus Consolidated Ry. Lighting & Refrigerating Co. . . , this court said:

"The notice in question . . . amounted to an urgent solicitation that these proxies should be executed and returned for use by one faction in its contest, and we think there is no authority for imposing the expense of its publication upon the company. It may be conceded that the directors who caused this publication acted in good faith, and felt they were serving the best interest of stockholders; but it would be altogether too dangerous a rule to permit directors in control of a corporation and engaged in a contest for the perpetuation of their offices and control, to impose upon the corporation the unusual expense of publishing advertisements, or, by analogy, of dispatching special messengers for the purpose of procuring proxies in their behalf."

The Appellate Division acknowledged in the instant (Fairchild) case that "It is obvious that the management group here incurred a substantial amount of needless expense . . . ," but this conclusion should have led to a direction [to] incumbent directors . . . to come forward with an explanation of their expenditures. . . . The complaint should not have been dismissed . . . due to failure of plaintiff to segregate the specific expenditures. . . .

The second ground assigned by the Appellate Division for dismissing the complaint against incumbent directors is stockholder ratification of reimbursement to the insurgent group. Whatever effect or lack of it this resolution had upon expenditures by the insurgent group, clearly the stockholders who voted to pay the insurgents entertained no intention of reimbursing the management group. . . . The insurgent group succeeded as a result of arousing the indignation of these very stockholders against the management group; nothing in the resolution to pay the expenses of the insurgent group purported to authorize or ratify payment of the campaign expenses of their adversaries, and certainly no inference should be drawn that the stockholders who voted to pay the insurgents intended that the incumbent group should also be paid. Upon the contrary, they were removing the incumbents from control mainly for the reason that they were charged with having mulcted the corporation by a long-term salary and pension contract to one of their number, J. Carlton Ward, Jr. . . .

There is no doubt that the management was entitled and under a duty to take reasonable steps to acquaint the stockholders with essential facts concerning the management of the corporation, and it may well be that . . . a contest warranted them in circularizing the stockholders with more than ordinarily detailed information. . . . As this court said in Lawyers' Advertising . . . "There is no impropriety in charging . . . expenses within reasonable limits. . . ."

Only such [expenses] as were reasonably related to informing the stockholders fully and fairly concerning corporate affairs should be allowed. The concession by the plaintiff that such expenditures as were made were reasonable in amount does not decide this question. . . . The cost of entertainment for stockholders may have been, and it is stipulated that they were, at the going rates for providing similar entertainment. That does not signify that entertaining stockholders is reasonably related to the purposes of the corporation. The Appellate Division, as above stated, found that the management group incurred a substantial amount of needless expense. That fact being established, it became the duty of the incumbent directors to unravel and explain these payments.

Regarding the $127,556 paid by the new management to the insurgent group for their campaign expenditures, the question immediately arises whether that was for a corporate purpose. The Appellate Division has recognized that upon no theory could such expenditures be reimbursed except by approval of the stockholders. . . . Upon the other hand, an act which is ultra vires cannot be ratified merely by a majority of the stockholders of a corporation. . . . In Davis vs. Congregation Beth Tephila Israel, it was held that a single dissenting member of a corporation might maintain an action to vacate an ultra vires agreement. . . .

In considering this issue, . . . we begin with the proposition . . . that it is beyond the power of a corporation to authorize . . . campaign expenses in a proxy contest. . . . As in political contests, aspirations for control are invariably presented under the guise of policy or principle.[1] . . . The main question of "policy" in the instant corporate election . . . concerns the long-term contract with pension rights of . . . , J. Carlton Ward, Jr. The insurgents' chief claim of benefit to the corporation from their victory consists in the termination of that agreement, resulting in an alleged actuarial saving of $350,000 to $825,000 to the corporation, and the reduction of other salaries and rent by more than $300,000 per year. The insurgents had contended in the proxy contest that these payments should be substantially reduced so that members of the incumbent group would not continue to profit personally at the expense of the corporation. . . .

These circumstances are mentioned primarily to illustrate how impossible it is to distinguish between "policy" and "personnel," . . . but they also indicate that personal factors are deeply rooted in this contest. . . . Some expenditures may concededly be made by a corporation represented by its management so as to inform stockholders, but there is a clear distinction between such expenditures by management and by mere groups of stockholders. The latter are under no legal obligation to assume duties of managing the corporation. They may endeavor to supersede the management for any reason, regardless of whether it be advantageous or detrimental to the corporation, but, if they succeed, that is not a determination that the company was previously mismanaged or that it may not be mismanaged in the future. A change in control is in no sense analogous to an adjudication that the former directors have been guilty of misconduct. The analogy of allowing expenses of suit to minority stockholders who have been successful in a derivative action . . . is entirely without foundation. . . .

The insurgents in this instance repeatedly announced to the stockholders in their campaign literature that their proxy con-

[1] In Cullom vs. Simmonds, 139 N.Y. 5. 2nd 401, a Stockholders Protective Committee, organized for the avowed purpose of ousting directors of R. Hoe & Company, was not granted expenses, even though successful. The Appellate Division held that the expenses were incurred solely to change personnel and not in connection with matters of corporate principle or policy.

254

test was being waged at their own personal expense. If reimbursement of such items were permitted upon majority stockholder ratification, no court . . . could pass upon which types of expenditures were "needless." . . . Whether the insurgents should be paid would . . . depend upon whether they win the [battle of proxies]. . . . It would be entirely irrelevant whether the corporation is benefited by their efforts. . . . The courts could not indulge in a speculative inquiry into that issue. That would truly be a matter of business judgment. In some instances corporations are better governed by the existing management and in others by some other group which supersedes the existing management. Courts of law have no jurisdiction to decide such questions, and successful insurgent stockholders may confidently be relied upon to reimburse themselves whatever may be the real merits of the controversy. . . . Under the judgment which is appealed from, success in a proxy contest is the indispensable condition upon which reimbursement of the insurgents depends. Adventurers are not infrequent who are ready to take advantage of economic recessions, reduction of dividends or failure to increase them, or other sources of stockholder discontent to wage contests in order to obtain control of well-managed corporations, so as to divert their funds through legal channels into other corporations in which they may be interested, or to discharge former officers and employees to make room for favored newcomers according to the fashion of political patronage, or for other objectives that are unrelated to the sound prosperity of the enterprise. The way is open and will be kept open for stockholders and groups of stockholders to contest corporate elections, but if the promoters of such movements choose to employ the costly modern media of mass persuasion, they should look for reimbursement to themselves and to the stockholders who are aligned with them. If the law be that they can be recompensed by the corporation in case of success, and only in that event, it will operate as a powerful incentive to persons accustomed to taking calculated risks to increase this form of high-powered salesmanship to such a degree that, action provoking reaction, stockholders' meetings [contests] will be very costly. To the financial advantages promised by control of a prosperous corporation would be added the knowledge that the winner takes all insofar as the campaign expenses are concerned. To the victor, indeed, would belong the spoils.

The questions involved in this case assume mounting importance as the capital stock of corporations becomes more widely distributed. To an enlarged extent, the campaign methods consequently come more to resemble those of political campaigns, but, as in the latter, campaign expenses should be borne by those who are waging the campaign and their followers, instead of being met out of the corporate or the public treasury. Especially is this true when campaign promises have been made that the expenses would not be charged to the corporation. . . .

It is the established law of this State that expenditures may be incurred by management limited to informing the stockholders fully and fairly concerning the affairs and policies of the corporation, which may well include an explanation of the reasons [for] its policies, nor is there any reason . . . stockholders who have neglected to sign proxies through apathy may not be solicited so as to insure a quorum . . . , but beyond measures of this character, the purely campaign expenses of a management group do not serve a corporate purpose, and paying them is ultra vires. The same is true of all of the expenses of insurgent stockholders. . . .

The judgment appealed from should be reversed so as to direct [the insurgents to pay the corporation $127,556] with appropriate interest, representing the moneys reimbursed . . . and an interlocutory judgment should be entered for an accounting to determine what part of the $133,966, representing expenses incurred by the old board, was improperly charged to the corporation and requiring [two members of the old board and two members of the new board] to pay [the amounts thereof in proportion to how much was approved by the old board and how much by the new board].

This minority opinion deterred lawyers for the ousted directors of New York Central from recommending a last-ditch defense of expenditures in the proxy fight against Robert R. Young. So the case was settled out of court.

APPENDIX II

Sewell Avery's Farewell

Here is my report on the Montgomery Ward stockholders' meeting of Friday, April 22, 1955, as it appeared in the *Philadelphia Bulletin* and other newspapers:

Avery's Days Are Numbered As Montgomery Ward Boss

By J. A. Livingston

Chicago——Sewell L. Avery, who, according to *Who's Who*, is 81, has lost control of Montgomery Ward & Co. But forty-three-year-old Louis E. Wolfson didn't take it away.

Before 2,500 Ward shareholders, employes and friends at Medinah Temple, Avery bared his own inadequacy for the job. A 14-year-old girl said to her mother: "He acts just like grandpa when grandpa doesn't quite understand what we're talking about at dinner."

Avery's fellow directors can no longer afford to retain him as chief executive officer out of friendship or loyalty.

You had to be there to understand why. The *Chicago Daily News* had a headline: "Avery Has Trouble With Speech." Austin C. Wehrwein wrote in the *Chicago Sun-Times*, "Insofar as it was possible to understand Avery, he seemed to be telling again his story of how he rescued the mail order house in the early 'thirties."

Brought on Own Undoing

Avery brought on his own undoing. A stockholder asked him: "How do you explain the 50% drop in Ward earnings since 1950?" Edmund A. Krider, president, jumped up and said, "I'll answer that." He explained that retailing had enjoyed a "bonanza" immediately after the war. Then competition set in. Avery would not let well enough alone. He decided to add to Krider's explanation. Here, as I've pieced it together, is what he said:

"There are several changes easily submitted there. The difficulty of these changes came about in the early days. I would say that the difficulty came about two years before 1932—which was the time chains were beginning. There was a development of time payments, Mr. Krider. The situation was brought about by the determination that these stores had difficulty in handling the mail order business. We had to make a correction.

"They had a plan ready and with $60,000,000 put this in the hands of the mail order people. This was a question of what stores were needed. Then we went out and got what stores we needed. When I came into the situation there was extreme difficulty. We went out to get the buildings. There was great difficulty. Houses had to be put up. We were expanded.

Summary Shows Net Worth

"The people that selected them without any understanding of the needs of the stores used $60,000,000. Put a number of stores on the wrong sites. The situation has carried on to this day from the purchase of these stores. We still have the difficulties because of them but to a lesser degree at this time. That is the state of the profits—the $60,000,000. I think that in view of the figures I have here the results are still remarkable indeed.

"We're still handling a number of these stores. We're reducing them. We have about 80 and are working under disadvantage. We're tearing down. It's a difficult situation. We probably have something like 80. We have little stores in bad places. That is our difficulty. That is the reason. That is the change. We are keeping the better stores and abandoning those that are unsatisfactory.

"In the meantime, what do you think of the performance of 24 years? A good modern store is available with $700,000,-000 and no doubt! In the war, 20,000 persons were taken from us. That affected our organization at a time when we had the benefit of taking on the kind of thing that mail order boys had to select a store and the merchandising of it. You all have the figures. We're entirely without debt." (Avery held up a printed summary of earnings and net worth which was distributed to shareholders.) "It's available for everyone to see.

"Would Step Down"

"When we get through with the high cost of construction because we can't build today at economic prices. Don't come to any easy conclusion that this is a weak situation. Our friend [meaning Wolfson] tells us what he will do. He hasn't been in the business. He has a hungry eye. If you've listened to my stumbling remarks you know we have $700,000,000. No doubt. Clear as a bell. Is there any question about that?

"The gentleman we have here as a guest doesn't know what he's talking about. When and how do you get $700,000,000? When you have no debt whatsoever and an organization that is the very best that we've ever had. I apologize for the nervous movement or difficulty of handling these matters. We have everything we need—many buildings with this thing.

And knowing we have $700,000,000 and are nervous about Mr. Wolfson and his picking that up. Thank you, gentlemen."

A stockholder then asked if there were "any plans for the honorable retirement of Mr. Avery." Avery answered: "My age is common knowledge on every page. I'm actually 82. I have been having during the year difficulty through a medical attack. It has been a burden for a year. Now I'm in good health and my head is no better than before.

"This is not a guess. I have a burden of some of the things that are threatening us. You can't buy what you want. I mean buildings. Because cost is so great. You get less and less for more and more. If I'm undesirable I will step down very pleasantly. I have a vigorous physical self. I can't for the life of me sit down. I won't lose anything if I leave this situation. I'm safe. If I'm unworthy of the job, I will very cheerfully retire. Thank you."

There were cheers. But these were cheers of sadness, not the exuberant, cheerful cheers which greeted Avery when he first walked onto the stage. Then he was champion. Now he was somebody everyone, even his friends and admirers, realized had to go.

Reprinted by permission of Publishers Syndicate

APPENDIX III

Shareholder Inter-Communication

A shareholder's proposal to other shareholders, if it is to get SEC approval, must be like a swain's proposal to a loved one, "proper." Otherwise, shareholder time, money, and energy would be wasted.

A "proper proposal" must relate to matters on which shareholders, as shareholders, have the power to vote. If, for example, the state law under which a corporation is chartered reserves to directors the declaration of all dividends, then a shareholder resolution that "all earnings and realized capital gains be paid as dividends" (actually proposed in 1955) is out of order.

Similarly, the proposal made by Judge Jonah B. Goldstein, representing the Grand Street Boys' Foundation, owner of 650 shares of American Telephone & Telegraph Company, to increase the dividend, was disallowed. On the other hand, a proposal that directors take steps to split the stock four-for-one was considered a "proper subject" and allowed to go to shareholders in 1957. (It was voted down.)

The SEC will permit the management to omit proposals of a political or philosophical nature. Thus a resolution that the Greyhound Corporation do away with segregation in its busses in the South was excluded on the theory that a corporation is run for the profit of shareholders, not for social reform; similarly a proposal that Radio Corporation refrain from hiring Communists and former Communists was excluded.

Nor will subjects which have a personal animus be permitted. Thus a shareholder of Sparks-Withington (Sparton Radio) wanted the company's proxy statement to describe the "police record, serious illness record, and any other physical defects" of proposed directors. This might have been excluded also on the ground that it hardly constituted a resolution or a proposal. Similarly, a proposal asking that a representative of the Bell System Pensioners Association be made a member of the company's Benefit Plan Committee was ruled a personal grievance. The proposer, an ex-employee, was interested in increasing his own pension.

Finally, the SEC has laid down a "substantial progress" rule. Shareholders may not resubmit the same proposal for the same company unless there is evidence of headway. The first time a proposal is made it must get 3 per cent of the vote to be resubmittable at the next meeting, otherwise it will be excluded for three years. On resubmission, it must get 6 per cent of the vote, or again it can be excluded for three years. If it gets 6 per cent of the vote, then the next time it must get 10 per cent of the vote, or again it may be excluded for three years.

The tally on excluded shareholders' proposals in the calendar year 1955 and the fiscal year 1956 (in effect, there is no overlap, since the proxy season—the proposal season—occurs in the first half of the year) follows on page 264.

Acting Dean David C. Bayne, S.J., of the University of Detroit Law School feels that the SEC has been too narrow in its interpretation of "proper subject." His views are given in a scholarly fashion in the University of Detroit *Law Journal*, April, 1957, in an article on "The Basic Rationale of Proper Subject." This issue of the *Journal* is devoted to the

	Calendar 1955	Fiscal 1956
Not submitted in time	6	6
Not a proposal	1	1
Proposal is a negation of a management proposal; in other words, shareholders would have a chance to vote on opposite side of question	5	..
Improper subject—not a matter for shareholder consideration under state laws	18	16
Personal grievance	3	4
Ordinary business—a matter for executive, not shareholder decision	4	6
Insufficient vote at a previous meeting	..	2
Exclusions	37	35

SEC proxy rules. It is well worth reading by anyone interested in the subject in depth.

Shareholders have the right to argue for their proposal in one hundred words. But the management is not limited in its rebuttal. To A. Wilfred May, executive editor of the *Commercial and Financial Chronicle,* a champion of stockholder rights, what is space for the executive ought to be space for the stockholder. May feels that the one-hundred-word limit does not permit "adequate education of rank-and-file shareholders" on matters which are frequently technical. However, the SEC was pragmatic. It cannot limit the number of proposals shareholders individually or collectively can make. It can merely rule out those which are duplicates or improper. So, it was forced to put a limit somewhere, otherwise proxy statements might become even more unwieldy than they are.

When the SEC first opened proxy statements to shareholders, corporation executives rushed memoranda, lawyers, and themselves in person to Washington. There would be no room for anything in proxy statements except crackpot shareholder proposals. They overestimated shareholder energy. Out of two thousand proxy statements filed with the SEC in 1956, only sixty-six (about 3 per cent) contained shareholder proposals. In all, there were 102 proposals. (Some proxy statements contained more than one.) In addition, forty-one other proposals had been made, of which six were withdrawn by the shareholders, either because the management agreed to the proposal or convinced the shareholder it was not needed, and thirty-five were excluded by the management with the SEC's consent for various reasons. In 1955, the tally was much the same: sixty-three out of 1,973 proxy statements contained proposals. Again 3 per cent. Of greater significance, seventy-eight out of 102 proposals in 1956 were the product of the "professional shareholders," the two Gilbert brothers and John Campbell Henry. In 1955, their proportion was almost as high. Moreover, in 1956, only nineteen shareholders, other than these "pros" sent out proposals; in 1955 only thirty-six. Institutional investors, as noted in Chapter XII, don't use shareholder proposals. They make their resolutions directly to management, knowing they'll be heard.

APPENDIX IV

BOILER ROOMS AND BUCKET SHOPS

When a householder in Fargo, North Dakota, or Wichita, Kansas, is summoned to the telephone and the operator says "New York calling," the householder instantly feels important. The caller says he has a great investment opportunity. "Your name was given to me by Mr.," and what comes after Mr. is a blur or grunt. Right then and there the householder from Fargo or Wichita had better hang up. Otherwise he is ripe for a taking. A fast-talking boiler room salesman is on the other end of the line.

A "boiler room" is a small, crowded office, usually in New York, but sometimes in Houston or Dallas (which smack of oil) or California (also oil, plus Hollywood). The drab walls are lined with desks on which sit telephones, shrouded with hoods. On the table are out-of-town telephone books. Names —"victims"—are selected at random. As soon as a prospect is nibbling, the salesman ducks his head under the hood to block out the chatter of other hard-pushing salesmen. Thus he can talk real quiet and confidential-like. The salesman quickly warms up to the glorious prospects of American Interstellar Oil, or some such company, and then puts on the pressure, the steam. Whence the term "boiler shop." In the summertime, boiler shops are intensely hot; salesmen often work in undershirts. Another figurative justification for the term "boiler room."

The SEC estimates some twenty thousand persons a year get taken by boiler room operators. In 1955, six boiler rooms in New York sold $30,000,000 in securities (not tremendous considering that new issues every year now total $9,000,000,-000). But they realized a $4,500,000 profit, and their victims lost $15,000,000. Here are some examples of gullibility from SEC files:

A retired Floridian, on the strength of three phone calls from New York, sent blue-chip stock worth $97,000 along with power of attorney to a firm which offered him two sure-fire oils and a manufacturing stock. His newly acquired shares soon were worth about $27,000. He suffered a depreciation of more than 70 per cent.

A man in Sioux City, Iowa, purchased two Canadian oils and one American oil for $94,500 cash. Present value: $54,500.

A doctor in Globe, Arizona, purchased a Canadian oil stock for $7,000. Present value: about $3,500.

A man in West Point, Mississippi, invested $13,790 in some oils and within six months—during a bull market—lost about $7,700.

Most of the victims seem to be men.

As soon as the SEC discovers a boiler room operator, an injunction is sought; steps are taken to revoke broker-dealer licenses; and criminal actions are started—to run the marauder out of business. Here is a good rule: Any time somebody tries to sell you securities over the telephone, tell him to put it in writing. Then he has to use the mails. If he writes, and if he is an out-and-out swindler, at least you have written evidence of the fraud.

A boiler room is not to be confused with a bucket shop. A boiler room salesman has every intention of committing a fraud—making a false representation over the telephone, which is contrary to law. Originally, a bucket shop, properly operated, was a type of betting establishment. The customer would come in, put up a modest margin and "buy" a stock. The bucketeer, however, would not place the order with a broker. He would count on the customer's being wrong. If the stock dropped below the margin put up, the customer lost everything. The bucketeer, of course, pocketed commissions on the stocks he didn't buy.

The New York Stock Exchange did much to "disfranchise" bucket shops in the late 1920's and early 1930's by requiring member firms to obtain approval of all direct wires to non-members. In this way, the Big Board did away with quotation services to bucketeers.

Bernard M. Baruch, in his autobiography *My Own Story,* tells how John W. (Bet-a-Million) Gates, a super-salesman of railroad equipment and a tremendous stock market operator, decided to give bucket-shop operators a "dose of their own medicine." He and some friends placed orders incognito with a bucketeer to buy stocks which had been relatively quiescent. Then they bid up the stocks on the Exchange. When they tried to collect their winnings, a new firm's name was on the door. "Only by threats of a suit and an exposé," said Baruch, "did Gates force the bucket-shop operators to pay part of their losses."

Bucket shops are now outlawed in most states. Boiler rooms have taken their place for the "get-rich-by-crook" boys.

APPENDIX V

Where the SEC Does Not Shine Its Light

Because of a quirk in the Securities Laws, some extremely large companies do not have to comply with SEC proxy rules, insider-trading disclosure, or make reports according to SEC accounting standards. The approximate number of shareholders, and the market value of the outstanding stock of some of these companies is given here; included are a few companies which, because they have registered $2,000,000 of securities, file annual and semi-annual reports with the SEC, and these are indicated by the letter X:

(Data from Standard Financial Manuals)

	Assets Circa 12/31/56 (millions)	Approx. Stock-holders Recently Reported	Common Stock Market Value 12/31/56 (millions)
Humble Oil & Refining Co. (u)	$1,433.0	8,400	$4,483.9
Creole Petroleum Corp. (u)	1,131.0	6,300	7,061.2
X Tennessee Gas Transm. Co.	1,006.0	63,800	435.0
X Texas Eastern Transm. Corp.	543.0	49,600	182.0
Great Atlantic & Pacific Tea Co. of America (u)	509.0	N.A.	148.0
Weyerhaeuser Timber Company	504.5	7,500	900.0
Singer Manufacturing Company (u)	444.8	8,264	175.0
X Duke Power Company (u)	420.7	2,500	272.3

(Data from Standard Financial Manuals)—*Continued*

	Assets Circa 12/31/56 (millions)	Approx. Stock- holders Recently Reported	Common Stock Market Value 12/31/56 (millions)
X Transcontinental Gas Pipe Line	401.8	26,000	131.0
American Express Company	353.9	25,300	73.0
X Southern New England Tel. Co.	296.6	46,500	213.0
X Kaiser Steel Corporation	292.6	6,900	162.3
Eli Lilly & Company	195.6	4,800	247.0
Time, Inc.	177.2	8,600	135.0
X Ralston Purina Company	171.2	4,600	198.0
M. A. Hanna Company	159.6	3,500	374.0
Sherwin-Williams Company (u)	153.8	5,500	152.1
Carnation Company (u)	133.7	2,100	72.8
Grinnell Corporation	116.9	4,200	56.0
Aetna Life Insurance Co.	3,070.2	23,600	516.0
Travelers Insurance Co.	2,823.7	30,800	680.0
X Insurance Company of North America (u)	675.4	17,000	506.2
Bank of America N. T. & S. A.	9,991.8	200,000	986.0
Chase Manhattan Bank	7,756.9	96,000	650.0
First National City Bank	7,427.0	63,900	680.0

(u) Traded unlisted on American Stock Exchange.
X Files annual and semi-annual reports with SEC.
N.A. Not Available.

Congress granted exemption from SEC regulation to "supposedly small" companies whose stocks are not listed—registered—in a stock exchange. That is how the above companies escape.

APPENDIX VI

The $300,000-and-Up Breadwinners

Business Week (May 25, 1957, pp. 114, 116) ranks America's top corporation breadwinners as follows:

1. Eugene G. Grace, chairman, Bethlehem Steel...... $809,011
2. Harlow H. Curtice, president, General Motors..... 695,100
3. Arthur B. Homer, president, Bethlehem Steel...... 669,176
4. Crawford H. Greenewalt, president, du Pont....... 600,886
5. Frederic G. Donner, exec. v-p., General Motors.... 577,625
6. Louis C. Goad, exec. v-p., General Motors........ 521,100
7. Robert E. McMath, v-p., Bethlehem Steel......... 514,340
8. J. W. Schwab, president, United Merchants & Manufacturers.................................... 386,588
9. Ernest R. Breech, chairman, Ford Motor........ 370,000
   Henry Ford II, president, Ford Motor............ 370,000
10. Henry B. du Pont, v-p., du Pont................ 354,000
11. Samuel Bronfman, president, Distillers Corp.-Seagrams 351,042
12. Charles M. White, chairman, Republic Steel...... 351,000
13. Walter J. Beadle, v-p., du Pont................. 350,831
14. Walter Dannenbaum, v-p., du Pont.............. 347,700
15. Albert Bradley, chairman, General Motors........ 341,300
16. Neil H. McElroy, president, Procter & Gamble.... 319,974
17. William S. Paley, chairman, Columbia Broadcasting 316,526
18. Delmar S. Harder, exec. v-p., Ford Motor........ 315,000
19. Frank Stanton, president, Columbia Broadcasting.. 312,335
20. W. K. Whiteford, president, Gulf Oil........... 300,061
21. Morse G. Dial, president, Union Carbide......... 300,000
22. Lewis D. Crusoe, exec. v-p., Ford Motor......... 300,000

This table, of course, omits stock options, when granted; also pension remittances, and post-retirement consulting fees.

APPENDIX VII

(From the *Philadelphia Bulletin* of January 27, 1955, and
other newspapers around the same date)

R. P. VANDERPOEL

STOCKHOLDERS LOSE CHAMPION
IN DEATH OF R. P. VANDERPOEL

By J. A. Livingston

They laid Robert P. Vanderpoel to rest Monday. But the
vigorous skepticism he left behind will never rest.

Vanderpoel was financial columnist for the *Chicago Sun-
Times* and, before that, financial editor of the *Chicago Herald
American*. But he started out as a teacher of economics and
English at Ashtabula Harbor High School in Ohio. And it
was as a teacher he died—helping people to understand busi-
ness and finance.

His death is a loss to the newspaper profession. Vanderpoel
was independent in thought, inquiring in approach, and direct. He meant what he said and, fully as important, could
say what he meant—free from the obfuscation of financial
journalese.

His death is a loss to small shareholders. He championed
their rights. He wanted annual meetings held in places convenient to stockholders. He fought for annual reports stockholders could understand and representation of minorities on
boards of directors through cumulative voting. He suggested
that directors own stock in companies they direct.

Opposed Free-Wheeling Options

He attacked free-wheeling stock-option, pension, and bonus
plans for executives. He urged the Securities & Exchange

Commission to grant shareholders wide latitude in communicating with other shareholders on corporation proxy statements. He believed in a single standard of corporate democracy, thus:

"When big businessmen go hat in hand to Washington, they emphasize the great number of shareholders who own their company. . . . It is a nice story. But when these little fellows try to make their voices heard, too often they are squelched. Some managements do not like voices prodding them each year."

His death is a loss to bankers and businessmen. By pointing out mistakes and successes, Vanderpoel helped men in power to assay themselves and their peers and thus do a better job. He was both their critic and conscience.

In his daily life Vanderpoel often dealt with big shots. Yet, the plush of Chicago clubdom didn't soften his touch on the typewriter.

Protested Avery's Management

He committed a supreme financial heresy. He questioned the notion that nothing but good comes from stock splits. He pointed out that it costs more in brokerage to buy or sell 75 shares than 25 shares. Does that help the stockholders, the company, or brokers? he wondered.

When executives began leaving Montgomery Ward in half-dozens, Vanderpoel protested against Sewell L. Avery's personal management of the company. This took guts in Chicago. To many persons there, Avery was the man who defied "that man in the White House"—an idol. But not to Bob.

Yet, when Louis E. Wolfson began his proxy fight to add Montgomery Ward to his collection of corporations, Bob did not rush to Wolfson's side because Wolfson was on his, Bob's, side. Instead he looked into Wolfson's intricate deal in Devoe & Raynolds Co.

First, Wolfson interests bought up working control of the B stock which could elect two-thirds of the directors. Then Wolfson's Merritt-Chapman & Scott Corp. made an offer to swap one and one-third shares of its stock for Devoe & Raynolds B, but only one and two-thirds shares for Devoe & Raynolds A. This aroused Vanderpoel.

Interested in Small Holder

The A stock was entitled to twice the dividends of the B stock. It rated as $2 par value as against the B's $1 par. And, historically, the A stock sold for twice the B stock, reflecting the dividend differential. Inference: The A stock should get twice as much in the swap as the B. But Wolfson interests owned the B.

Commented Vanderpoel: "If Wolfson is to 'always guard the rights and welfare of the small stockholder as well as I guard my own,' as he has pledged, he can not propose a deal such as this." Bob wasn't against Avery or against Wolfson. He was for the small stockholder.

Just after Christmas, he sent me a note expressing concern about the blithe spirit of the New Year.

"Isn't it true," he asked, "that at a time such as the present, it is very difficult for anyone to be other than optimistic? If you are in government, pessimism loses votes; if you are in business, it loses sales; and if you are a newspaperman, I fear it loses readers. And so we build up more and more optimism until something occurs to knock the props from under the boom and then we wonder how we could have been so foolish. Best wishes for 1955."

To the last, he was the helpful, inquisitive skeptic, who'll be survived, as befits a teacher, by the questions and consciences he left behind—in other people. So, it's "au revoir" to Bob, not goodbye.

Reprinted by permission of Publishers Syndicate

BIBLIOGRAPHY

In the course of preparing this book, certain reading was routine: *The Wall Street Journal*, *New York Times*, the *Philadelphia Bulletin*, *Washington Post*, *Business Week*, *Fortune*, *Harvard Business Review*, *Barron's*, the *Financial World*, *Nation's Business*, the *New York Journal of Commerce*, the *London Economist*, and other periodicals dealing with economics and finance. I used several encyclopedias, including the *Britannica*, *Compton's*, and the *New International*, and constantly referred to *Standard & Poor's* and *Moody's* manuals, and reports of the Securities and Exchange Commission and the New York Stock Exchange.

Not all books or reports in this bibliography have been cited in the text or footnoted. Such recent works as *Proxy Contests for Corporate Control*, by E. R. Aranow and Herbert A. Einhorn, and George A. Hills' *The Law of Accounting and Financial Statements* were insurance; I wanted the feeling of being abreast of the latest work and thought in major fields associated with stockholder rights and powers. I mention here only those works which were consulted for *the specific purpose* of writing *The American Stockholder*:

Aranow, Edward Ross, and Einhorn, Herbert A., *Proxy Contests for Corporate Control*, Columbia University Press, 1957

Arnold, Thurman, *Folklore of Capitalism*, Yale University Press, 1937

Baruch, Bernard M., *My Own Story*, Henry Holt & Co., 1957

Berle, Adolf A., Jr., and Means, Gardiner C., *The Modern Corporation and Private Property*, The Macmillan Co., 1932

Berle, Adolf A., Jr., *The Twentieth Century Capitalistic Revolution*, Harcourt, Brace & Co., 1954

Bollinger, Lynn L., *see* Butters

Burnham, James, *Managerial Revolution*, The John Day Co., Inc., 1941

Butters, J. Keith; Thompson, Lawrence E.; and Bollinger, Lynn L., *Effects of Taxation*, Harvard University Press, 1953

Clews, Henry, *Fifty Years in Wall Street*, Irving Publishing Co., 1908

Dennison, H. F., and Galbraith, J. Kenneth, *Modern Competition and Business Policy*, Oxford University Press, 1938

Dewing, Arthur S., *The Financial Policy of Corporations*, 3d revised edition, The Ronald Press Co., 1934

Dodd, David L., *see* Graham

Drucker, Peter, *Concept of the Corporation*, The John Day Co., 1946

Drucker, Stanley W., editor, *Corporate Democracy*, compilation of "Dicta," 1952–53 *Virginia Law Weekly* articles

Einhorn, Herbert A., *see* Aranow

Emerson, Frank D., and Latcham, Franklin C., *Shareholder Democracy*, Western Reserve University Press

Galbraith, J. Kenneth, *see* Dennison

Gilbert, Lewis D., *Dividends and Democracy*, American Research Council (Larchmont, New York), 1956

Glover, J. D., *The Attack on Big Business*, Harvard University Press, 1954

Graham, Benjamin, and Dodd, David L., *Security Analysis*, McGraw-Hill, 1951

Hills, George A., *The Law of Accounting and Financial Statements*, Little, Brown & Co., 1957

Holbrook, Stewart H., *The Age of Moguls*, Doubleday & Co., 1954

Karr, David, *Fight for Control*, Ballantine Books, 1956

Keynes, John Maynard, *The General Theory of Employment, Interest, and Money*, Harcourt, Brace & Co., 1936

Kimmel, Lewis H., *Share Ownership in the United States*, The Brookings Institution, 1952

Kulski, W. W., *The Soviet Regime, Communism in Practice*, Syracuse University Press, 1954

Latcham, Franklin C., *see* Emerson

Leffler, George L., *The Stock Market*, The Ronald Press Co., second edition, 1957

Loss, Louis, *Securities Regulation*, Little, Brown & Co., 1951

———, *Securities Regulation*, 1955 Supplement, Little, Brown & Co.

McCormick, Edward T., *Understanding the Securities Act and the SEC*, American Book Co., 1948

Medbery, James K., *Men and Mysteries of Wall Street*, Fields, Osgood & Co., 1870

Ripley, William Z., *Main Street and Wall Street*, Little, Brown & Co., 1927

Rothschild, V. Henry, II, *see* Washington

Securities and Exchange Commission, *The Work of the Securities and Exchange Commission*, published by the SEC, 1957

Thompson, Lawrence E., *see* Butters

Warshow, Robert Irving, *The Story of Wall Street*, Greenberg, 1929

Washington, George Thomas, and Rothschild, V. Henry, II, *Compensating the Corporate Executive*, The Ronald Press Co., 1951

Williams, Charles M., *Cumulative Voting for Directors*, Harvard University Press, 1951

Among the reports which provided historical background were:

Regulation of the Stock Exchange, Senate Committee on Banking and Currency, 1914

Stock Exchange Practices, Senate Banking and Currency Committee, 72d and 73d Congress, 1932–34

Investment Trusts and Investment Companies, Securities and Exchange Commission, 1939–41

For legal material, I have consulted case books and articles in many of the law journals published by leading universities, notably: *The California Law Review, Columbia Law Review, Detroit Law Journal, Georgetown Law Journal, Harvard Law Review, Michigan Law Review, Pennsylvania Law Review, Stanford Law Review,* and the *Virginia Law Review.*

—30—

Index

Index

279

Index

Index

Silberstein, Leopold D. Wolfson, Louis E.; Young, Robert R.
Radio Corp. of America, 85n, 88, 151, 166, 226, 262
Railroads, 191, 223, 224, 225; *see also* individual companies
Ralston Purina Co., 270
Reader's Digest, 70
Reda Pump, 48
Reed, Philip D., 106
Regional meetings, *see* Meetings
Remington Rand, 92
Red Cross, 234
Reports
    annual, 94, 102, 104, 194n, 203, 272
    post-meeting, 78, 84-85, 94
    "10-K" to SEC, 95; *see also* Securities and Exchange Commission: rules, companies exempted
Republic Steel, 76, 83, 223, 237, 271
Retired persons, *see* Stockholders
Retirement compensation, *see* Executive compensation
Reuther, Walter, 18, 220
Reynolds Tobacco Co., 187
Rhinelander, Laurens H., 50n
Richfield Oil, 203
Rickenbacker, Eddie, 84
Richardson, Sid W., 44, 46, 134-35, 140, 149
Ripley, Professor William Z., 95n, 172, 191
Robinson-Hannegan Associates, 138
Rockefeller, John D., Jr., 34, 45-46
Rockefeller, John D., Sr., 164, 180
Roosevelt, President Franklin D., 19, 126n
Rosenfeld *vs.* Fairchild, 145-46, 249-57
Rothschild, II, V. Henry, 226
Royal Typewriter, 85n
Runyon, Damon, 200
Safeway Stores, 246
St. Joseph Lead, 85n
Salaries, *see* Executive compensation
Sarnoff, David, 88
Saturday Evening Post, 22, 106
Schram, Emil, 23

Schwab, J. W., 271
Schwartz, George L., 37
Scott, Congressman Hugh, 122
Scott Paper Co., 87, 107, 217, 226
Sears, Roebuck & Co., 61, 152, 155, 239
Seattle Gas, 85n
Securities Act of 1933, 19, 126n, 197, 200n, 207, 211
Securities Exchange Act of 1934, 19, 57, 126n, 200n, 201, 208, 213n, 214n
Securities and Exchange Commission, 13, 19, 20, 21, 48, 68, 69, 75, 81, 126n, 137, 156n, 171, 173n, 190, 194, 195, 197-216, 223, 232, 234, 240, 243, 244, 262, 263, 265, 267, 268; *see also* Proxy; "Full disclosure"
    rules, companies exempted from, 211, 212-14, 269-70
Securities Regulation, 21, 69
Select Committee on Improper Practices in the Labor or Management Field, 202n
Seligman, Daniel, 239n
Senate Banking and Currency Committee, 126n, 215
Senate Judiciary Subcommittee, 230
Servel, 83
Shanks, Carroll M., 223-24
Share Ownership in the United States, *see* Kimmel, Lewis H.
Shareholder Democracy, 20n, 69
Sherwin-Williams Co., 270
Shepherd, Howard C., 223
Short selling, 208
Silberstein, Leopold D., 20, 40, 48, 101, 162n, 204
Sinclair coal properties, 185
Singer Manufacturing Co., 212, 269
Skouras, Spyros P., 87
Sloan, Jr., Alfred P., 28, 109, 110, 127
Smith, Governor Alfred E., 121, 128
Smith, A. Weston, 107
Smith, Adam, 182n
Smith, B. E., 191
Smith, C. R., 84
Smith, Frank L., 44n

Index